PEACE & WAR

A Maiden City Childhood

By Gerry Murray

Published 2018 by NonieG Publications

ISBN 978-1-5272-2952-5

Front cover image © Helen Murray Photography

Contents

Preface

For a number of years, I have been very much aware of the saying that within each one of us there is a story to tell. I fondly remember the words of Mark Twain; 'Every person is a book and each year is a chapter.' Family and friends had often told me that I had a great memory of personal events in my life, as well as of what had been happening on a wider local, national and international stage. With their encouragement, I decided to write and this memoir is the result. Paper never refuses ink and I have enjoyed what I would call this labour of love on which I have spent many weekends. My mind was bubbling over with memories and the first choice I had to make was to select a time frame for this memoir.

There are many periods in one's life that become identifiable as specific compartments. They often range from first childhood memories onwards. For me, the period from early childhood, right through to finishing secondary school education, is an easily identifiable part of my life. This is the story of those years spent in the Maiden City. In speech, locals refer to the city as either Derry or Londonderry. To me, it was simply home.

In writing a memoir, I am very conscious that I am writing a version of those years from my own personal perspective. I readily accept that someone else might have an alternative version and I would encourage them to write their own personal memoir. Unlike many of my contemporaries, I thoroughly enjoyed school days, from Primary One at the Holy Child School in Creggan, through the Christian Brothers at the Brow of the Hill and on to St. Columb's College in Bishop Street. Tony Blair, on becoming Prime Minister in 1997, famously set out his priorities with the words, 'Education, Education, Education.' He was light years behind my parents' generation, for whom the education of their children was a canon of faith. It should therefore be no surprise that educational experiences feature so much in this memoir.

Anyone with a working knowledge of the history of Northern Ireland would appreciate that the years covered in this memoir can be easily divided into two separate eras. There is the first period from my birth to 1968, when world moved from the post-war austerity and rationing to the Swinging Sixties. This is followed by what has become euphemistically known as the years of 'The Troubles,' when the country was plunged into decades of political instability, murder and mayhem. My final year at school was to prove the most bloody of the entire period of the Troubles and there appeared to be little prospect of resolution to increasingly bitter communal divisions.

In some ways, it may have been easier to write two memoirs but I felt that it was important to contrast life before the Troubles started in 1968 with went thereafter. Confucius may have uttered the expression, 'May you live in interesting times,' but that would be to understate the experiences of my teenage years. Just over a century before the Northern Irish Troubles began, Leo Tolstoy wrote his classic work, *War & Peace*. I have chosen the title to reflect that my childhood was, by contrast, spent growing up in an era of Peace &War, in that order.

In my mid-teens, it seemed to me that Derry/Londonderry was the epicentre of much that was happening, politically, in Northern Ireland and I had a ringside seat to witness it. In the following pages, I try to capture, for readers, some of those important landmark moments in modern Irish history and I hope that readers will appreciate that there was vibrancy to growing up in Derry and a pride in the city that crossed sectarian divisions, especially when it came to supporting the local football club, Derry City F.C.

The city in which I grew up has changed almost beyond recognition in the intervening years. Whilst the spires of its two cathedrals still dominate the skyline, the city centre and waterfront are barely recognisable from the darkest days of the Troubles. It has been a slow and tortuous process and there is much unfinished business.

In writing this book, I have not only delved into my memory but have checked facts from as many records as possible and I have been assisted by the recollections of many of my contemporaries, whose contributions often helped sharpen my memory of events and individuals. I have been given good counsel by Pat Mc Art, a friend from my years of writing for *The Derry Journal* and Martin Cowley, who covered the Troubles for *The Irish Times*. They have both read early drafts of the book and provided much welcome suggestions. My thanks are also due to *The Derry Journal* for its permission to use a photograph from my days at the CBS in Feis Doire Comcille and also one of the CBS Rice Cup team. A word of thanks is also due to the staff of the Central Library, who helped me in my archival research of the period and to Dr. Wesley Johnston of Colourpoint Creative for his advice in bringing this book to publication.

In particular, deepest thanks are due to my wife and publisher, Nora, for her encouragement and many suggestions on the book. A special word of thanks is due to my daughter Helen for her tireless commitment to producing the pictures that accompany this text. Of course, I cannot omit mention of all my children, Maoliosa, Katherine, Ceallach as well as Helen, all of whom have been persistent in the encouragement that they have given to me to see this book completed and published.

Gerry Murray
July 2018

PART ONE
PEACE

Chapter One
Early Memories

To 'Derry of the little hills' & 'a dour, cold city to an outsider' I arrive, a month after Queen Elizabeth's visit

On Saturday 15th August 1953, I was born in the city of Belfast. In a private nursing home, at number 1 Rosemount Gardens, I made my entry into the world. It is a red-bricked Edwardian terraced house, in a quiet street off the Limestone Road. It is now converted to flats. The year of my birth was an excellent one for champagne producers, with a vintage described as a low, ripe, concentrated fruit, with exceptional balance and harmony. These are attributes that I would have wished for myself. I later discovered that I had the same birthday as Napoleon Bonaparte and I could well have taken his motto, *To Destiny,* as mine also. The day before I was born, the Soviet Union announced that they had produced the Hydrogen Bomb, thus ensuring that I would grow up in the shadow of the Cold War that dominated the global stage.

I was born within a decade of the end of the Second World War, it was hardly surprising that some former military figures had emerged as political leaders. In America, General Dwight Eisenhower, Allied commander for the Normandy landings, had been elected President on a Republican ticket, in 1952. Winston Churchill, war-time Prime Minister, who was swept from power, in 1945, in Britain, had made a come-back, winning the 1951 General Election, and had been restored to 10 Downing Street. Meanwhile, in Northern Ireland, Viscount Brookeborough, from Churchill's 'dreary steeples of Fermanagh and Tyrone,' and whose military service had been in the First World War, was celebrating his eleventh year as Prime Minister. A few months after my birth, he was returned to power in a General Election to the Stormont Parliament, in which twenty-five of the fifty two seats were uncontested. South of the Border, his nemesis, Eamon de Valera, the last surviving commandant of the 1916 Rising, was again Taoiseach or Prime Minister, as his Fianna Fail party had won the General Election of 1951.

Eight days after my birth, I was christened at Holy Family Catholic Church in nearby Newington. The middle name given to me on baptism was Jude, the patron saint of hopeless cases. I oft wondered why I had been so favoured with such an apparent burden. I was to find that it was a name that did not run in either my father's or mother's families. When the Beatles had a hit with their song, *Hey*

Jude, I felt a buzz at this strange name. Only years later, in the late 1980s, did I discover that I had been adopted. Through a tortuous search, I uncovered the full story as to why it was in Belfast that I was born and how I acquired the middle name Jude. In the words of an Irish maxim, 'Sinn scéal eile,' which translates as 'that's another story,' and a very interesting story at that. However, it is not a story that I intend to recount, detail, in this memoir.

My birth mother was an unmarried girl from a small village, just over the Border in County Monaghan. When it was discovered that she was pregnant, she was sent to the convent of the Sisters of the Nazareth Order in Belfast. So, that was how it came about that it was in the city of Belfast that I was born. I was not destined to spend any of my childhood years in Belfast, a place with which I had no real connections. Within a week of my birth, I was taken from Belfast to the Nazareth Nuns' nursery in Fahan in County Donegal, ten miles from the Maiden City of Derry. From there, it was to Derry I was brought a few weeks later by my adoptive parents. A year earlier, the novelist, John Steinbeck had visited the city, as he searched for his roots in the county. Writing in Collier's Magazine, he described Derry as 'a dour, cold city to an outsider – dark angular buildings and uncrowded streets waiting for something – a city of protest…' What was I getting myself into? A few weeks before I was born, the newly crowned Queen Elizabeth made a three day state visit to Northern Ireland and inspected a guard of honour of Royal Navy sailors in the Maiden City's Guildhall Square. Sure if this city was good enough for the newly-crowned Queen, it must surely have been good enough for me. Given Steinbeck's comment of a city of protest, it must have been reassuring to her Majesty that she was feted in her visit, although *The Derry Journal*, the mouthpiece of Derry Catholics, was sullen and resentful to her visit. Of course, lying in my mother's womb in far off Belfast, I was completely oblivious to such commotion and resentment.

Whilst *The Londonderry Sentinel* was reporting that the flag-bedecked Guildhall Square was a mass of red, white and blue, *The Derry Journal* was busily giving prominence to the marches of the annual marches of the Ancient Order of Hibernians, at which Communism was denounced as a menace to the Catholic Church. South of the Border, Sligo Corporation passed a resolution protesting at the singing of the Red Flag by a number of delegates at a recent trade union conference in Sligo Town Hall, and blamed Communists from Belfast and Liverpool.

In the outside world, the year 1953 was memorable in the sporting world; the year of the *Matthews Final*, at Wembley, as Blackpool's Stanley Matthews finally received an F.A. cup winner's medal. His side came from 3-1 down to defeat

Bolton Wanderers in a seven goal thriller and although it is called the *Matthew's Final*, I much later learned that the star was Blackpool's Stan Mortenson, who scored a hat trick. Of the twenty two players on the pitch, eighteen were English and the remaining four were Scots. The two managers were English. That's a far cry from the modern game. On the day on which I was born, the final Test between England and Australia began at the Oval, with the previous Tests having resulted in draws. I might have been a lucky mascot for Leonard Hutton's side, as the home team won the final Test and thus the Ashes. On the parochial sporting scene, Glentoran won the Irish League, while Linfield won the Irish Cup. Kerry was crowned All-Ireland Gaelic football champions for the sixteenth time, beating Armagh in the final. England was the Five Nation's Rugby Union champions and was only denied the Grand Slam by an Irish team that held them to a 9-9 draw in Lansdowne Road, in Dublin. For those who preferred faster sports, these were the years when Juan Manuel Fangio dominated Formula One motor racing. However, in both 1952 and 1953 the winner was Ferrari's Alberto Ascari. For those who preferred horses to cars, the year saw Gordon Richards ride the 5/1 joint favourite, *Pinza*, to victory in the Derby, a race he had been trying to win since 1924. His victory came four days after he had been knighted by Her Majesty, the Queen. As there was no room in competitive sport for sentiment, he pipped the Queen's horse to win. Meanwhile in the Grand National, only five of the thirty one horses completed the field and Bryan Marshall rode the 20/1 outsider, *Early Mist*, to victory.

For those more inclined to sedentary relaxation, films seemed to be dominated by plots set in the Second World War with the release of *From Here to Eternity,* starring Burt Lancaster and Deborah Kerr, and *The Cruel Sea*, starring Jack Hawkins, based on Nicholas Monsarrat's novel of the same name. The first movie version of *The War of the Worlds* also made its appearance. Novels published that year included *Casino Royale* by Ian Fleming, *Lucky Jim* by Kingsley Amis and *Battle Cry* by Leon Uris. Frankie Lane was crooning his way to the top of the hit parade with *I Believe*, followed by Mantovani's Orchestra's version of *Where is Your Heart* from *The Moulin Rouge*.

As a baby, I was adopted by Johnnie and Mary Murray and raised in the Creggan Estate in the Maiden City of Derry. Creggan from the Irish, *An Creaghan*, meaning a stony place, was a sprawling post-war housing estate built on a hill, overlooking the river Foyle. Over two thousand years ago, Creggan was covered with trees and heavily wooded. Its first inhabitants would have been subsistence farmers and fishermen on the river Foyle, which had a plentiful supply of salmon and oysters. The Creggan that the writer, Cecil Frances Alexander, surveyed from the Bishop's Palace was one she described with the words, 'There is a green hill far away, without a city wall.' It was on this 'green hill far away' that public housing commenced a century later and the housing estate, on which I would live for over a quarter of a century, was built.

When the Troubles started in Northern Ireland, in the late sixties, I enjoyed saying that I had made a wise choice to get out of Belfast at such an early age. However, I used to wonder why I was born in Belfast, of all places and when I asked was told that my father had been working there in the post office, which I accepted unquestioningly. I was almost unique in Creggan as an only child, in an age when Catholic families were quite large. My first memories of childhood are of sitting on a swing in a back garden in Linsfort Drive in the Creggan Estate, surrounded by boys and girls none of whom was a sibling. I was the only child of Johnny and Mary Murray. They had been going out together in the 1930s when my father, who lived in Bridge Street in Derry, was in the British Army. His family had their roots in Ardmore a few miles outside Derry. He completed his seven years' service in the Royal Inniskilling Fusiliers August 1939 and their wedding plans were thrown off course when he was immediately called up when war broke out a month later. He left Derry the following month and only returned in 1945, having seen service in Malta and the Middle East. He ended the war as a P.O.W. and spent eighteen months in a stalag, having been captured in the battle of Leros in the Dodecanese Islands in November 1943.

My father and mother were married in St. Eugene's Cathedral in 1946, and rented a flat in at 5 Upper Magazine Street, before eventually securing a Housing Trust flat in Linsfort Drive in the Creggan Estate, in the early 1950s. Quite a high percentage of the houses and flats were allocated to ex-servicemen. Harold Macmillan was busy telling the British electorate, '*most of our people have never had it so good*' and a flat in Linsfort Drive was a major improvement in the housing that they had endured in the first decade of their marriage.

My mother had worked in Tillie and Henderson's shirt factory, overlooking Derry's Craigavon Bridge. She often told me that, after the war, my father spent his remaining army days as a military policeman, in Derry, and she would wave to him as he patrolled the bridge. They were married shortly after his soldiering ended and he became a postman. As I later discovered, there were many postmen in Derry who were ex-servicemen. I have a photograph of my father, resplendent in his Post Office uniform on his delivery run the Strand Road. His normal working day was to start at the sorting office, in Post Office Street, shortly after 4 a.m. and he worked until noon, unless he had to work overtime. He used to take me with him to the sorting office and out with him in the post office van making deliveries around the city. Dessie McLaughlin was a message boy and he used me to take me for a run on his motor bike around Guildhall Square and along the back of the quay. In later years, he became a well-known travel agent in Derry.

My mother gave up work to look after me and returned when I was well into primary school. They were wonderful parents, who really put me at the centre of their universe. They wanted the best for me and as I grew up, they took a great interest in my education and studies. My father was my first teacher and my first reading book was *The Belfast Telegraph*, where I started reading the headlines and, as I progressed, the first paragraph of the lead story. Maybe, this was also an introduction to politics in which I developed an interest from an early age. Given his ex-army life, my father was always keen to ensure that I was always well dressed and groomed. 'Boots polished, face washed and hair combed,' were values that he instilled. On a Saturday, he swapped his post office uniform for an impressive suit, natty tie and trilby for his weekly outing to George Tracey's Electric Bar and the bookies nearby. As my mother said, he was dressed like a 'Burton's dummy' as he cut an impressive figure. In his army days, he had been a boxer and retained his passion for the sport. One of the first sporting events I attended was when I accompanied him to an amateur boxing night in Derry's Guildhall, where Ireland opposed Scotland. We were up in the balcony from where I had a spectacular view of a great, raucous, night as the home team won.

The city to which I came as a baby was captured by the poet John Hewitt in his poem, *Ulster Names,* where he wrote of a city with its walls, famous for its sieges and its oakgrove, made famous by Colmcille. It was a divided city, whose citizens could not even agree on its name. Its politics was a straight and dogged fight between the Nationalist Party that had only one objective, a United Ireland, and the Unionist Party that supported Northern Ireland remaining a part of the United Kingdom. There was a simple sectarian division as most Catholics supported the Nationalists, whereas almost all Protestants were Unionists. The Catholics called the city Derry, while the Protestants referred to it officially as Londonderry although they may have used the term Derry in everyday conversation. Each side had its own newspaper, *The Derry Journal* for Catholics and *The Londonderry Sentinel* for Protestants. I read *The Sentinel* during the football season, as it provided good reports of Derry City football games and its action shots of the games were a special addition to a Derry City scrapbook that I had made. I did not stop at the back page and I thus became eventually became aware of Protestant/Unionist views on current developments. This was an asset in the development of my political consciousness, as I became aware of what 'the other side' was thinking. The playwright, Brendan Behan once disparagingly said that the city *got the name*

Londonderry from a company of London-based swindlers in the seventeenth century, whose intention was to drive the native Irish off the land and to settle the place with English and Scots. The non-contentious alternative name for the place was to call it the Maiden City, a name given to the city as it had survived three sieges in the seventeenth century, without its walls being breached.

The city in which I grew up traces its origins to a monastery, founded in the 6th century, which sat high on a hill, which became the heart of the walled city more than a thousand years later. The founding of the monastic settlement, Doire, the Oak Grove, was credited to Saint Columba, or Colmcille. The first name for the settlement was Daire Calgach. Daire/Doire was the old Irish word for an oak grove. Calgach was an ancient warrior and Caledonian leader, who claimed the area of North West Ulster to be his. By the 12th century the settlement was known in the Annals of Ulster simply as Doire Cholmcille, in dedication to its monastic founder. With Derry being divided on a religious basis, it is hardly strange to relate that both the Church of Ireland and the Roman Catholic Church have a claim to the site of the original Columban monastic churches. Historical and archaeological study tends to favour St. Augustine's, within the city's walls, as having been an ecclesiastical site for almost fifteen hundred years. The claim that the location of the Long Tower Church was the original monastic site only gained momentum in the closing years of the nineteenth century, thanks mainly to Father William Doherty, later the administrator, who organised the celebrations of 1897, celebrating the thirteen hundredth anniversary of the death of Colmcille.

Derry, or Londonderry, as it was renamed in the early seventeenth century after its plantation by London companies, is a city built on hills, located at the eastern end of a small range of hills, occupying an important position between the Foyle and Swilly valleys, in the North West of Ireland. Street names resonated with kings and aristocrats, William and James as well as Marlborough, Sackville, Clarendon and Tyrconnell. In what became known as the Bogside were streets named after British military heroes, Wellington and Nelson. The origins of the modern city are not in any doubt, as it was London companies which undertook the rebuilding of the city and its walls, in 1610, as part of the Plantation of Ulster. Derry was the last walled city built in Ireland and was long regarded as the jewel in the crown of the Ulster Plantation. Three years later, the city was officially renamed by Royal Charter and the building of the walls was commenced. The city's coat of arms features a skeleton seated on a mossy stone beside a three towered castle on a black background. The top third depicts the coat of arms of the City of London, a red cross and sword on a white background. The castle is thought to relate to a 13th or 14th century keep, but there are many theories about the skeleton. The most popular one is that of a Norman knight starved to death in the castle dungeons in 1332. The city's motto introduced me to my first words of Latin, *Vita, Veritas, Victoria* which translates as *Life, Truth, Victory*. My first memory of seeing the coat of arms and the motto of the city was on Craigavon Bridge, where it can still be seen today.

Amongst the earliest colonists of the city were orphan boys sent over as apprentices from Christ's Hospital in London. It was events in the closing years of the seventeenth century that marked the city as of historic importance to Irish Protestants. Thirteen apprentices shut the city's gates, in 1688, to deny entry to soldiers of the Catholic King, James II. This event triggered a siege that was only lifted in August of the following year. 'No Surrender,' words hurled by the city's defenders in the face of King James, have resonated for Ulster Protestants in the subsequent centuries. The Jacobite army and its French allies, who besieged the city, in 1688/89, had their main encampment on what is now Creggan Estate from where they would fire across the Bogside area into the Walled City itself. With the partition of Ireland after World War I, Londonderry, city and county, were included in the new state of Northern Ireland, which was made up of the six counties of Antrim, Down, Armagh, Tyrone, Fermanagh and Londonderry. The Donegal hinterland was included in the twenty six county Irish Free State.

From the earliest years, Derry Catholics, who made up a majority of the city's citizens, deeply resented being on what they saw as the wrong side of the Border. Londonderry's Protestants, by contrast, were determined not only to ensure that the city remained within Northern Ireland but also that political power in the Corporation should be in Protestant hands. Electoral boundaries were drawn in such a way to ensure that the city's Protestant minority elected twelve members to the Corporation, while the Catholic majority elected only eight members, a position that was established in the 1920s and which was unchanged when I was born. The Corporation was run by the Unionist Party and one had to go back to 1920 to find the last Nationalist Mayor of the city. Similarly, Northern Ireland was run by the Unionist Party, since the inception of the state in May 1921. The Nationalist Party had only ever succeeded in having one piece of legislation passed, the Wild Birds' Protection Act, in 1931.

My home town had therefore two names, Derry and Londonderry. Unlike the lyrics of a song about New York, the names did not reflect a belief that it was 'so good they named it twice.' As a postman, working in a sorting office in the days before post code and electromechanical sorting machines, my father often said that Nationalists addressing letters as Derry, rather than Londonderry, always ran the risk of their letters being sent, by mistake or otherwise, to Derby, in the English Midlands. His practical advice was to write the word 'Local' across the corner of the letter to indicate the intended destination. He also told me that there never was a County Derry as counties in Ulster were a result of the Plantation by the English government in 16th and early 17th centuries and that County Londonderry was specifically created, in 1613, as a result of the merger of various lands. It amused him that the Gaelic Athletic Association, whose structure was firmly built on a county system, was recognising the lasting influence of the Plantation and the English system of administration of Ireland.

Once you got over the political divisions, which many of the city's inhabitants could never do, it would be difficult to deny that my adopted city was a beautiful place in which to grow up. It twas *'Derry of the little hills,'* as the poet, Francis Ledwidge wrote, while stationed at Ebrington Barracks, in 1916. Creggan, built on one of those hills had a panoramic view of the city. The view from the top of Bligh's Lane was magnificent. The skyline was dominated by the spires of the city's two cathedrals, one dating to the seventeenth century, the Anglican cathedral and the other, the Roman Catholic cathedral dating to 1873. There were other domes clearly visible, as the copper domes and spires of the Guildhall, Austin's department store and St. Columb's College stood out in pale green due to oxidation. With the clearance of the slums in Nailors' Row and Fahan Street, the city's seventeenth century walls were clearly visible with the ninety foot high Walker's Pillar looking over the Bogside, with the statue of the former Governor of the city pointed towards the river Foyle, looking for any sign of ships to break the boom and relieve the city. In the distance, Altnagelvin Hospital, opened in 1960, dominated the landscape.

The city is divided by the river Foyle. While the west bank has become almost exclusively Catholic as a result of the Troubles, it was, apart from the Creggan estate, very mixed right up to the early 1970s. The area bounded by Abercorn Road and Bishop's Street was almost exclusively Protestant and the same applied to Rosemount Avenue, Oakfield and Belmont. The Northland and Glen public housing estates were thriving Protestant areas. By the eve of the outbreak of the Troubles, in 1968, there were twelve thousand Protestant electors on the west bank of the River Foyle. A decade later, this figure had fallen to four thousand and continued to dwindle to around a thousand. A sign of the growing self-confidence in the Protestant community can be gauged by the fact that a new Church of Ireland church, St. Peter's was opened on the Culmore Road in 1966. The Protestant Exodus from the west bank began within a few years, in my last school years. It did not seem imaginable in my early childhood. It is one of the great untold stories of the period, which for many was conveniently airbrushed from their narrow narrative of the Troubles.

The city had a thriving sporting and arts life and many schools of distinction, with high reputations for academic achievement. Maybe, it would be truer to say that it was a tale of two cities, where Catholics and Protestants stuck within their own communities, by and large. In the post-war years, the demand for public sector housing and jobs exceeded supply, a phenomenon that was common throughout Britain and Ireland, but was given a special edge for Derry Catholics, who believed that the lack of houses and jobs was deliberately driven by the Unionist government at Stormont. The shirt factory jobs for women eased the financial position in many homes. In the mid-1950s, the opening of the Birmingham Sound Recorder (BSR) factory in Bligh's Lane, on the edge of Creggan, saw jobs for men, the number of which exceeded seventeen hundred, until the factory closed completely in 1967. At its peak, the BSR was supplying turntables and auto-changers to most of the world's record player manufacturers. The largest employer in the city was the American Dupont Corporation, a major success in the efforts to attract foreign inward investment. The problem was that there were not enough jobs being created and unemployment rates in Derry were among the highest in Northern Ireland. The demand for jobs and houses was never far from the surface. Looking back, the situation was akin to a story we read at school of the little Dutch boy who stuck his hand into a hole in a dyke to save his town from flooding. Northern Ireland had many dykes and, with the benefit of hindsight, it is almost safe to say that there was certain inevitability that at some time the dykes would break. What was unknown in the late 1950s and early 1960s was the scale of the possible eruption.

My mother enjoyed singing and taught me songs, some of which I still vividly remember, as I sang along with her the lyrics of *Heart of My Heart*, and *Sing Little Birdie*, the British entry in the Eurovision Song Contest of 1959. She loved taking me by the hand everywhere with her. I remember weekly visits to Lipton's in Bishop Street, where I was always given sweets by the shop assistants, whom I simply knew as Mary and Wee Anne. Derry had a lot of, what appeared to me to be, large shops and by far my favourite was Woolworth's on Ferryquay Street. I was greatly impressed with its dark mahogany counters and especially the sweet counter, behind which stood Bridie Collins, who lived in Carrickreagh Gardens, on the Creggan Estate. She looked like a nurse, in her uniform with her hair tied back behind a white starched half cap, the same you see golfers wearing to keep the sun out of their eyes.

One day, we were walking around Woolworth's and I saw large numbers of children carrying little flags, the same as were hanging from a lot of the buildings in the street and in the city centre. I pleaded with my mother for one but the pleas fell on deaf ears. I could not really understand the logic for such a refusal. Outside, there certainly was music in the Derry air as bands marched towards the Diamond. The bands were so diverse. There were the brass bands resplendent in their uniforms, the bagpipers and the flute bands that jauntily skipped through the city centre. It was my first sight of an Orange march and I was fascinated by the music, the bands and the men in bowler hats wearing orange sashes. Some of them were carrying ceremonial swords and were holding aloft banners with a great diversity of scenes and events. I could not quite understand what a 'Temperance Lodge' was and why there were banners depicting Britannia or Queen Victoria standing over the kneeling figure of a black man, who was wearing only a loin cloth. The 'Burning of Latimer and Ridley' featured quite a lot, and I hadn't a clue who they were. I later discovered that they were Anglican bishops martyred in England in the mid sixteenth century. Then, there were the banners with simply the Crown and the Bible and the proclamation, 'the secret of Britain's greatness.' Pride of place seemed to be reserved for what I thought were poor men doing some kind of penance. They were carrying massive drums strapped across their chests, which I was told were called Lambegs, and were beating these mercilessly. Quite a lot of these poor souls were sweating profusely but were encouraged by the onlookers to beat their drums harder. I wondered what they had done to deserve such punishment. I was told by my mother that I could watch but not cheer and of course, I did not have a flag to wave! To placate me, she took me across the street to Battisti's ice cream parlour.

At some stage in the 1950s, we moved a short distance from the flat in Linsfort Drive to an upstairs flat in Carrickreagh Gardens, where I lived until I was nine years old. It was a block with four two bedroom flats, two on the ground floor and two above. We lived in one of the upstairs flats. A coal fire provided hot water but there were no such luxuries as central heating. The modern conveniences that are taken for granted such as a fridge, a washing machine and a vacuum cleaner were light years away. Mind you, we didn't need a vacuum cleaner as we had no carpet. It was linoleum on the floors. A gas cooker was the source of all meals, operated by putting a shilling into the meter.

The street always seemed to be busy with milkmen, breadmen and coalmen making their deliveries and the gas man emptying the shillings from the meters. The milk float from the Old City Dairy was powered by electricity and had three wheels. We would often get a run in it to the top of the street. Then there was the *Belfast Telegraph* delivery boy, who made a daily appearance around tea time. In days before councils provided residents with the environmentally friendly brown refuse bins for food scraps, we had the 'Brock Boy,' who would arrive with his cart. He knocked on the door and took away scraps of potato skins and rotten food to feed to the pigs. There was occasional excitement in the street with the arrival of the rag man, who would generally give you a few balloons for old clothes that would otherwise have been dumped. Occasionally, he gave us a few coppers. His name was Seamus and he had a donkey with baskets to carry the clothes. We would follow him up Carrickreagh singing the chorus of Donkey Riding, a song we had learned at the Holy Childs' School:

Hey ho, away we go
Donkey riding, donkey riding
Hey ho, away we go
Riding on a donkey.

I quickly made friends with Arthur and Charles Duffy who lived in the same block. At the time, their dad was in the Royal Navy. I remember that one Christmas, they got Grenadier Guard uniforms and paraded up and down in front of our block as though they were on duty at Buckingham Palace. My father showed them how to bear arms and stand to attention like real soldiers. It would have been unthinkable in the 1970s for a Creggan parent to buy a Grenadier Guard uniform for a son and even less likely to see the boy parading around Creggan, resplendent in a red military jacket and wearing a Busby! By that time, the Grenadier Guards were on the streets of Creggan and had been billeted in St. Cecilia's School on Bligh's Lane, after their arrival in the city in 1969. Another Christmas, in the early Sixties, I got a tricycle from my parents and a cousin bought me cowboy outfit, complete with a replica Colt 45 and a sheriff's badge. So the Duffys and I were the young custodians of law and order.

One day when we were on patrol, we saw Mr. Robb, one of our neighbours, walking down the street in a real uniform, a high collared, dark coloured tunic. We saluted him and he returned our salute. I later asked my mother if he was a policeman and was told he was a B Man, a term with which I was completely ignorant. In later years, I discovered that the B Specials were a well armed reserve constabulary and were exclusively Protestant. Calls for their disbandment were regularly voiced by political leaders across the entire nationalist spectrum almost since the foundation of the state. Yet, before the outbreak of the Troubles in the late 1960s, it was a fact that B Specials lived in the Creggan beside their Catholic neighbours. Unknown to me, Mr. Robb also had a reputation as a wrestler and was known in the ring as *Tiger Robb*. In Carrickreagh, we played with Shirley

Robb and the Gallaghers, who were also Protestants, and there was no sectarian bitterness whatsoever. When William Gallagher left Foyle College, he got a job in the Corporation and worked in the Guildhall. I remember my father saying that he would not have got that job if he had been a Catholic. However, I think it is fair to say that I was not aware of any particular tensions between the two communities in Derry in the years preceding the Troubles,

At that time, Carrickreagh Gardens was on the periphery of Creggan but within a few years the Northern Ireland Housing Trust was busy building more houses, as Creggan spilled over into another estate called Foyle Hill. At the top of Carrickreagh, all we could see was a massive building site and the layout of a new road from the Brandywell to Foyle Hill. Derry is built on hills and even at a young age I was greatly impressed by the magnificent view from Foyle Hill across the river as it wound its course from New Buildings. Land had been vested by the Corporation for building these estates even when the War was raging, in 1944. In the quarter of a century from the end of the Second World War, the two estates were eventually to house over eighteen thousand, in what was the greatest housing development in the history of the city. This vast sprawling area was poorly served with amenities. Along Central Drive there was a line of ground floor shops, which were part of Housing Trust flat complexes. Officially, they were called Aran Court and Clare Court but we just called them 'the shops.' In the alleyway behind the shops many a teenager was knee-capped by the IRA in the 1970s, by which time most of our Protestant neighbours had moved out of Creggan.

I was often sent errands there and remember every detail. There was Hegarty's Butchers, with O' Hare's Chemist and Post Office next door and then Hunter's Bakery and Dan Jackson's Grocery. Between this block was the continuation of Bligh's Lane, an old dirt track that became a walkway that went to Creggan Heights. On the next block were Johnny Coyle's all cash store, another grocery owned by Harry Doherty and Mickey Quigley's fish shop, better known as Mickey Fish's. I have many memories of Dr McCabe's surgery, as I seemed to be there often. Dr. Jim McCabe was a tall, impressive man and the walls of his surgery were lined with degrees and certificates. I thought him the most clever and best educated person that I met. He was very innovative as he was one of the first general practitioners to establish a surgery in a housing estate, long before the advent of health centres.

Next door was Dr. McCabe's surgery and then Mc Cool's Newsagents and Frankie Ramsey's fish and chip shop. Hegarty's butcher shop did a roaring trade five days a week but was usually quite empty on Fridays, when there would be a queue outside Mickey Fish's to buy herrings, whiting or red fish. Friday was a day of abstinence for Catholics, and no meat was allowed. This rule was rigidly adhered to when I was growing up. For us, the attraction was that Friday night was usually a meal of fish and chips, with long queues also outside Frankie Ramsey's fish and chip shop. The last addition to the facilities was the establishment of a public house, the Telstar Bar, named after the communications satellite went into space and relayed the first transatlantic television pictures in 1962.

In addition to the shops at Central Drive, there was a regular mobile shop, the All Cash Stores, that toured Creggan and I remember that one of the Doherty brothers, who worked in it had the phrase, 'truly fantastic', to describe literally everything in life. It was from the mobile shop that I acquired my first hobby, collecting flags of the world, which were cards, the size of playing cards that came with packets of bubble gum. There were eighty cards in the collection and on the front of the card was the country's flag, while the back of the card gave details of language, population, capital city and a few phrases. For a long time, I tottered on the edge of a full collection as I awaited Poland, which I eventually got by swapping five of my surplus cards with a boy at school.

My Saturday morning usually began with a listen to Junior Favourites on the radio, hosted by Ed Stewart, better known as Stewpot. My favourite piece of music was *Puff the Magic Dragon*. There were other radio shows that played musical requests, many of which were for BAOR. I asked my father was this anything like BOAC, the airline, and he told me that it meant British Army On the Rhine. Within a few years the Rhine Army would be in Creggan! A Saturday morning lie on was invariably interrupted by mother telling me to get up and go a message to the shops. She usually gave me a note for the butcher, wrapped in a ten shilling note, which I handed across the counter, received my order and the change wrapped in the original note. I then proceed to Mc Cool's and bought comics, *The Beano* and later graduated to *The Valiant*. In the pages of *The Beano*, I was introduced to such colourful characters as Roger the Dodger, Minnie the Minx, Biffo the Bear, the Bash Street Kids, Lord Snooty, Dennis the Menace and his dog, Gnasher. I am sure that someone could do a Ph.D. on the differences between *The Beano* and its rival, *The Dandy*. *The Valiant* had more war stories such as *Captain Hurricane* and introduced me to the detective stories of *Sexton Blake*.

Within a few years, I had graduated from *The Beano* and *The Valiant* to *Charles Buchan's Football Monthly* and began a hobby of collecting football programmes. On a Saturday night, I would be back in Mc Cool's to buy *The Ireland Saturday Night* with its report on all the sporting events of that day, years ahead of *Match of the Day* on television. I avidly read Malcolm Brodie's analysis of Irish League games and the brief reports on the major games in England. Games featuring Celtic and Rangers, in Scotland, always received massive coverage, a first indicator that these teams then had a greater following than many English first division teams. The exceptions were Manchester United and Tottenham Hotspurs, especially as the latter was captained by Danny Blanchflower, who also captained Northern Ireland and who led Spurs to the first Double of the twentieth century as they won both the League and F.A. Cup in the 1960/61 season.

Creggan estate was almost exclusively Catholic and this presented the Catholic Church with the need to ensure the provision of a new church, as well as adequate schooling. At the time, Creggan was part of the Cathedral parish and a new church was planned to be built on what was appropriately called 'the Bishop's Field,' which lay in the middle of the estate. I remember my mother taking me to see it being built. Her brother, John, was one of the crane drivers on the site and for a few minutes I pedalled my tricycle around what would become the centre aisle of St. Mary's Church, which was consecrated in May 1959 and with which I would have many associations in the coming years. Bishop Farren was a man who had no difficulty in mixing religion with politics. In blessing the site for a new church in 1954, he reminded his audience, 'It is an extraordinary thing that we should be building our Church here because this land of Creggan was once Bishop's land before the days of confiscation and plantation.' He returned to this theme five years later, on the opening of the new church. 'The new Church of St. Mary's will be a link connecting Catholic Derry of today with the Catholic Derry of years before the English invasion. Instead, however, of receiving restitution of their land of which they were robbed by the Confiscation, the Catholics had to buy it back at the cost of £400 an acre.'

I have memories of visiting my grandparents. My father's father was still alive and lived in Bridge Street, which is just off Carlisle Road, in the city centre. He was a veteran of the First World War, after which he worked in Brown's Foundry, in Foyle Street. The house in Bridge Street was a tall three storey building, which housed many of the Murray family. There were plenty of maiden aunts and two of my married aunts, Bridget and Martha also lived in the house with their husbands when they were married. Granda was very much into the Ancient Order of Hibernians, which my father called 'the Green Orangemen,' which I did not understand. It was a fraternal, Catholic lay organisation, whose heyday was in the opening decades of the 20th century. My granny Mc Brearty lived in Elmwood Street, a street of terraced houses sloping down to the Lecky Road, which sat in the shadow of the Long Tower church. I remember her singing to me when I went to visit her and she always gave me sweets. The song I remember was also a skipping song:

"My Aunt Jane, she called me in,
She gave me tea out her wee tin,
Half a bap with sugar on the top
And three wee brandy balls after that."

Her house had no bathroom and the toilet was outside in the back yard. My first friendships were with the Seamus and Brian Carlin who lived in number 12. Brennan's fish and chip shop on Stanley's Walk backed on to Elmwood Street and I would often be sent in the back gate to order what was definitely the best fish in Derry. One of the first bonfires I saw was in Elmwood Street, on 15th August, and for some reason I thought it was especially for my birthday but was quickly disabused of such notions.

The McBreartys had to Derry from west Donegal in the 1840s and Granda McBrearty had been a docker and had been very involved in brass bands right through to middle age. Granny Mc Brearty died when I was six. She had been looked after by my aunt Peggy, who was not married. I later learned that the landlord tried to evict Aunt Peggy from the house, when granny died, but a very good solicitor, Claude Wilton, represented her and won her the right to remain. A few years later she married an English sailor, Ted Outhwaite from west Yorkshire. He left the navy and got a job in the power station at Coolkeragh. I remember their wedding reception as it was the first one I attended. It was held in the Melville Hotel on Foyle Street. In those days, it was more a wedding breakfast than an all day affair as the newlyweds made the short journey to the Great Northern Railway station at the end of Foyle Street, to catch the noon train for their honeymoon in Dublin. Ted and Peggy had a daughter, Joan, and she and her mother came to stay with us in Carrickreagh when Joan was born, as their house in Elmwood Street did not have a bathroom. I remember my mother using the large bottom drawer of a chest of drawers in her bedroom as a bed for Joan. When I looked at Joan, I really wanted a sister. Everybody else at school seemed to be getting one and I felt left out.

The first school I attended was the Holy Child School, which had opened in 1956. On Monday August 17th, Bishop Neil Farren dedicated the school and concelebrated Mass in the Assembly Hall. It was the first time that a public Mass had been celebrated in the Creggan Estate. *The Derry Journal*, of the following day, described it as a 'Red Letter Day.' The estate, which had started to take shape in the late 1940s still had neither church nor schools. The Journal went on to say that the school was, 'Designed with the object of making a strong appeal to the child mind and there are some revolutionary features. Instead of having a large playground, the playing area is broken into several intimate units.' The school was supposed to cater for 384 pupils but quickly became oversubscribed, due to the vast numbers of infants on the estate. It was forced to operate on a dual basis of 'morning children,' who started school at nine o' clock and 'evening children,' who came to school at one o' clock. In addition, many of the children on the estate attended St. Eugene's in Francis Street, run by the Sisters of Mercy or its counterpart in the Long Tower, both of which were known as 'The Wee Nuns,' before transferring to the nuns' primary schools that were known as 'The Big Nuns.'

At the Holy Child, there were three forms, infants, juniors and seniors and three classes in each form. I was enrolled as a morning child as my parents thought it better that I got used, from an early age, to rising early in the morning as a good preparation for life. Our first day was assembly in what appeared a very large hall as we were sorted into classes. We returned to the hall regularly for P.E. lessons which mostly consisted of hoopla hoops and bean bags. The assembly hall also housed the school piano and for singing lessons we gathered round the piano. In class, I sat beside Deirdre O' Hara, who lived beside my aunt in Dunaff Gardens and Charles Duffy, who lived next door to me in Carrickreagh. My first teacher was Miss Daly, who told us she was from the country. In fact, Marian hailed from Fermanagh and one of her brothers, Edward, was ordained and became a curate in Derry, where he would eventually become bishop. My memories of Miss Daly's class are of painting, at which I did not excel and singing at which I excelled. She encouraged us in community singing rather than solo performances. I do recall being admonished by her for one solo effort that I gave, which was a rendition of *Silent Night*. My crescendo in the last lines was 'Sleep in heaven with police,' which I was informed was inaccurate. No wonder she preferred us merrily singing as a group and I well remember '*Paul's Little Hen*,' and its fate when it met the fox, who was not the magnificent one, created by Roald Dahl:

> "*Paul's little hen flew away from the farmyard,*
> *Ran down the hillside and into the dale.*
> *Paul hurried after but down in the brambles,*
> *There sat a fox with a great bushy tail.*
>
> *Cluck! Cluck! Cluck!*
> *Cried the poor little creature.*
> *Cluck! Cluck! Cluck!*
> *But she cried in vain.*
> *Paul made a spring but could not save her.*
> "*Now I shall never dare go home again.*"

Of course, religious instruction also featured heavily as we were due to make First Communion in our second year. I could recite the Our Father and Hail Mary. I greatly impressed my teacher by telling her father had taught me that Lucifer used to be an angel before being banished from Heaven for being too proud and thinking himself equal to God. Aside from being a poor hand at painting, however, I was a wizard at multiplication tables and arithmetic because of my father's instruction. These attributes must have impressed as I was selected to skip junior class and advance to seniors, where my new teacher was Miss Harvey. However, I had to go back to the Juniors' class every Tuesday for religious instruction for first Communion. I looked forward to that big day in our lives but somewhat dreaded the prospect of our first confession. Although, in canon law, we had attained the age to have what was called 'the use of reason,' I had difficulty in putting together any coherent list of mortal sins that I may have committed. Having rhymed off the Ten Commandments, few of which I understood, I did not appear to have broken any of them and was told that I could confess any venial sins such being disobedient at home or in class. This was quite a relief.

With first confession now out of the way, I made my First Communion in St. Mary's Church. Dressed in short-trouser suit, hair stuck down with Brylcreem rather than Corporation water to hide my 'Bull's Lick', I must have looked angelic. Those were the days when I had a head of hair. I should add that the natural parting of my hair was from right to left. My mother tried her utmost to ensure that my hair would be parted 'the right way;' from left to right but my Bull's Lick continued to be an ever-present a distraction. After Mass on first communion Saturday morning, we were marched back to the Assembly Hall of the Holy Child School for cream buns and lemonade, before heading off to be presented to relatives and gleefully accept donations. I opened my first bank account at the Trustee Savings Bank with the money I had collected that day, which amounted to almost eight pounds. I regarded it as a fortune.

The move up to the Seniors' class seemed a challenge, as the leisurely days of juniors were quickly left behind. We started on a well trodden educational experience that emphasised the 'Three Rs,' reading, writing and arithmetic. From reading the headlines of the *Belfast Telegraph* at home, I had gone beyond reading material even before going to school. For Christmas 1957, I was given two cowboy annuals, which I still have, *Roy Rogers* and *Gene Autry* with stories with titles such as *Apache Blood, Pioneers of the Old West and The Valley of the Bones*. The reading material at the Holy Child's was less blood-curdling as our reading book series was *Dick and Dora*, with their beloved pets, Nip and Fluff. At school, I enjoyed painting although my efforts were woeful. Religious instruction took the form of stories from the Bible and learning Catechism by heart. Catholic schools used the Maynooth Catechism of 1951, neatly arranged in sections covering the Unity and Trinity of God, Creation, Actual Sin etc. We were put through our paces learning the section called *The Creed*, of which the following were some of the questions and tenets of faith:

'*Q. Who made the world? A. God made the world.*
Q. Who is God? A. God is our Father in Heaven, the Creator and Lord of all things.
Q. Where is God? A. God is everywhere but in a special way He is in heaven, where He is seen by the angels and saints.
Q. If God is everywhere, why do we not see Him. A. We do not see God, because He is a spirit and therefore cannot be seen with bodily eye.
Q. Does God see us? A. God sees us for nothing is hidden from his all-seeing eyes.'

I was always intrigued by the last question and at home would look intently at the large picture of the Sacred Heart that hung above the fireplace, as it did in almost every Catholic household. When I moved from side to side, it seemed that the eyes of Jesus followed me around the room, tending to confirm the Catechism that we had learned at school. As we were being prepared for First Communion, one of the Creggan priests, Fr. McLaughlin, came into class and asked us questions from the Catechism, which provoked a Pavlovian response. One day he asked could anyone tell him a story from the Old Testament and I proceeded to give a version of one of my favourites, *Joseph*, without an amazing multi-Technicolor dream coat. This was many years before Andrew Lloyd Webber made it into a musical. For my effort, I was given a three penny bit, which I spent on sweets. I think that Lloyd Webber got considerable more for his endeavours.

I had one break in my schooling at the Holy Child's which was when I had to go into Altnagelvin hospital to have my tonsils removed. Altnagelvin was the first general hospital to be built in the United Kingdom after the Second World War. It was a bit like a holiday adventure as the hospital seemed to be miles from Derry and we had to take two buses to get to it. The first thing I remember was the hideous sculpture that greeted me when I got off the bus from the Guildhall. It was of Princess Macha and was regarded as a major and prestigious piece by Banbridge born artist, F.E. McWilliam. The statue is still there, and every time I visit the hospital, I am reminded of the time when I had my tonsils removed. What was termed 'Modern Art' adorned the walls on the ground floor. To me it seemed like something we could have done at school by taking a bucket of paint and splashing it over a canvas and then drawing squares. My antipathy to modern art was thus established at a young age and has remained with me throughout my life. The happy memory of Altnagelvin was that ice cream was prescribed as a stimulus to recovery.

It wasn't just the hospital with which I had early experiences of the National Health Service. All the sweets and chocolate, on which I was weaned, without understanding of their affects, took an early toll on my teeth and I had to go to Mr. Charlie Gallagher's dental surgery in Clarendon Street to have four teeth removed. Clarendon Street was then known in Derry as the street of the doctors and dentists, many of whom had their surgeries on the ground floor of their three storey Edwardian terraced buildings and lived on the upstairs floors. Mr. Gallagher applied gas very liberally to me, presumably in the hope of knocking me out. It worked and when the removal of the offending teeth was completed I felt that I was vomiting buckets of blood as I came around and that I was going to die. I survived and Mr Gallagher remained my dentist until he retired. As a young man, Charlie Gallagher had been a very good Gaelic footballer and played for, and captained, his native Cavan. As a dentist, he had a sharp turn of phrase and stories abounded about him. One female patient reputedly told him that she did not know what was worse; having a tooth out or having a baby. Quick as a flash Charlie replied, 'Well dear, if you make up your mind, I will adjust the chair accordingly.'

A few years later when I was at primary school, I had my next brush with the National Health Service, when I had to attend Altnagelvin Hospital again, this time to have a wart removed from my back. This was mild compared to a medical visit at school when we all had eye tests and I failed miserably, being told that I would need glasses, especially for reading books and making sense of what was written on the blackboard. This all seemed reasonably straight forward until I was also told that I would have to use a special eye ointment for two weeks before wearing glasses. An appointment was duly made with Harris Rundle, an optician in Shipquay Street, and I began a course of ointment. I thought I was going to go blind as the ointment made my eyes very bleary and removed whatever ability I had to read books or blackboard. It was with some delight that I finally got my first pair of wire framed glasses, later popularised by John Lennon, although I think that his spectacles did not come via the National Health Service.

Chapter Two
Early Years at the Christian Brothers

A headed 'goal' in Celtic Park – 'the British Grenadiers' – Money for the Black Babies – Emptying the ink boats & playing Conkers

Two years at the Holy Child passed quickly and admission to a primary school became a major issue. Given the phenomenal growth of the Creggan and Foyle Hill housing estates, it seems strange to relate that there were no primary schools factored into this development. The nearest primary schools were the Rosemont Boys' and Girls' schools, situated just outside of Creggan. My parents wanted me to go to the Christian Brothers' School, the CBS, which was situated at the Brow of the Hill, along the Lecky Road and a considerable distance from Creggan. My father, and his father before him, had both attended the school. By the time it came my turn to transfer to a primary school, the CBS had a high reputation for achieving good results in the Eleven Plus exam, which was the passport to a grammar school secondary education.

The Christian Brothers was a religious community, founded in Ireland at the beginning of the 19th century by Edmund Ignatius Rice, a rich merchant. The order came to Derry in 1854, as educators of Catholic boys from poor backgrounds. When the first principal, Brother Larkin, opened the doors, on 13th March, he expected a small intake. Instead 290 boys turned up and with the two Christian Brothers, who accompanied him to Derry, taught classes of almost one hundred pupils. They set high standards for generations of pupils and prided themselves on the academic results they achieved. So good was their reputation that inevitably there were more applicants than places available and my application was rejected. Rosemount Boys' Primary School was much nearer to Carrickreagh, about fifteen minutes' walk, but my father really wanted me to go the Brothers. He arranged an interview with the principal, Brother Byrne and took me along. He also brought a photograph of his class from the 1920s and proudly told Brother Byrne the lineage of relations that had attended since the school was established. He must have made a big impression as a few weeks later I was told that I would be following his footsteps. At the Christian Brothers I would spend the next five years of schooling.

The main school building had at one time been the home of Alderman Hogg, a wealthy merchant, whose quarry gave the city the name 'Quarry Street,' and formed part of his large demesne. In 1846, it became a seminary and the residence of the Catholic Bishop of Derry, Most Rev. Dr. Mc Ginn, who named it the 'Brow of the Hill.' The classroom we first entered had been the dining room of the seminarians and the classrooms upstairs were the study hall. Although the school was run by Christian Brothers, by the beginning of the nineteen sixties the majority of the teachers were laymen.

In our very first week at the Christians, as we simply called the school, we were abruptly introduced to corporal punishment in the form of the leather slap, which could be administered for anything from the lowest misdemeanour, like talking in class, to getting homework wrong or missing football practice. I think that the Christian Brothers were not unique in their use of the strap and it was futile to complain at home about its use as it was an accepted tenet of faith. My father once tried to comfort me, when I complained that I had been slapped for something I had not done by telling me that he had similarly been punished in his school days, for robbing a birds' nest, when he had been innocent. I was told to remember the times when I should have been slapped but was not!

Our first teacher was a Mr. McLaughlin, who used the strap liberally in first term. By contrast, Brian Sharkey was a model teacher and I enjoyed my year under his tutelage. In Primary 5, I was taught by Tommy Carr, who, as principal in the early 1970s, was seriously injured when the IRA left a booby-trapped bomb in the school grounds. The only Christian Brother who taught me for a substantial period was Brother Keane, who took us for two years, covering the year of the Eleven Plus, referred to as the 'the Qually,' and the year preceding it.

When I went to the Christians, one of the first changes to my daily routine, apart from a long walk to school, was that I had to either take a lunch or go to my Aunt Peggy's house in Elmwood Street. She was the youngest of my mother's sisters. There were plenty of Creggan boys at the Christians, including classmates who also transferred with me from the Holy Child's School. Many of us were good friends such as Brian Barr, Nigel Cooke, Gerry McLaughlin and Damien Conaghan. While most of my classmates lived in the area that later became known as the Bogside, there were quite a few from Creggan and the Waterside. My contemporaries at the Christians came from all over Derry City. My class was an interesting mix. Eamon McAteer was a son of Eddie McAteer, the Nationalist MP at Stormont, while Declan McGonigle was the son of Stephen McGonigle, McAteer's Labour and Trade Union opponent in Stormont elections. Colm Keenan was the son of Sean Keenan, an IRA leader who was interned in both the 1940s and 1950s.

Over lunchtime, we sat in class together eating our sandwiches before going to the large play yard, overlooking the Lecky Road, at the bottom of the long school walk. The school was set amidst what I would have called a forest of trees and in the autumn of each year, we would eagerly engage in playing conkers, a game I hardly ever see played by youngsters nowadays. There were plenty of horse chestnut trees within the school grounds and when the green outer casing of the seed turned brown, it revealed the conker inside. To make the conkers harder, I used to bring them home and have my mother bake them for a few minutes in the oven. Through the centre of the conker I would then drive a nail and thread a string with a knot tied at the end and now my conker was now ready for competition.

We had established rules of engagement. Each player would take turns at trying to hit the opposing conker by wrapping the conker string around one hand, taking the conker in the other hand and swinging it down hard on the opposing conker. As my conker had no history of competition, it was readily challenged by boys who boasted that theirs was, for example, a 'tenner', meaning that was the number of its victories together with the previous scores it had acquired from its vanquished opponents. I would then take great pleasure as my untested, but well hardened and prepared conker, did battle and split the opposing conker in two after a few well-timed hits. Suddenly, I would have an 'elevener' and would be the envy of my classmates. The sweet sense of victory would never last too long as my recently vanquished classmates queued up to smash my conker in duels of attrition. In spite of the best home baking, every conker had a finite life span. Someone once asked our teacher if William the Conqueror was so named because of a prowess at conkers, which brought a blistering response. Another childhood game, which we played, and that seems to have all but disappeared was marbles, which again had its own strict rules. You had to be fully aware of terms such as 'scoots', 'high drops' and 'everything or nothing' to make any progress in playing.

There were no canteen facilities in the Christians and on days when I didn't go to Aunt Peggy's, I usually brought a packed lunch, together with a thermos flask of either tea or soup. Of course, I remember our daily one third pint of milk, the crates of which were delivered at the top of the school. Harry Devenny, from William Street, who was a few years older than me, was in charge of despatching the milk to the various classes and divided out the milk quotas and crates to the two boys from each class who were sent to complete the delivery run. Occasionally, we got orange juice either together with, or as an alternative, to milk. We were not that keen on the milk, half of which was thick cream, and seemed to us like the slops that the dairy was going to discard.

In our early years, we were taught the consequences of failure in regular tests, in that if you got a lower mark than gained in the previous exam, you were slapped. In an arithmetic test I succeeded in getting all ten questions right, thus gaining top mark of 100%. Next time round, I got one question wrong but still had the top mark in class. My punishment was a slap on each hand and an admonishment for falling from the dizzy heights. I still have a prize that I won, *The Boys Book of Soccer*, given to me by Mr Sharkey for competence in Arithmetic. It was the 1955 Annual, not the most up-to-date version, as it was presented to me in 1962. However, this did not stop me from enjoying its contents, which included famous dates in Soccer History. The first entries were the story of the formation of Notts County, the oldest club in the English League, in 1862. The first FA Cup Final was played a decade later, in which a team called Wanderers beat the Royal Engineers 1-0.

In our first year at the Christians the rigours of the Three Rs were intensified and great emphasis was placed on cursive handwriting and the difference between capital and small letters in writing. Each desk had an inkwell and we started writing with a rather primitive nib pen, mounted on a slim wooden handle. I am sure that the desks were the ones at which my father had sat and that the pens were also recycled from his days. I enjoyed writing with this modern version of a quill. My mother told me that this should be the only time in my life when I should be 'emptying the ink boats,' which was a Derry expression for signing on the dole, the local expression for being unemployed. However, she also reminded me that one of the safest jobs in Derry would be working in the dole office, as it was unlikely ever to be closed down! One Christmas I asked my parents for a real fountain pen and was delighted when I received a Parker Duofold, which I kept for special occasions of writing and used it when sitting my Eleven Plus.

One of my real adventures in my primary school days was when I was invited to go with our neighbours, the Whites, to Belfast, on a day trip. They were then living in number 19 Carrickreagh, having moved in after one of the former occupants had committed suicide. They had one son, Tony, who was also at the Christian Brothers. Mr. White worked for a building company and was one of the few Creggan residents to have a car. I was really excited about going to Belfast, where I had been born but had only ever heard my father refer to as 'an Orange hole,' a term with which I was totally unfamiliar. It was my first journey away from Derry and I remember seeing the motorway, the M2, and being astounded at the number of lanes it had in each direction.

My abiding memory of the day trip is the time we spent in Smithfield market and my visit to a pet shop, where I bought a mouse, while Tony bought a tortoise.

I was given a shoe box to house my new purchase, to ensure that I did not lose it on the return journey. On the way back, I christened my new pet Mousie and was as proud as Punch when I showed him to my mother. Needless to say, her reaction was not what I would have hoped. 'Keep that thing away from me,' she thundered and I felt poor Mousie was being rejected. My father was much more stoical about my acquisition, to the extent that he undertook to build a little wooden cage for Mousie, which he duly did. Mousie looked out at the world through the thin wire mesh, except when I transported him around the place on my shoulder. I had the notion that I could teach him to perform acrobatics but this did not come to pass. My biggest challenge was what to feed him and I decided that Doherty's sausages would be ideal. He seemed to revel in this diet and began to fatten up until one morning, about six months after he arrived, I found him lying in his cage, tiny legs pointing to heaven. He was dead as a door nail. I think I overfed him and was distraught, a sentiment not shared by my mother, who advised that there should be no replacement. Thankfully, my mother did not report me for cruelty to animals. Tony White and I held a solemn and sombre funeral service and buried Mousie in the back garden, deep enough in the soil to prevent any cat feasting on his corpse.

From the seemingly ridiculous to the sublime as I recall another early experience at the Christians, when we stood and prayed for Irish army soldiers, killed in a far-off country in Africa, called the Congo. They were peacekeepers and we were told that they had been butchered by savage tribesmen. We were told by the Brothers that their funerals in Dublin were the largest seen in Ireland since those of Charles Stewart Parnell and Michael Collins. We weren't at all clear as to the identity of these famous Irishmen.

The Christian Brothers placed a great emphasis on what could be called an Irish nationalist education and all things Irish. Sporting activities were confined to Gaelic games, with football prevailing over hurling. All of this was at a time when Derry could easily have been defined as a soccer city. Gaelic games were more prevalent in the county, well outside the city boundaries. For the Gaelic Athletic Association, the GAA, soccer, rugby and cricket were 'foreign games', which its members were forbidden from playing. Our Gaelic football lessons took place at Celtic Park, about a ten minute walk away from school. It is now a magnificent stadium that has been developed by the GAA but then its playing surface was either bone hard on dry days or a quagmire in the rain. The changing rooms were more like a cow byre, with a tin roof, a couple of wooden benches and no lockers, showers or toilet facilities. Along the way to Celtic Park, I was sent to collect the key from Johnny Brown, who lived a few doors away from my aunt Peggy, in Elmwood Street. Beside Celtic Park was the Alpha Tennis club, which appeared to have more attractive changing rooms than ours. Their tennis courts were well lined, whereas there were no markings on the Celtic Park pitch.

Football practice was far from enjoyable, with its emphasis on kicking and catching and trying to block an opponent's shots. With eagle eyes, Brother Keane would be on the lookout for shirkers and woe betide the boy who dribbled the ball, soccer style, rather than pick it up. Brother Keane would chase us around Celtic Park, leather strap in hand, shouting, 'none of your Brandywell stuff here', and would literally and liberally slap the backside of any boy dribbling the ball. The Brothers were in awe of the football played by Kerry, the aristocrats of Gaelic football, who were regularly in all-Ireland finals at Croke Park and were the masters of the art of the kick and catch game. The Brothers waxed lyrically about the great Kerry teams and players like the rugged Paddy Bawn Brosnan, whose training was on the fishing boats in Dingle, and highly talented Mick O' Connell from Valentia Island. No one in class was excused from football practice.

After our sessions of catching, kicking and blocking we played a match. I played at left corner forward and the highlight of my playing days was to score two goals in Celtic Park. For the second goal I palmed the ball into the net past Dessie Baldrick. A few minutes later, Nigel Cooke headed the ball into the net, for what looked to me a great goal. However, Brother Keane, apoplectic with rage at this soccer tactic being employed, disallowed the goal and hit Nigel a right slap with the leather strap on the backside. Rather than acquiesce in his punishment, Nigel tried to explain, most logically, that if he had caught the ball and brought it down to shoot, the chance to score would have been gone. This just enraged Brother Keane even further and Nigel was duly sent off. It was a shock to us soccer followers to learn that the rules of the GAA did not permit a player to head the ball. To the best of my knowledge, the GAA has not changed that rule to this very day. Terry Duddy got a belt of the strap for cheering the disallowed goal. Matters got worse on another occasion. I have a vivid memory of Danny Mc Closkey from Waterloo Street, being put over a desk and walloped on the backside with a leather strap for missing a football session in Celtic Park. It didn't seem fair but no one complained lest they receive the same treatment. I think the Brothers looked scornfully on our attachment to soccer and would have thought that we were very likely to go round singing the lyrics of a song, *Football Crazy*, sung by Jamie Mc Gregor and Robin Hall:

> *He's football crazy*
> *He's football mad*
> *And the football, it has robbed him*
> *Of the wee bit of sense he had.*

Our early musical education at the Brothers came courtesy of the BBC. We listened to *Singing Together*, the annual series of radio programmes of popular music for schools, which encouraged us to join in with the singing. We even had booklets of the lyrics, provided free to the school by the BBC. For many of us, this was our only musical education. There were always plenty of sea shanties such as *Bill Bone's Hornpipe* and *The Mermaid. Green Grow the Rushes Oh* and *The Twelve Days of Christmas* were great exercises in memorising litanies as well as giving great pleasure as we belted them out. Looking back, there were many Irish songs included in the repertoire of songs we sang in our primary school days, like *Brennan on the Moor, the Minstrel Boy, the Mallow Fling* and *Molly Malone*. We were almost in tears as we sang *Robin Adair*, a lament by a distraught widow on the death of her husband. There were songs from all the nations of the British Isles, and our spirits were lifted by a very bloody version of *Men of Harlech*, with lyrics such as:

'Tis the tramp of Saxon foemen
Saxon spearmen, Saxon bowmen,
Be they knights or hinds or yeomen,
They shall bite the ground
...Hurl the reeling horsemen over,
Let the earth dead foemen cover...'

For the Scots, there was the *Skye Boat Song*, remembering Bonnie Prince Charlie. For the more discerning ears, Kathleen Ferrier gave a beautiful and moving rendition of *Blow the Wind Southerly*. We also lustily sang *Sweet Lass of Richmond Hill, the British Grenadiers* and *Waltzing Matilda*. I wonder what the Christian Brother made of us singing the following lyrics:

'Then let us fill a bumper and drink a health to those
Who carry caps ad pouches, and wear those louped clothes.
May they and their commanders live happily all their years.
With a tow, row, row, row, row, row, for the British Grenadiers.'

Some of the boys who sang these words would, in their late teens, become members of the IRA and would be shooting at the same British Grenadiers when the Troubles erupted in Derry!

Within a few years of our introduction to *Singing Together*, we had musically advanced to the point where we participated in the school choirs in Feis Dhoire

Colmcille. Feis is an Irish word for arts and cultural festival and the plural of 'feis' is 'feiseanna.' In the divided society of Northern Ireland, there were two feiseanna in the Maiden City. The Londonderry Feis was established in 1900 and Feis Dhoire Colmcille was in 1922. Both were held in the Guildhall, which was about all they had in common. For the Londonderry Feis, the Union Flag was prominently displayed on the stage and the national anthem, *God Save the Queen*, was sung at the end of each day's performances. For Feis Dhoire Colmcille, the hall was bedecked in green banners but there was no Irish Tricolour as any display of it was banned under government legislation. The Guildhall is a magnificent red sandstone building of neo Gothic architectural design, which had been opened in 1890. While it was not a museum in the 1960s, it had a collection of chandeliers and marble sculpture, including a full-sized statue of Queen Victoria in ceremonial gown and robes. It was the first statue of the Queen to be unveiled in Ireland. The many stained glass windows told the city's history from the monastic settlement of St. Columba through Gaelic resurgence in the 16th century to the siege of Derry in 1688/89. As primary school boys, we took very little interest in such splendour but were well aware that during the famous siege, dogs, cats and rats were the staple diets if not luxuries of the city's starving inhabitants and that the price of a mouse was sixpence.

The Christian Brothers did not participate in the Londonderry Feis and focused all their efforts on Feis Dhoire Colmcille. It was approached with the usual competitive focus, as the Brothers expected us to win every competition and carry off the accolades of the adjudicators. The Feis was held annually during the Easter school holidays. Looking back, it is interesting to recall that while we had no knowledge of either music or Irish we formed quite good choirs. The techniques were simple. Firstly, adopting a method known as tonic sol-fa, the notes of the chosen piece were written on the black board and we learned them off by heart. When we were sufficiently competent in this, the Irish lyrics were written up in phonetics and we proceeded to master the piece. One piece stands out in my memory from all others. For the three part choir, the chosen piece was a Jacobite anthem, *Rosc Catha Na Mumhan*, written in the 18th century by Piaras Mac Gearailt and translated into English as *The Battle Cry of Munster*. For a week, every afternoon after school ended, we sang out the notes, which started:

Do Re La Ti Do La So Mi Do
Re Mi Fa Mi Re La So Fa Mi Re Do La
So La La Ti Do Fa La So Fa So Mi Do
Re Me Fa Me Re La So Fa Me Re Re Re

Having mastered the notes we proceeded to the phonetics of the Irish lyrics and soon were singing away like native speakers, without knowing a word of the meaning. This was quite an achievement and it was only years later that I discovered the translation of the lyrics.

> *D'aithníos féin gan bhréag ar fhuacht*
> *'S ar anfa Thétis taobh le cuan*
> *Ar chanadh na n-éan go séiseach suairc*
> *Go gcasadh mo Shéasar glé gan ghruaim*

> *Measaim gur subhach don Mhumhain an fhuaim*
> *'S dá maireann go dubhach de chrú na mbua*
> *Torann na dtonn le sleasaibh na long*
> *Ag tarraingt go teann 'n-ár gceann ar cuairt.*

> I knew it well by the chilly weather
> And the fury of Thetis by the shore,
> And by the tuneful singing of the birds
> That my Caesar free from gloom would return.

> I feel the news is welcome to Munster,
> And for the downtrodden race of victors.
> The crashing waves on the sides of vessels,
> Drawing baldly on a visit to us

The theme was the promise that a French fleet was on its way over the seas to free Ireland and bring back the Wild Geese, the Jacobite army that left Ireland after defeat in the Williamite Wars. Ireland being Ireland, the music was also later in an Orange folk song, *Boyne Water*.

Although we competed in solo singing competitions, these were regarded by the Brothers as a warm-up for the main event, the choirs. I still remember standing alone on the stage of the Guildhall's Main Hall singing out *Casadh an tSugain, the Twisting of the Rope*. Again, without knowing the meaning of the Irish lyrics, I started off *Do casadh cailin deas orm in uaigneas na dtra,* which translated into English as *A lovely girl met me in the loneliness of the beach*. Maybe the Brothers deliberately kept the translation from us, lest we might have had impure thoughts! A few years ago, I was watching the film, *Brooklyn*, and in the middle of it was a rendition of that very song I sang solo in the Feis, just over half a century earlier. I participated for two years in the choirs and we swept the boards in all three categories, the Gregorian Chant, Three Part and Unison. Anything less would have been regarded as failure and the Brothers didn't do failure.

Tommy Carr was our singing teacher and he drilled us with military precision in preparation for the Feis. In a similar way, Brother Keane coached the school team, featuring my classmates, to victory in the Rice Cup, a Gaelic football competition played against other Christian Brothers' Schools in Northern Ireland. In whatever we did, the Brothers ensured that we were competitive and winning meant everything. When the Brothers were not drilling us in the arts of Gaelic football, singing and teaching us the three Rs with an eye on the Eleven Plus, they were very strong on religious instruction and weekly collections for the Missions. Each morning, class began with prayers and my fondest memories are of the celebrations in honour of Our Lady in the month of May. We built a Marian shrine and were encouraged to bring in flowers on a daily basis to adorn it. Each morning, we would stand and sing '*Bring Flowers of the Rarest-The Queen of the May*,' a most uplifting hymn of celebration with lyrics '*Oh Mary, we crown thee with blossoms today/ Queen of the angels and Queen of the May*.' A month later, we were singing *Saint Columba, Saint Columba, holy patron of our town*,' Columba being one of our own, as opposed to St. Patrick who came to Ireland as a slave from Wales. Of course, we also regularly prayed for the conversion of 'pagan England' and were reminded that one of the original verses of the hymn *Faith of Our Fathers,* was dedicated to this very sentiment;

> "*Faith of our Fathers! Mary's prayers*
> *Shall win our country back to thee:*
> *And through the truth that comes from God*
> *England shall then indeed be free.*
> *Faith of our Fathers. Holy Faith!*
> *We will be true to thee till death*"

As part of our religious instruction we were taught about Purgatory and Limbo as well as Heaven and Hell. Our concept of heaven was cherubic angels singing and spending the rest of the time filling the sky with clouds. Hell was simply taken from Dante's *Inferno*. The half way house was a place called Purgatory, where souls, not ready to enter heaven, were cleansed of the non-mortal or venial sins that prevented them being united with God. Limbo was the place to which the souls of babies, who died, without having been baptised, were consigned. I felt it was very wrong to deprive the souls of such babies of entry to heaven as they had never done anything wrong in their short lives. Eventually, the Church abolished Limbo. As a combination of my education with the Christian Brothers and being an altar boy, I was drawn into Catholic rituals such as praying for the holy souls in Purgatory. We were told that such prayers, especially around the feast of the Holy Souls, would earn indulgences for such souls and help them on their journey to heaven. There were plenary and partial indulgences to be earned and after we had prayed for the souls of our departed relatives we were encouraged to pray especially for those souls, who had no one to pray for them. I felt good going home from St. Mary's Church at the thought that I had helped a few souls on their journey towards heaven. A few years later, I was shocked to learn that the Medieval Church had engaged in selling indulgences, much the same way as Lloyd George sold peerages.

The Christian Brothers had many schools in underdeveloped countries in Africa and South America and were eager to make us aware of the conditions of children in these schools. They encouraged us to raise money to support them. This was long before many charities had been established for the relief of what became known as the Third World. Each morning, my mother gave me a penny or two, which was not to be spent on sweets but given for what we called 'the Black Babies.' We had collections in class as well as raffles. In our first years, the row in class that contributed the most money would get off homework at the weekend. Quite an inducement, given the amount of homework the Brothers regularly gave us, even though it detracts from the concept of altruism. I am sure the Black Babies did not mind. During the Troubles, it was often said that the rioters were somewhat loath to target black soldiers, which may have had something to do with the school time memories of the Black Baby collections.

As part of our religious instruction, we were taught about the Christian martyrs of the early church and for more modern times we learned about a man called the Curé of Ars, a French priest, who jousted with the devil and performed many exorcisms. The Brothers regaled us with stories of titanic battles between the two of them, with the devil often throwing the Curé around a room as he tried to make him submit. The devil was a living being, not a figment of the imagination. The Curé, John Vianney was canonised a saint in the mid 1920s. The world that the Christian Brother set out before us was one of good versus evil; everything was black and white with no grey matter in between.

Chapter Three
The Altar Boys and Life Beyond School

Thuribles, Incense, Gregorian Chants and the FA Cup

My introduction to the Latin verses of the Gregorian chant coincided with the opening of a new part of my life, as St. Mary's recruited a new intake of altar boys, including a number of us who were at the Christian Brothers. I have heard Christy Moore, an Irish folk singer; jokingly talk about becoming an altar boy. He said it was akin to being initiated into a secret society, with its own language and rituals. Whilst secret societies have abounded in Ireland over the centuries, I would certainly not consider the altar boys to be one of them.

Fr. George McLaughlin was our teacher and, at our initial training session, he said the first words that would be addressed to us as altar boys and the response we would make:

Priest: *'Introibo ad altare Dei.'*
I will go to the altar of God.
Server: *'Ad Deum qui laetificat juventutem meam.'*
To God, Who gives joy to my youth.

We were unaware of the English translation and its beautiful sentiments and our only desire was to ensure that we started off with the correct Latin response. We then progressed to the first major hurdle, which was to master the Confiteor, the Confession. In reality, the altar boys almost went prostrate and the Confiteor was more mumbled than said aloud. It was only after the Latin responses had been mastered that one was judged suitably qualified. One of Fr McLaughlin's particular methods of questioning us was to pose the question, 'What are the opening words of the second half of the Confiteor?' The quick fire response, 'Ideo precor beatam Mariam semper Virginem,' (therefore I beseech Blessed Mary ever-Virgin) would impress Fr. George and indicate the respondent as potentially a team captain.

In learning the Latin responses, I was greatly helped by my father who had served Mass while in the army and he gave me an old, slightly battered Missal. The inscription, on the inside cover, told that it had been given to him by an army padre for whom he clerked Mass, in Malta, during the siege of that island for two years from 1940. I noticed that at the end of the Mass, the Missal had prayers for the King and asked my father why we did not have prayers for the Queen at the end of Mass in Derry. 'It's a long story, son,' he replied. Having mastered the Latin, it was time to be kitted out as a prospective altar boy, which meant being taken to the Good Shepherd convent in the Waterside to be fitted for a black soutane that extended to my ankles and white cotton surplice with three quarter length sleeves and which extended to above the knee.

I looked like a junior priest and was now ready for my big day, our first Mass. We were arranged in teams and had our first outing at ten o' clock Mass one Monday morning. There were four functionaries in the team with the main jobs being Server and Helper. One boy, all altar servers were boys in those days, was given the task of ringing the bell at the Consecration and the last task was to ensure that the button was pressed to ring the clock informing the congregation that the priest and his entourage of altar boys was about to appear on the altar. For my first Mass, I was the helper and performed my duties under the watchful eyes of my proud mother and all my aunts. I am sure the thought passed their minds that maybe one day I would become a priest.

Sunday Mass was a central feature of Catholic life and men and women, boys and girls dressed up in what was known as their 'Sunday best'. There were five Sunday Masses in Creggan, beginning at eight o' clock and the parish had four priests. The celebration of the Mass is one of the central pillars of Catholic devotion. At school, we had been told about the Penal Laws in Ireland, when the celebration of the Mass was illegal and priests caught saying Mass were summarily executed. There are Mass Rocks throughout the country, where priests and people risked life and limb to celebrate Mass. From a young age, we had learned the story of a Father James Hegarty, the parish priest of Fahan, who had lived on the run in a cave, saying Masses throughout Inishowen at Mass Rocks. Eventually captured, he was beheaded by the Redcoats just outside Buncrana, on the banks of Lough Swilly. A visit to Buncrana was never complete without going along the shore walk, where, a mile from the town his grave and a rock named after him were to be found. The rock had a crack in the image of a cross. Going to Mass was, for us, something to connect us to the past generations who risked their lives and liberty. For some, the Mass was a symbol of resistance to English rule, although we were also vaguely aware of English Catholic Recusants who risked life and liberty to protect Catholic priests on the run.

My days as an altar boy were very enjoyable. We progressed from weekday and Sunday Mass servers, to occasions such as High Masses, at Easter, when we were under the watchful eye of Bishop Farren. For these occasions, St Mary's borrowed red soutanes from the Cathedral. You were lucky if you got one that fitted and the secret was to bring a spare belt to hitch up a long soutane rather than trip over it. For High Masses and Sunday Devotions the smell of incense wafted around the altar and the atmosphere was heightened by the singing of traditional Latin hymns such as *O Salutaris Hostia* and *Tantum Ergo*. There were more solemn occasions such as funerals. The highlight of the year was the altar boys' excursion to Portrush. We got a day off school and our adventure started with all the altar boys assembled in St. Mary's, for ten o' clock Mass, when the unfortunate servers of the Mass were subjected to the critical eyes of their peers.

After Mass, a large coach waited to transport us on our day away. Fr McLaughlin and the sexton, Harry Hamilton, came along to ensure order. First stop was the strand at Portstewart for a game of football, followed by lunch in a restaurant along the Promenade. Lunch over; we headed to Portrush, or more specifically to Barry's Amusement Arcade, where we spent a few leisurely hours on bumpers and the roller coaster. The gaming machines were off-limits. Exhausted, we would troop on to the coach for the return journey home with Fr. McLaughlin leading the Rosary. The only other excursions that I went on were day trips with my parents to Buncrana, in county Donegal. Great James Street and Patrick Street were bursting with buses of the Londonderry and Lough Swilly Railway Company for trips to either Buncrana or Moville and invariably we went to the former. The bus ride was great fun, especially if you were on the top deck of the double decker and had a really different view of places such as the asylum on Strand Road/Asylum Road as we could see over the high wall for the first time. The main attraction for many day trippers in Buncrana was Cullen's Amusement Arcade but for me it was the adjoining putting green. Buncrana always seemed to be teeming with day trippers from Derry, whereas Moville was much quieter. My father told me that the most famous thing about Moville was that it had been the home of the ancestors of General Montgomery, Monty of El-Alamein fame, although the seaside town did not seem to go out of its way to remember one of its most famous sons.

Each year, the altar boys were witnesses to the annual parish retreats, when priests from religious orders came to preach a week of fire, brimstone and eternal damnation for souls of sinners. There was a week for the men and one for the women. Each day began with Mass at 6.30 a.m. for those who were working, with an alternative at ten o' clock and Devotions in the evening, at 7.30 p.m. While the missionaries were delivering their homily, the altar boys were busily playing football outside the sacristy, with the only condition imposed being that we did not make much noise. On wet evenings we sat in the sacristy and could not fail to hear the missionaries preach about all sorts of vice, like communism and socialism and the flames of hell that awaited those who departed from the path of righteousness. I felt that the missionaries would have been very happy to burn heretics at the stake. It was a throwback to days of learning the Catechism' *Question 31 – 'How did God punish the angels who rebelled?' Answer-'God punished the angels who rebelled by condemning them to the everlasting pains of hell.'* The end of the women's retreat was an occasion of high fashion in Creggan. Many women, my mother included, made the special purchase of a new hat and it was a very stylish congregation that thronged around Bishop Farren, who attended the closing ceremonies. I remember that at the end of the retreat women were falling over themselves to kiss the Bishop's ring. He was like a temporal ruler dispensing favours to the masses and he seemed to enjoy every minute of it.

The liturgy of the Latin Mass seemed to have remained unchanged for centuries and dated back to the late sixteenth century. About the time I became an altar boy, the Catholic Church was undergoing its most radical change in centuries as Pope John XXIII opened the Second Vatican Council. All I remember is the pomp and splendour of the opening ceremonies in Rome and thereafter we were blissfully unaware of what was happening.

This wave of modernity chimed with the musical sensation as a Belgian nun, Sœur Sourire, made the top ten in the pop charts with her song, *Dominique,* which was about Saint Dominic, a Spanish-born priest and founder of the Dominican Order, of which she was a member. The refrain, which introduced us French, ran:

Domi-nique-nique-nique s'en allait tot simplement,
Routier, pauvre et chantant

However, what I associate most from that era was not the pop song but the changes ordered by the Council, in particular, the introduction of Mass in the vernacular. This change coincided with our time to leave the altar boys and it looked as though altar boys were being made slightly redundant. It was to be the congregation, and not the altar boys, who would now say aloud the Confiteor, as well as the Gloria, the Credo and Pater Noster. To make matters worse for the altar boys, almost all responses were now in English. There remained some vestiges of the Tridentine Mass as, for example, the priest gave the final blessing in Latin-'*Benedicat vos Omnipotens Deus, Pater et Filius et Spiritus Sanctus,*' to which the response remained '*Amen.*'

Quite a lot of life in Creggan revolved around the Church and, as an altar boy, I was only too well aware of the events such as confraternities, sodalities, benedictions, novenas and devotions that were the staple diet for the parish. Then there was the Pioneer Association, promoting abstinence from alcohol and the Legion of Mary. Fr. Carolan organised the annual sports day in a field behind Creggan Heights and encouraged us to join St. Mary's Boys' Club. My membership was short-lived as I was neither interested in boxing competitively or doing gymnastic exercises over a vaulting horse. The Church controlled education and my father said that the priests controlled the Nationalist Party in the same way that the Orange Order controlled the Unionist Party. A couple of times a year, there was a stipend collection for the upkeep of the priests of the parish. During Mass, the donations on a street by street basis were read from the altar, naming individuals and their contribution. I was quite horrified and felt that people were being shamed into making a high contribution, when it should have been a very personal and confidential matter. It was certainly an era, in which the Church seemed to rule with a rod of iron. As altar boys, we used to enjoy winding up Fr. Carolan by telling him stories such as we had seen a sailor leave a certain house as we were on our way to morning Mass. Quick as a flash, he would be into his car and off seeking out the phantom trail and by the time he had returned to the sacristy, we had cleared off home.

Apart from life at school and being an altar boy, what was beginning to dominate our lives was the novelty of television. My primary school days saw the most revolutionary change in family entertainment that century, with the first television sets beginning to appear. My mother and my father took me to a television shop at the corner of Butcher Street and Magazine Street. It was filled with very bulky television sets all broadcasting BBC on black and white screens. One of my earliest memories is of my father and a number of postmen gathered around a television in the flat Carrickreagh Gardens watching an FA Cup Final on BBC. I have vague memories that the first Cup Final I watched was Wolves beating Blackburn Rovers 3-0, with Dave Whelan, a Blackburn defender breaking his leg, which ruined the game as substitutes were not allowed. By the following year, my knowledge of the game was quite advanced and I watched Tottenham Hotspurs, captained by Northern Ireland's Danny Blanchflower, attempt to become the first team in the 20th century to do the elusive Double, win the League title and FA cup in the same season. They succeeded, beating Leicester City and retained the cup the following year by beating Burnley in the final. The only thing I remember from the 1962 final was the singing of 'She's A Lassie from Lancashire' sung by the northern hordes who had descended on the capital. The Spurs' supporters answered with their song, 'Glory Glory, Hallelujah,' which I recognised as *John Brown's Body*, an American civil war marching song that we had learned at school.

In subsequent years, FA Cup Final day on BBC became a day to remain glued to the television screen from early morning. There was 'The Road to Wembley,' showing the goals from the games that each of the finalists had played. This was followed by 'Meet the Teams,' with a profile of each player. The BBC did not go in for in-depth analysis of the up-coming game; it was the days before the professional pundits were to dominate the screens. Fans were interviewed along Wembley Way before the game and a man in a white suit conducted 'community singing,' which ended with *Abide With Me*. Before the kick-off, the teams were introduced to a member of the Royal Family and *God Save the Quee*n was sung without incident or interruption. At three o'clock on the dot the game was underway. I remember the commentators talking about the '*Wembley hoodoo*,' as the turf often accounted for serious accidents.

It was the FA Cup Final of 1963 that introduced me to Manchester United and made me a life-long fan. I was vaguely aware, from my father, of the famous Busby Babes, the team of the Munich air disaster but had never seen Manchester United. All changed as I got my first glimpse of my new hero, Denis Law, recently signed from Torino for £115,000, then a British record. Holding the cuffs of his jersey, he strutted around the pitch like a king. The final was against Leicester City, who was again to lose, this time 3-1, with Law scoring the opening goal, beating Gordon Banks, England's keeper. It was United's first trophy since the air crash and represented the start of the glory days that culminated in winning the European Cup five years later. Denis Law is the only Scotsman ever to have won the prestigious Ballon d'Or, European Footballer of the Year.

Apart from the annual F.A. Cup finals, I always enjoyed watching Grandstand on BBC on a Saturday afternoon, especially as David Coleman peered over a machine called the tele printer and read the football results as they came in. The machine typed each character of the results, one-by-one. I was usually holding my father's football pools, as I watched the results come in on the screen. I waited with baited breath for the last digit to appear in a score line. It was a forlorn hope that he would eventually get the eight draws he needed to win the jackpot. Coleman was a good presenter, who kept my attention. Not only would he give the scores but he would also give a commentary on the affect of the result on a team's position and a summary of their last few games. My love affair with Manchester United could not have been better timed as the following year the BBC started broadcasting *Match of the Day*, featuring highlights of first Division games with United regularly on the box. In the 1960s, I nursed a great sympathy for Leicester City as they lost all three F.A. Cup Finals in which they appeared in a space of eight years.

Apart from the F.A. Cup Finals, the BBC also introduced me to rugby union and the internationals in the Five Nations that were broadcast live each year. It was the era of the four Home nations and France. On a black and white television screen, it was sometimes difficult to make out the difference between the red jerseys of Wales and the green ones of Ireland. The first iconic figures were players such as Ireland's captain Tom Kiernan, England's leader Dickie Jeeps and Cliff Morgan of Wales who went on to be an outstanding commentator Even at a distance of over fifty years, I can still visualise one of the great individual tries scored by an Englishman, Andy Hancock, when he ran the length of the Twickenham pitch to score against Scotland. My other abiding memory of rugby international is the commentary of Bill McLaren, the teacher turned broadcaster, who had an encyclopaedic knowledge of rugby, a sport he genuinely loved.

There was one serious interruption to my regular Cup Final day television routine, when ITV introduced professional wrestling to be shown as an alternative to the BBC coverage of the build-up to the game. My mother preferred the sporting spectacle of watching Mick Mc Manus, dubbed by commentator, Kent Walton as 'the man you love to hate,' wrestle with Jackie Pallo in front of a host of screaming women, rather than Community Singing from Wembley stadium. It was pure theatre as Pallo's peroxide blonde wife, Trixie, bedecked in a fur coat, would be the focus of the camera as she remonstrated with the referee and Mc Manus. Wrestling had started its television appearance late on a Wednesday night after the Ten O' Clock News and my mother was hooked from the start. My father was aghast and dismissed it as pure showbiz and not competitive sport. Soon, names such as Big Daddy, Giant Haystacks, Johnny Two Rivers, the Mohawk Indian, and the tig-tag team of the clean cut Royal Brothers joined Mc Manus and Pallo as regulars on our screen.

Before I leave the subject of FA cup finals, I have a salutary piece of advice for clergymen. In 1977, I was, as usual, at home on Cup Final day, sitting in front of the television screen, roaring on United as we tried to put the disappointment of the previous year behind us. Although hot favourites, we had lost to a late Southampton strike. Now Liverpool stood in our way. The game was goalless at half time, when our doorbell rang and there stood Fr. Seamus Kelly the administrator of St. Mary's, who had chosen that afternoon to make his house visits to Fanad Drive. My mother warmly welcomed him and ushered him into the living room, where I was watching the match. 'Turn that TV off,' she said and I had no option but to comply. I inwardly groaned when she offered him tea but was delighted when he demurred, saying he had plenty of houses to call with that afternoon. I thought that only a priest from Gaelic football playing County Derry would be so witless as to plan house visits in Creggan for Cup Final Saturday. Thankfully, it was a fleeting visit and he left before the second half started, going next door to Devine's house, where I knew there was a large group of United and Liverpool fans watching the game. I later learned that Rosie Devine did the exact same as my mother and had the television turned off for the priest's visit. By the time it was switched back on, three goals had been scored within five minutes, with United taking the lead and Liverpool equalising within two minutes only to see Jimmy Greenhoff reply with what was to prove the United winner. Years later, just before I got married, I went to see Fr. Kelly about obtaining what are called 'letters of freedom.' I could not resist telling him the story of the 1997 cup final at which he laughed heartily and undertook never again to make parish visitations on that said afternoon. For any clergyman in a working class parish, knowledge of soccer was essential for bonding with most male parishioners.

Television was more than just soccer and my first viewings were the *Watch With Mother* series, which I watched with my mother. I don't remember the Monday programme, *Picture Book* but can still sing *Andy Pandy's coming to play, tra la la la la la la,* which greeted me on a Tuesday afternoon. Andy was a puppet, who lived in a picnic basket, came to life and would be joined by his friend Teddy and a rag doll called Loopy Loo, who had her own song, '*Here we go Loopy Loo*.' Wednesday saw Bill and Ben, *The Flowerpot Men*, who lived at the bottom of an English garden. Between their flower pots was Little Weed, a sunflower with a smiling face. In each programme there was the song; *Was it Bill or was it Ben*? Looking back, it was a poor educational programme as Bill and Ben both spoke a strange from of the English language which was called Oddle Poddle. Thursday was *Rag Tag and Bobtail*, a hedgehog, a mouse and a rabbit. It was the down-market BBC version of *The Wind in the Willows*. On Fridays we watched *The Woodentops* with Mother and Father Woodentop, their twins, Jenny and Willy, Baby Woodentop and of course their dog, Spotty. They lived on a farm and had a cow called Buttercup. Such political correctness extolling the virtues of a nuclear family would never pass in today's BBC. They spoke what was called 'received pronunciation,' Standard English, unlike Bill and Ben. However, Father Woodentop, being a farmer, had, what I would later discover was, a West Country accent.

Long before watching the film version of *Tom Brown's Schooldays*, I was introduced to the BBC's Billy Bunter of Greyfriars School, a very greedy and obese schoolboy. My general knowledge improved by watching Geoffrey Wheeler as the quiz master in *Top of the Form*. With its jaunty theme tune *Marching Strings*, it featured mainly grammar schools and was a junior version of *University Challenge*. There was one unforgettable time when this question was posed: 'What do a pair of trousers and a billiard table have in common?' The correct answer was pockets but one unfortunate boy answered 'balls,' which caused quite a titter of mirth but was expertly glossed over by the quiz master.

When I was at the Christian Brothers, the new attraction on a Saturday evening became *Dr. Who*, the Time Lord who travelled in a Tardis, which was a British police box. Before the intrepid Doctor appeared on our screens, I had been introduced to time-travelling through the film, *The Time Machine,* based on the novel, by H. G. Wells, of the same title and written in the closing years of the nineteenth century. Its hero, George, invented a time machine that allowed him to travel through time and eventually arrived thousands of years in the future to rescue the Eloi from their oppressors the Morlocks and fell in love with Weena. The nemeses of Dr. Who were the Daleks, described by their designer as resembling 'human-sized pepper shakers.' They had a single mechanical eyestalk, mounted on a rotating dome and a gun mount that spat out a death ray. They were intent on taking over the world and their favourite term was 'Ex-ter-min-ate,' delivered in a harsh staccato tone to anyone who stood in their way. The doctor was in many a tight corner but always managed to escape and good prevailed over evil.

My introduction to grown up television was the weekly episode of *Dixon of Dock Green*, which was on BBC every Saturday evening just after the Six O' Clock News. The series ran for about twenty years and the star was Sergeant George Dixon, who personified the local Bobby, whose beat was Paddington Green in London's East End, an area in which he also lived. 'Evening all,' Sergeant Dixon would say at the beginning of each episode and then given the outline of the story for that evening's episode. As the music faded at the end, I could hear my mother running the bath for my weekly scrub. The only departure from normality was one night, when, by mistake, she liberally sprinkled my back with Vim, a scouring powder rather than talcum powder.

I had progressed from the *Watch With Mother* series and became particularly drawn when I was about seven, firstly, to *The Lone Ranger* and later to *The Adventures of Robin Hood* and *Ivanhoe*. All were paragons of virtue, upholding right against wrong and evil. The Lone Ranger was the American Wild West equivalent of Count Zorro and never appeared without wearing his mask and always won against countless odds, never losing his hat or mask in any fight. His trusted accomplice was Tonto, an Indian, who addressed our hero as 'Kemosabe,' an American Indian term meaning faithful friend. The show started and ended with the Lone Ranger riding off on his steed, Silver, to the strains of what I eventually found out was the *William Tell Overture* by Rossini.

Independent Television, ITV, had been established in the mid-1950s and challenged the BBC, which was the state sponsored broadcasting corporation. The funding of ITV depended upon advertising and for the first time, programmes were interrupted by what American television stations called 'a word from our sponsors.' It was quite annoying to have the ad men intrude, especially when they brought with them the most banal of slogans to recommend their products. We became used to being told that *Daz* 'washes whiter and it shows,' and that *Maltesers* were 'the chocolates with the less fattening centres,' rather than inhabitants of Malta. Of course, the political incorrectness of the period also saw the Robertson's Golly with the ad telling us to 'look for the Golly, the Golly on the jar,' and you got an enamelled mascot badge of the delightful golly if you collected so many labels from the jam jars. There were even golly dolls. Within decades, as political correctness prevailed, Robertson's retired the golly.

The advertising boom inspired some of my contemporaries to outdo the ad men and two home-made ad slogans stand out in my mind. Andrews Liver Salts and Bisto gravy granules were to be found in almost every household. The schoolboy parody of the Andrews ad ran as follows:

> *When the bottom falls out of your world*
> *Take Andrews*
> *And let the world fall out of your bottom*

Similarly, the parody of the Bisto ad was:

> *If you suffer from diarrhoea, take Bisto*
> *Because Bisto browns, seasons and thickens all in one go*

Of course, our initial viewing of ITV was to see how it would challenge the BBC's imported all-American hero, the Lone Ranger. This was done by the creation of very strictly English heroes, beginning with Richard Greene, starring as Robin Hood. We were treated to the weekly half hour series, in which Robin was the defender of Anglo Saxon England. The king, Richard the Lionheart was away on the Crusades and his wicked brother, John, was attempting to usurp the throne. John's enforcer was the Sheriff of Nottingham, against whom Robin jousted and avoided capture. At some time we had seen Errol Flynn play the swashbuckling Robin in the film made before the Second World War, with Olivia de Haviland as Maid Marian and Basil Rathbone as the Sheriff of Nottingham. The ITV programme had a very catchy theme song that we sang as we pretended to be the Men of Sherwood:

Robin Hood, Robin Hood, Riding through the glen
Robin Hood, Robin Hood, With his band of men
Feared by the bad, Loved by the good
Robin Hood, Robin Hood, Robin Hood

Alan-A-Dale was Robin's wandering minstrel, oft sitting on a riverbank and singing *Greensleeves* and strumming on a mandolin. I remember him clearly because one day in a school quiz we were asked which English King had reputedly composed *Greensleeves*. Quick as a flash, I stuck up my hand and shouted out, 'Richard the Lionheart.' I was stunned when told that I had given the wrong answer and that it was reputedly Henry VIII who composed the love song for Anne Boleyn. I protested that Alan-A-Dale had sung it in *Robin Hood,* only to be told that I should not believe everything I saw on television. The Lionheart was dead over three hundred years before Henry VIII ascended the throne. While some may have accepted the artistic license used by programme makers, I could not forgive them for making an eejit of me in front of the whole class. My interest in the programme waned and I was relieved to acquire a new hero, Roger Moore playing Ivanhoe, a character created by Sir Walter Scott in the early 1820s. Like Robin Hood, the programme had a very bouncy theme song:

Ivanhoe, Ivanhoe
Side by side we're proud to ride with Ivanhoe
At his call we spring to help him ride along
The song we sing is free and joyous song
Ivanhoe, Ivanhoe

The Ivanhoe theme was very like that of Robin Hood, set in the reign of Richard the Lionheart. We learned that Richard, while returning from the Crusades, had been kidnapped for ransom by Duke Leopold and that Prince John was intent on retaining for himself the money raided to pay the ransom. Like Robin Hood, Ivanhoe had a girlfriend, Lady Rowena and on a weekly basis set about righting wrongs and securing justice that was being denied by the Normans. It was only natural that in the 1960s the next logical progression in these historical dramas for children was the series, *Richard the Lionheart.*

Richard, played by a genial Irish actor, Dermot Walsh, seemed to spend an inordinate period of his reign in the Holy Land, trying to recapture Jerusalem from the Muslims. Sultan Saladin may have been his enemy but Richard had more problems with his supposed allies and I was treated to the spectacle of medieval chivalry, as the Sultan sent his personal physician to heal Richard. The series further increased my interest in history and a desire to find out more about the Crusades. Many years later, reading W.L. Warren's life of King John, I discovered the obvious truth that the television and film productions about the period were exceptionally one-sided. Richard was not a hero and John was far from being a villain. The debate still rages as to how accurate to historical reality are films and television productions.

My mother became a great fan of television but was very selective in the programmes she watched. *Crossroads* and *Coronation Street* were her favourite early evening viewing and she quite enjoyed American soaps such as *Dr. Kildare* and *Peyton Place*. One series, in particular, captivated not only her imagination but that of the whole country. It was called *The Fugitive*, starring David Janssen, as Dr. Richard Kimble, a physician who was falsely convicted of his wife's murder and sentenced to death. Needless to say, he escaped that fate, as the train taking him to death row was derailed and he escaped. Thus began a four season airing of his flight from the chasing Police Lieutenant, Philip Gerard. Kimble's story was that the real killer was a one armed man. The final episodes were run on TV in August, 1967. There was utter suspense as to whether Lieutenant Gerard would finally catch Kimble or 'the one armed man' would prove to be the real killer. I leave it to my readers to work out the ending, without recourse to the internet. The more relaxing programme for my mother was undoubtedly *Come Dancing*, on BBC. It was introduced by Peter West and featured weekly ballroom dancing competitions from regions of the UK. My mother enjoyed dancing, herself and was taken by the sight of the women dancer sin their wonderful sequin ball frocks.

By the time I was an altar boy, we had moved from Carrickreagh Gardens to Fanad Drive, a street on the Creggan Estate that had been built by the Housing Trust in 1949. The surrounding streets had names associated with the bays and headlands of County Donegal, Malin, Dunree, Leenan, Melmore and Dunaff. It was said that the names related to places that a Corporation official had visited on walking tours of Donegal. After sixteen years of marriage, my parents had secured a house, as opposed to the flats in which they had lived since getting married. The house was at the end of a block of four and was just opposite St. Mary's Church. It was spacious compared to the flat in Carrickreagh, although it was a two up two down house and only the living room had any heating in the form of a coal fire. No sooner had we moved in than my father was busy decorating and painting the house from top to bottom. I often went with my mother and him to Dickey's Paint & Wallpaper shop in Great James's Street as they choose wallpaper for each room. My mother was also busy painting her front door step with a paint called Cardinal Red. She was delighted with the move to Fanad Drive. Each morning, as she opened her bedroom curtains, her view was of the St. Mary's Church and the Secondary School, which had been opened a few years earlier. It was with a bounce in her step that she returned to working in the shirt factories and this second income ensured that we were very comfortable. She became a member of the newly established Derry Credit Union, which superseded the Provident as a source of borrowing money and, with her new-found income, started as a regular saver. She worked firstly in the Rosemount Factory and then with Ben Sherman. The shirt factories were then introducing time and motion procedures that meant the women were paid on the quantity of work done. Each evening, I would improve my mental arithmetic by helping my mother to add up the tickets of the work done that day.

Moving to Fanad Drive introduced me to a new circle of friends. Jim and Gerard Deeney were pigeon fanciers and their speciality was 'homing pigeons' that returned to the nest. You could hear Johnny Mc Gilloway playing his drums at any hour of the day or night, while the Browns were also very musical with John being a good accordionist. John and Hughie Devine could build the best go-kart possible from planks of wood, axles and the wheels of prams.

One of my first memories of conversation with these new friends centred on boxing and the name Sonny Liston, who had just beaten Floyd Patterson to become world heavy weight champion. One morning, I was awakened by what sounded like a ball being hit against a wall but the beat was so quick as to suggest that it was the sound of a punch bag being used for boxing training and so it turned out to be. One of our neighbours, Nobby Lynch, who was just over five feet tall and was called Popeye by us, behind his back, had been a keen boxer in his army days and had a punch bag installed in his back garden. He had a fearsome reputation, behind which he was a very kind man, eager to show us his boxing skills and let us try his punch bag. I became almost addicted to Nobby's punch bag and asked for one for Christmas. To my delight, I became the proud owner of what was called 'Freddie Mills Junior Trainer,' a punch bag, mounted on a four foot high metal rod that was secured to a red wooden board. The present even included a pair of boxing gloves, featuring the initials F.M. With glee, I placed my punch bag in the back garden, stood on the red wooden base and merrily punched away the time, just like Nobby. My Father was a keen boxing fan, having been a boxer in his army days. I enjoyed seeing him watch a fight on the television as he jabbed, ducked and weaved just like the boxers. However, he told me that he really enjoyed listening to radio broadcasts of fights, especially if

Eamon Andrews was the commentator, as Andrews had been an amateur boxer himself and conveyed the bouts with precision and eloquence.

Gerard Deeney boxed at St. Mary's Boys' Club and seemed very knowledgeable on the sport. I was forced to update my knowledge from my father, who had been a big fan of Patterson. Within a few years, the boxing conversations centred on the new kid on the block, Cassius Clay, who beat Liston to win the crown and, in the re-match, knocked him out in the first round. There was great debate as to whether the fight had been fixed and the fast-talking Clay, the 'Louisville Lip' who had by then changed his name to Muhammad Ali, saying that Cassius Clay was his slave name. The only fight televised live was when Clay, as he then was known, fought Henry Cooper at Wembley Stadium, in June 1963. It was a great spectacle and Cooper felled his opponent in the fourth round with his trade mark, which my father told me was called ''Enry's Ammer,' a good Cockney phrase. The savage left hook landed bang on Clay's jaw and he hit the canvas. In our small living room, my father was up on his feet, just like the 35,000 spectators at Wembley. As Clay got to his feet he was literally 'saved by the bell' and was dazed as he was led back to his corner. Alas, Cooper suffered from easily cut eyes and, in the next round, Cooper took a direct hit on his left eye, which immediately spouted blood. The referee had no option but to stop the fight and declare Clay the winner. Clay's excuse for having been knocked down was that he had been looking at Elizabeth Taylor who was ringside. Years later, in a television interview, he confessed that Cooper hit him so hard, 'That his ancestors in Africa felt it.'

For me, the move to Fanad Drive cut ten minutes off my daily walk to the Christian Brothers. I also found a new route home. I could amble along the Lecky Road towards the city centre. I caught the Creggan bus in Guildhall Square and it stopped just outside our front door. The early 1960s saw the major housing redevelopment along the Lecky Road and surrounding streets as sub-standard terraces of houses were demolished and landmarks such as the cattle market disappeared to make way for highrise flats in Rossville Street. The Greyhound Bar at the corner of Wellington Street and Barr's pawnbrokers also disappeared as did the Cinder Field, on which football was regularly played. The terraced streets were replaced with high quality homes that would have been the envy of anyone living in Victorian houses, which had multiple occupancy, no bathrooms and outside toilets. What I did not realise at the time was that most of this house building was to re-house families and made no great inroads into the long waiting lists, which numbered over a thousand families at the time. House-building could not keep pace with the Derry's growing population. The housing crisis was most manifest by the existence of Springtown Camp, a collection of Nissan huts that had housed American servicemen during World War II and which were occupied by homeless families when the Yanks departed.

In Creggan, we had the luxury of plenty of massive playing areas. There were greens that extended all along Greenwalk, where we played many enjoyable football matches over the years. On the other side of St. Mary's church, there was the Bishop's Field that provided many football pitches. It was the era of no offside, when coats were used for nets and it was twelve half and twenty four the winner, in terms of goals required, or you just played until it got dark. If you arrived when a game had started, you got a side only when someone else turned up and levelled up the sides. There were plenty of wide open spaces for games of football, as opposed to narrow streets.

On many a warm summer day, when we had finished a game of football, we would lie on the ground and look up to the sky, mesmerised by the jets that passed high overhead en route to, or from, America. We used to wonder if the pilots had seen us. Our interest in sky travel was greatly augmented in the spring of 1961, with the news that Yuri Gagurin, a Russian astronaut, had become the first man to journey to outer space, when his Vostok spacecraft completed an orbit of the earth. At school, we learned that he had been dubbed 'the Columbus of inter-planetary space,' and, overnight, his picture was on the front page of every newspaper and magazine. I avidly read the account of the orbiting of the earth in the *Belfast Telegraph,* as well as following the BBC news. Together with President John F. Kennedy, he was one of the first global celebrities and that summer he came to Britain and was interviewed on television. The Russians had certainly put one over on the Yanks, which simply ensured that no stone would be left unturned in Washington to gain revenge and redeem national pride.

Shortly after we had moved to Fanad Drive, in 1962, I made my Confirmation, on Ascension Thursday, 31st May. The Brothers prepared us well for the day, including a trip to the Palace Cinema in Shipquay Street to see a Spanish film with subtitles, *Miracle of the White Suit.* The story line was about Marcos, a seven year old boy living in dire poverty, whose dream was to have a white suit for his First Communion. The Brothers were trying to instil into us both piety and recognition of how lucky we were. We had learned that confirmation was the sacrament 'through which the Holy Ghost is given to us, with all his graces and his seven gifts, to make us strong and perfect Catholics and soldiers of Christ.' The outpouring of the Holy Ghost was the same as had been granted to the apostles, at Pentecost, which made them fearless preachers of the Word of God. The seven gifts were wisdom, understanding, counsel, knowledge, fortitude, piety and fear of the Lord.

Ascension Thursday was a sunny day and we had to arrive at school early for the year photograph, before being marched to St. Eugene's Cathedral for a ceremony that seemed to go on for hours, as every Catholic child in the city of Confirmation age, received the Sacrament that day. We each had a card on which was written our name and the Confirmation name we would be taking. The name I took was Martin, after St. Martin de Porres, who had been canonised that year, and whose picture I had won in a class raffle. My sponsor was, by coincidence, Fr. George McLaughlin from St. Mary's. The Confirmation ceremony involved the bishop giving us what could either have been a touch or a blow on the cheek to remind us that we were becoming soldiers of Christ. We were told that he might also ask us to recite the seven gifts of the Holy Ghost and failure to give the correct answers would see us removed from the ceremony in disgrace. With some trepidation I slowly walked up the long main aisle of the Cathedral, repeating over and over to myself the seven gifts and was somewhat disappointed when the bishop simply gave me a tap on the cheek and, without asking any questions, anointed me with the oil of chrism and made me a soldier of Christ. With the ceremony over, our minds turned to more materialistic matters such as doing the rounds of relations and receiving our financial rewards. By tradition you did better on the collection round after First Communion than Confirmation. Second time the novelty factor had obviously worn a little thin!

A few weeks after Confirmation, I had the opportunity of again meeting Bishop Farren, when he came to the Christian Brothers to unveil a plaque, commemorating the bi-centenary of the birth of Edmund Ignatius Rice, the founder of the Christian Brothers. After the unveiling, resplendent in our Confirmation suits, which were not white, we trooped up Hogg's Folly to the Long Tower church for a Mass of thanksgiving for the work of our founder. At the end of the Mass, we formed a guard of honour for the bishop. Together with Bernard Coyle, one of my classmates, I was selected to make a presentation to him of a small gift, which I think might have been a scroll. He smiled benignly, accepted our gift and made off in his car, which seemed to me to be the biggest limousine I had seen. The next time I saw it was when it was a People's Taxi, operated in Creggan by the Official Republican movement in the early 1970s.

Chapter Four
The Eleven Plus Years

From Brooke Park Library to Windsor Park Stadium and a few civil wars along the way with Corporal Zeal-for-the-Lord Relf

Even at an early stage of our education at the Christian Brothers, we were aware that there was a focus on a public examination, the Eleven Plus, which we would sit in our final year. It was widely called the *Qually*, as success qualified one for a grammar school education. Preparations were meticulous and started a full year in advance of sitting the papers. Throughout our school days at the Christians, academic teaching was predicated upon bring successful in the Eleven Plus examination. This may have had something to do with nineteenth century Ireland in which teachers' salaries were boosted on the basis of the examination success of their pupils. It probably had more to do with the sweeping social changes that the 1947 Education Act had introduced, in Northern Ireland, by making places at grammar schools and universities freely available to bright working class students.

In September 1963, we arrived back at school for our Primary Six year and were told we would have Brother Keane for the next two years. Brother Harney taught the other P6 class and the two classes were allocated adjoining classrooms in what was the most modern part of the school. It was a recently built unit, with plenty of large windows and thus bright light and was situated on an elevated site from which we had magnificent views of the hills of Derry sloping towards Celtic Park and Creggan. There were only two classrooms in the new unit and it almost appeared that we were in an incubator unit, quarantined from the rest of the school as we embarked on a course of study to prepare us for the Eleven Plus. The preparations were intense, to the extent that we went to school on Saturday mornings and weekly sat a mock exam. It was hardly a surprise that the Brothers generally achieved over 80% success rate in the Eleven Plus exams. Little did we know it at the time but the next seven years of schooling was being shaped out by this one public examination. In the greater scheme of things, and unknown to us, we were on a production line that aimed to see us successfully through Junior, Senior and A level exams as a preparation for university.

Singing Together ceased to be a Friday exercise and we progressed from the *Wide Range Reader* reading books. Instead, Brother Keane had a well-stocked library at the back of the classroom and encouraged us to use it and to join the local library at Brooke Park, which I duly did. One Saturday morning, my father brought me to the library, which was in a wing of a large 19th century building known as Gwyn's Institution and he enrolled both of us. When I was a child, my mother had often brought me to Brooke Park, with its duck pond and large cannon that dated to the 19th century. I used to marvel at the imposing statue at the main entrance to the park on Windsor Terrace. It was of Sir Robert Alexander Ferguson, a former MP for the city, but was simply called 'The Black Man,' on account of the statue's colour. He had been the MP for the city for thirty years until his death in 1860. The park was a gift to the city by a prosperous 19th century benefactor, James Hood Brooke.

Gwyn's Institute had been founded as an orphanage and had become a museum in which was housed the coach from the celebrated incident of Half Hanged Mc Naughton. The story, according to my mother, was one that went back to the 1760s, as follows: John McNaughton was a friend of the Knox family, which lived in Prehen House. Mary Ann Knox fell in love with him. However, her father forbade any talk of marriage and the two love birds planned to elope. When Mary Ann was travelling to Dublin with her father, McNaughton held up the carriage and in an ensuing exchange of shots, McNaughton accidentally killed Mary Ann. He was sentenced to hang for his crime but according to the ballad, "The rope it broke, not once but twice/ By the laws of man you can't hang thrice/ The people cried, 'Let him go free/ Don't hang him on the gallows tree." Legend says he was offered the opportunity to escape but declined, as he did not want to be remembered as Half-hanged Mc Naughton! The story captured my imagination, especially as my mother also told me that the famous coach was said to haunt the Prehen Road after midnight.

Having enrolled in the library, I usually went there once every couple of weeks. The librarians were very helpful, especially one called Violet, who knew my father. In returning books for him I would ask Violet if she could get detective novels for my father as he enjoyed these. I enjoyed wandering around the library and going beyond the narrow confines of the children's' section. Between Brother Keane's and Brooke Park's selections, I became increasingly attached to the adventures of *Biggles* and historical novels rather than Enid Blyton's *Favourite Five*. There were four books, in particular, that still stand out in my memory, two of which were set in the England of the civil war of the seventeenth century, the third was *Tom Brown's Schooldays* and the final book was a short history of the American Civil War. The English Civil War based novels were *The Children of the New*

Forest and *Simon*. The former followed the fortunes of the Beverley children, in hiding from Cromwell's Roundheads. The latter followed the experiences of a young Roundhead soldier and one of its characters had a name that one could not forget, Corporal Zeal-for-the-Lord Relf, who was tried for desertion and found guilty. Rather than being hanged he was given 100 lashes, demoted to private and transferred from the Ironsides to a regiment called the Pioneers, who were regarded as the scum of the New Model Army. While Brother Keane was delighted that I had taken to making good use of all the available library facilities, he had little sympathy for the Roundheads and at the mention of the name Cromwell, his eyes would tighten and with a withering look he would express an opinion that Cromwell would burn in Hell for what he did in Ireland. He then proceeded to tell of the slaughter of Catholic civilians by Cromwellian troops in Drogheda and Wexford.

On the shelf of library books in one of our classrooms in the Christians, I stumbled upon a short paperback history of the American Civil War. It immediately ignited my interest in the subject, in general, and the character of Abraham Lincoln, in particular. Stories illustrated the ignorance of conscripted farm boys, who, receiving marching orders, did not know their left leg from their right leg. The Union Army solved this problem by tying a clump of hay to the left leg and a clump of straw to the right and then barking out the marching order, 'hay foot straw foot.' The book had a simple statement that slavery was the cause of the war. Yet a century later, we still had television images of race riots in American cities and a phenomenon known as the Civil Rights movement. From an early stage, I instinctively identified with the Union rather than the Confederates, which may have had something to do with the fact that the Confederates were fighting to retain slavery. I had enjoyed Mark Twain's novels of *Tom Sawyer* and *Huckleberry Finn* but found *Uncle Tom's Cabin,* by Harriet Beecher Stowe, hard going. However, I was fascinated to learn that when Abraham Lincoln met the author he allegedly greeted her with the words, 'So, you're the little woman, who wrote the book that started this Great War.'

At the Christian Brothers' primary school, there was very little English history taught and most of it consisted of the story of the Norman conquest of Britain with the gory details of King Harold losing his eye and throne at the battle of Hastings. The Brothers, most of whom were from southern Ireland, had a greater desire to glorify insurrections against British rule in Ireland and remind us of the Penal laws imposed after the battle of the Boyne. Two ditties stand out in my mind from their schooling:

"Up a long ladder and down a short rope
To hell with King Billy and god bless the Pope
And if that won't do, we'll cut Billy in two
And send him to Hell wrapped in red, white and blue."

It dawned on me that the 'red, white and blue' was the Union Jack flag that my mother had denied me in Woolworth's some years earlier. The complexities of the wars of the seventeenth century were never alluded to, nor were we informed that a *Te Deum* had allegedly been sung in the Vatican, at the command of the Pope, to celebrate William's victory at the Battle of the Boyne, in 1690. Fast forward a period of just over two centuries, and we learned that:

Edward Carson had a cat, it sat upon the fender
And every time it saw a rat, it shouted No Surrender.

Any history we learned was from the Christian Brothers' own publication, *Our Boys*, which was particularly praiseworthy of the 1916 Easter Rising, as many of the insurgents had been educated by the Brothers. I recently came across one of these panegyrics, written by Seamus G. O'Kelly and published in 1965. It was called *The Glorious Seven*. The title was named after the seven signatories to the Easter Proclamation of 1916 and was not to be confused with the iconic western, *The Magnificent Seven*. The introduction began with the words 'As the Saviour of Mankind rose from the dead on the first Easter Sunday morning, so did the Irish nation rise from the living tomb when the guns spat lead from the G.P.O. on Easter Monday 1916 and the Tricolour fluttered free from the Headquarters of the Provisional Government of the Irish Republic...The Irish nation had re-awakened. The blood spilled in Easter Week had nurtured and brought back to life the soul of Ireland.'

I remember my father, whose father had been a Redmond volunteer, saying that the Brothers never mentioned that the leaders of the Rising had never had a single vote cast for them in any parliamentary elections. By contrast, John Redmond and the Irish Parliamentary Party had succeeded in getting the Home Rule Act on the statute book at Westminster. As we were preparing for the Eleven Plus, Brother Keane would keep us in class for an extra hour's grind, at the end of which he would give us a ten minute pep talk on Irish nationalist history and often play rebel songs on a record player. We were regaled with tales of Patrick Pearse and the Easter Rising, Kevin Barry, who was hanged in Mountjoy Jail and the War of Independence. From listening to Brother Keane, I had no impression that almost five hundred died during the Easter Rising, the vast majority of them being innocent civilians, which included forty children. His focus was exclusively on the fifteen leaders of the Rising, who were tried by court martial, found guilty and executed by firing squad by the British Army in Dublin in the wake of the Rising, and Roger Casement, hanged a few months later in Pentonville Jail in London. Michael Collins was held up as a hero until he signed the Treaty that ended hostilities with Britain but started a civil war in Ireland.

One of my classmates, Colm Keenan, seemed perfectly in tune with all of this republican sentiment. He would often bring books into class with tales of heroic deeds of republican icons such as Dan Breen and Tom Barry and their flying columns fighting the British army in Munster half a century earlier. Tom Barry even wrote a book extolling his exploits, *Guerrilla Days in Ireland*. Colm lived just off the Lecky Road, where my mother had spent much of her early years and knew his father. She took a dim view of me associating with Colm and told me that his father was an IRA man and had been in jail quite a lot. Brother Keane's records were the first time that I heard of the IRA. I was scarcely aware of the IRA campaign in Northern Ireland, from 1957 to 1962. It had petered out, due to insufficient support. However, Brother Keane's gramophone played rebel songs, such as *Sean South* and *The Patriot Game*, which were tributes to two IRA men killed on an abortive attack on a police station in County Fermanagh in 1957. All the republican heroes were dead and ballads were mawkish stuff, all about dying for Ireland. By the 1970s, all romance with republicanism should have ended when killings in the name of Ireland became an almost weekly occurrence. Before the Troubles erupted, the only tangible sign of rebellion was in the annual act of defiance of Tommy Carlin, who lived on Central Drive, at the top of Fanad Drive. Every Easter Sunday, he flew a large Irish Tricolour of green, white and orange from a flagpole outside his house. A few times the police came and confiscated it. There was no rioting and the whole thing seemed stage-managed. When the Troubles erupted Tommy Carlin became one of the founders of the Provisional IRA in Derry and was blown up making bombs in a house in Creggan. Colm Keenan became one of the first IRA members shot dead by the British Army.

In the early 1960s, it was hard to imagine what would happen in Derry before the decade was out. Progressing through school, being an altar boy and playing football occupied most of my time. I had little interest in local soccer until my father took me to the Irish Cup final, in 1964, when Derry City played Glentoran at Windsor Park. It was one of the first games I attended and was a never-to-be forgotten experience. It was the first time that Derry had been in the final since the late 1950s. The omens were good in that on the previous occasions that

Derry had won the cup, they had defeated Glentoran in the final. However, my father told me that this time Glentoran were runaway league leaders and a few weeks before the final they had beaten their arch-rivals, Linfield, 8-1. They also beat Derry City 4-3 in a recent league game. It was thus with hope, and some trepidation, that we boarded the football special train, early Saturday morning. The train had a cafe and bar and I gorged on crisps and lemonade. My father had something stronger, called 'a half and a bottle.' Windsor Park, the home ground of Linfield, was also where Northern Ireland played their international games and was a magnificent stadium compared to Celtic Park.

It was a good walk from York Street railway station and even if you did not know the directions, all you had to do was follow the crowd. Outside the ground, I was treated to that American delicacy, a hot dog and more lemonade. I hoped there were plenty of toilets inside. We were high up on a terrace behind one of the goals, which I later learned was known as the Spion Kop. There seemed to be more Derry fans than Glentoran supporters, which seemed strange as Glentoran came from just across the river Lagan in east Belfast. The game was tight with few chances. Just as a replay loomed, Derry scored two goals in quick succession through Matt Doherty and Joe Wilson. Windsor Park erupted and at the final whistle there was a pitch invasion by delirious Derry fans. The train journey back home was a boisterous one, with much singing and drinking and later that night the team held the cup aloft from an upstairs window in the City Hotel. I have always been very thankful to my father for taking me to the final, which was a great bonding event between us. In his twilight years, when Derry re-entered senior football, I had great pleasure in taking him to Brandywell and, just a few weeks before he died, we went to a League Cup final, in Sligo, that Derry won. On that occasion, on the way home we stopped at Barnesmore Gap, a mountain pass in the Blue Stack Mountains just outside Donegal Town, and in Biddy's, a well-known hostelry, we toasted Derry City's victory. My father had a bottle of Harp lager and a chaser of Irish whiskey. The wheel of life had gone full circle.

I had been well and truly initiated into soccer and the following season I became a regular at Brandywell with Nigel Cooke, who had headed the disallowed 'goal' at Celtic Park. I sported a red and white striped football scarf and carried a football rattle or corncrake that would probably now be banned as a dangerous weapon. I think it was modelled on Gas Rattles that had been used in the First World War, to alert soldiers in the tranches of gas attacks. After a few games, I decided to leave it at home. My first year as a regular attendee at Brandywell coincided with one of Derry's best teams ever and the Irish League was won for the first time in the club's history. Every match day Saturday, after our morning shift at the Christians in preparation for the Quallie, Nigel would call for me and we would make our way to Brandywell via the City Cemetery. We opted for the reserved terrace, which cost one shilling and sixpence and was sixpence dearer than the unreserved terrace. However, it had the better view as there was a six foot slope on the Brandywell's playing surface and it was better to watch the game from the elevated position than looking uphill. True to the medieval history we were watching on television, Nigel christened our vantage area the 'snobs' side,' while the unreserved terrace was the 'peasants' side.'

The best games were against Linfield, Glentoran and Coleraine and these were usually very tight affairs. Linfield was then the largest club in Northern Ireland and usually brought a lot of travelling support with them to Brandywell. Their fans usually sang Orange songs and really enjoyed their renditions of '*The Sash*' and '*Derry's Walls*.' Victory over them was thus most enjoyable. Glentoran was usually a very classy outfit, playing a delightful game of passing football. Coleraine was the local derby with no quarter given and had the spicy ingredient as Tony O'Doherty, from Creggan, was one of Coleraine's top players and was also a Northern Ireland international. There was one game, however, against a mediocre Bangor side, when the focus of attention, if not adulation, was on the visitor's manager. Charlie Tully was a legend who had played for Glasgow Celtic. He held the unique distinction, in his Celtic days, of having scored directly from a corner kick, only for the referee to order the corner to be re-taken. He promptly scored again with the re-taken kick.

These were the halcyon days for Derry City F.C. and they translated into a feel good factor for the city a as a whole. The Swinging Sixties had hit Derry and as proof of the city's status the Embassy Ballroom featured top British pop stars including Lulu and Adam Faith. Mary McDaid, my cousin, went to see him and told me she was disappointed as he was a bit of a midget who needed a large box and massive heels to make him appear a tall star. However, he fully redeemed himself by sending a signed LP to a fan who lived in Fanad Drive and who had a major heart condition.

It was during my primary school days that I began going to the local cinemas with my friends from school and Creggan. I would watch films in Technicolor rather than the black and white of the TV. One film in particular, which I watched at home, passed completely over my head. It was called *The Boy with the Green Hair*! There was the recently built ABC in Newmarket Street, the Palace on Shipquay Street, the City on William Street, better known locally as the Flea Pit, and the Strand on Strand Road. One of my favourite films was *The Three Hundred Spartans*, telling of the heroic defence by the Greeks of Thermopile, against overwhelming Persian forces and their betrayal by one of their own. At the Christians, one of the teachers, Terry Mc Donald, who was a dab hand with movie films, entertained us with showings at the end of term and often on Saturday mornings. The partitions between classrooms were opened back and a large screen appeared overhead on which was projected an exciting western or Tarzan. By this stage, we had graduated to the new film sensation, James Bond, played by Sean Connery, secret agent 007 as created by the novelist, Ian Fleming. There was a new film every year starting in 1962 with *Dr. No* and followed by *From Russia With Love, Goldfinger* and *Thunderball.* James Bond was constantly saving the world from SPECTRE, the **S**pecial **E**xecutive for **C**ounter-intelligence, **T**errorism **R**evenge and **E**xtortion. There were amorous adventures along the way, which we considered soppy as we were more impressed by the range of gadgets and vehicles that James had at his disposal to get out of awkward situations, such as a dagger shoe and a cyanide cigarette. I really liked his Austin Martin DB5, with its pop out gun barrels behind the front indicators, bullet shield behind the rear window and a 3-way revolving front number plate.

At the end of my primary school days there was another spy series with caricature heroes and villains. *The Man from Uncle* made its debut. It starred Robert Vaughn as the American agent, Napoleon Solo, who, teamed up with Soviet agent, Ilya Kuryakin, played by David Mc Callum. Their assignment was to protect the world from an evil organisation called *Thrush.* Ian Fleming, the creator of *James Bond* was involved in creating these new characters, who worked for UNCLE, an acronym for the **U**nited **N**etwork **C**ommand for **L**aw **E**nforcment. The programme was more of an American version of the British television series, *The Avengers*, which starred Patrick Mc Nee and Diana Rigg as John Steed and Emma Peel.

No sooner had I started my Primary Seven year at the Christians than the Olympic Games began in Tokyo. The BBC commissioned the German composer Helmut Zacharias to compose a theme tune to be played at the beginning of every programme from the Games. He came up with *Tokyo Melody*, which did not have any words but contained vocal harmonies which give the music a distinctly Japanese flavour. London time was eight hours behind Tokyo and I used to get up a bit earlier for school to see some of the events before heading to school. I well remember my pin-up girl, Ann Packer, winning the 800 metre sprint, early one morning. She also won a silver medal in the 400 metre sprint. Her roommate was Mary Rand, who had the almost unique distinction of winning Gold, Silver and Bronze medals at those Games. The star of the field events was the Welsh long-jumper, Lynn Davies, 'Lynn the Leap, who won the gold medal. My father followed the Boxing, especially the fortunes of the Irish contingent. Jim Mc Court from Belfast won a bronze medal. My father was particularly impressed by the American winner of the heavy weight title, Joe Frazier, who a few years later, in 1970, would become the undisputed heavyweight champion of the world, a crown he successfully defended against Muhammad Ali, in what was called the "Fight of the Century," in 1971.

In September 1964, we returned to the Christian Brothers for our final year at primary school, where we sat the Eleven Plus papers, in the autumn. As we headed towards this, the biggest academic test of our lives to date, nothing was left to chance. We were obliged to give up being altar boys as the Christian Brothers would not allow us to be absent from school to serve Mass at ten o' clock. Our day with destiny finally arrived a few weeks after the 1964 General Election. For the *Qually*, there were three papers, one in verbal reasoning, one in composition and comprehension and the third in arithmetic. We had continued in Primary Seven with Brother Keane and we had been preparing for the big day for over a year. In the run-up to the examination we would go to school on a Saturday morning and sit mock papers until the real ones came to us as second nature. In one day, our fate was decided in an exam, which was unique in that there was no provision for a re-sit. When we finished the last paper, it all seemed a bit of an anti-climax but Brother Keane told us that we had just completed an exam that would define our lives. He was always keen to stress that success in the Eleven Plus would open the door of opportunity to a grammar school education that had been denied to our parents.

Brother Keane was very optimistic of great results for his class and no sooner had we basked in the joys of completing the *Qually*, than he set about preparing us for grammar school, months before we received our results. He said this would give us a head start on boys from other primary schools. Without fuss or fanfare, we were introduced to French, Irish, Geography, Algebra, Geometry and Trigonometry. French and Irish mainly consisted of the present tense of the verb to be, with being able to recite the Lord's Prayer, thus ensuring that I could now bless myself in four languages, English, Latin, Irish and French. Our geography lessons consisted of learning the provinces and counties of Ireland. We were given a special reminder that Donegal, Cavan and Monaghan were Ulster counties, although not in Northern Ireland. County Derry was never called Londonderry, although there had never been a County Derry, only a County Londonderry. On the blackboard were drawn, what we learned to be, right angles as well as acute and obtuse angles. More excitingly on the football pitch, the Christian Brothers team featuring many of my class mates, Peter Jackson, Jim Murray, Dennis Feeney, Paul Kearney, Maurice Brennan and Joe Doherty, won the Rice Cup, competed for by Christian Brothers' primary schools from all over the North.

One day, Brother Keane announced that there was going to be an American submarine docking in Derry that weekend and that it would be open for public visits on the Saturday afternoon. This was something not to be missed. During the Second World War, Derry quay had been crammed tight with British, American and Canadian warships. Now, here was an opportunity see inside a submarine. The last time submarines had docked on the Foyle was when the German U-boat fleet surrendered in 1945. Together with Peter Jackson and Paul Mc Clintock, I set off to see the submarine, which was berthed far down the quay, near to where Sainsbury's now stands. The long walk was certainly worthwhile and we were given an extensive tour, even seeing the torpedoes. Living conditions looked just as overcrowded and claustrophobic as they did in the movies and there was a feeling that, if anything went wrong, you would slowly suffocate to death. The young sailors said that it had been their ambition in joining the navy to be submariners and they did not really mind the fact that they would often be under the seas for months on end. While the visit was very enjoyable, it reinforced my prejudices as a landlubber. The nearest I would ever come to being a sailor was to sing Gilbert & Sullivan's *The Monarch of the Seas!*

When the New Year dawned, our focus was increasingly on the day that was drawing nearer, when the results of the Eleven Plus, were due to arrive. It was the Saturday morning that most parents dreaded. In my case, I did not have to wait until the arrival of the postman. As my father was a postman, he had often taken me with him to the main sorting office or around the city in the delivery van and most of the local postmen knew me. After school on the Friday afternoon, I called in to the main sorting office and was met by Don Stewart, one of my father's work colleagues, who asked me what I doing there as my father had finished work at lunchtime. I explained that I was very excited about my results and asked if there was any chance that they were already in the sorting office. About five minutes later, he returned and handed me a bulky envelope, saying 'you've passed.' I wondered how he knew. He read the expression of both awe and delight on my face and told me that the bulky envelopes contained a lot of forms to be completed about choosing secondary school.

I thanked him profusely but he was most concerned that I keep the results a secret, to be shared only with my parents, until the next morning. I almost danced a jig out of the post office, caught the Creggan bus in Guildhall Square and rushed into the house to tell my father. He was pleased, but not surprised, at my success. When my mother arrived home from the shirt factory, she was euphoric with joy. There was never any question as to where I would be going, St. Columb's College, simply known in Derry as 'The College', whose main buildings backed on the Christian Brothers. For many years it had been out of bounds to all except one of my class mates, Noel Quigley. He lived in Corporation Street and had permission to go through the College grounds as a short cut to the Christians, rather than take a very long detour down the Dark Lane and Hogg's Folly and along the Lecky Road and then the climb up the Brow of the Hill. He described the College to us in terms of the land of milk and honey, with two large football pitches, a handball alley and a concert hall.

On the Monday morning I returned to school, as normal, and discovered that over eighty percent of our class had passed the *Qually* and were destined for the College. Brother Harney had the same success rate in his class. We did not have to wait until September to set foot inside the hallowed grounds of St. Columb's, as we were 'invited' to sit an entrance exam, which was supposedly designed to allocate us to the various graded classes in first year. So, one Saturday afternoon in June, we entered the College, via the rear entrance, as it was the only one we knew, and were herded in to what was called the Senior Study for a series of papers on composition, comprehension and arithmetic, precisely the same subjects examined in the Eleven Plus. In total, there must have been well over one hundred and fifty of us in the College that day, boys from primary schools all over the city, meeting for the first time. The director of operations, that afternoon, was a Mr. McMahon and he had a booming voice that could be heard all over the study. Three months later, I discovered he was to be my Maths teacher.

My last year at the Christians ended with Derry City winning the Irish League and thus qualifying for the European Cup as one of the champions of Europe. Across the water, my beloved Manchester United won the English League, on goal difference, ahead of Leeds United. I had visions of Derry City playing the Red Devils in next year's European Cup. The F.A. Cup final was contested between Liverpool and Leeds United, who, under Don Revie's managership, wore an all-white rig as they attempted to become the Real Madrid of English soccer. Liverpool won the cup 2-1 and I remember a news headline, which was, 'Hail the Beat Leeds,' with pictures of the Liverpool football team and that city's most famous pop stars, the Beatles. The pop group, and not the football team, was now established as, what we now call, a global brand. The nearest we had come to pop mania was when all the altar boys were given free tickets to see Chubby Checker perform in St. Columb's Hall, where we usually went to see the annual pantomime. Obviously, Checker, who was a well-known American singer who popularised a dance style called 'the Twist,' had not sold the hall out and we were there to make up the numbers. After that evening, we were all masters of the Twist but did not have many opportunities to show off our newly-found dancing abilities.

I also have many happy memories of other evenings in St. Columb's Hall of pantomimes featuring Frank Carson and musical evenings which featured my cousin, John Carlin. One such evening stands out in my mind as John played a Burlington Bertie from Bow character and gave a rendition of 'Champagne Charlie is My Name' before leading the chorus in the *Toreador's Song*. I was always very proud of my Carlin cousins, John and Neil, who were great singers. Neil went with the Gaelic Singers to America in the 1950s and subsequently sang with the Sadler's Wells Opera Company in Britain.

The summer of 1965 was very leisurely. I counted the days until I started the College proper as a first year or 'Yap,' as we would be called by our seniors. Endless days of football were interrupted by long walks to Grianan Fort, which was over an hour away from Creggan on foot. I also have an abiding memory of going to the ABC cinema to see *Zulu*. In the queue, I met a boy who had been sitting beside me at the 'entrance' exam, Mario Hegarty, who lived near the Long Tower church and had attended its primary school. We exchanged stories about our interests and, unlike me; he was a keen Everton fan. He was destined to be in the same class as me in the College.

At that time, my father had renewed a friendship with an old army buddy from Belfast, Davy Mc Quade, and he and his wife Aggie would often come to Derry for the weekend and stay with us. Davy drove a Morris 1000 and in it I often travelled around county Donegal. Davy and my father organised a re-union of some of their fellow soldiers from their army days. A bus load of veterans from Belfast and Derry headed off to Willie Porter's pub, the Cruishkeen Lawn, in Buncrana to reminisce and drink. Among other things, I remember father and Davy talking about Alec Robinson, better known as the Buck Alec, who lived in Belfast and had been a ruthless loyalist paramilitary, boxer, wrestler and was reputed to have been a bodyguard for Al Capone. The Buck also fancied himself as a lion-tamer and he famously kept three toothless lions, monkeys and other animals in his back yard. That summer, my mother and I spent a week with Aggie and him in their home in Mossley, in the countryside outside Belfast. It was a village which revolved around a large mill that had been established in the eighteenth century. Davy told me that Trevor Thompson, Glentoran's centre forward, was a manager at the mill.

It was July and preparations were underway for the Orange celebrations of the Twelfth, the day Ulster Protestants celebrate the Williamite victory at the Battle of the Boyne. On the eleventh night, Davy took me around the bonfires on the Shankill Road, the heart of loyalism. The bonfires were much bigger and higher than anything I had seen in Derry on the 15th of August. We even visited his brother, Johnnie, who lived on the Shankill and who was a Unionist councillor on Belfast Corporation. Johnny was a docker and, like my father and Davy, was ex-army, having been at Dunkirk. Later that year, he was elected as a Unionist an M.P. for the constituency of Woodvale. He defected to Paisley's Democratic Unionist Party in 1971. One amusing story told to me about Johnny's years on Belfast city Council was about a debate on the development of the Waterworks. One councillor suggested that the Council introduce a gondola as an attraction. Johnny piped up, 'why don't we get two and then we could breed them?'

I remember sitting in his living room where the wall was dominated with a large picture of the Queen and the cushions were embroidered with images of King William, Prince of Orange, crossing the Boyne on his white charger. I thought I should fart on King William but refrained as the whiff would have embarrassed my mother. I think that I was probably the only Catholic youngster from Creggan to have had the privilege of sitting in Johnny Mc Quade's home, where I was regally fussed over by his wife, Cissie, with cream buns and lemonade. The next day, the Glorious Twelfth, I was taken to the parades, which in those days, passed without incident. I really enjoyed the brass bands, of which there were many. The bands generally tended to become much louder as they played a tune, which I was told was called *The Sash My Father Wore*, which I had heard being raucously being sung around the bonfires on the Shankill Road the previous night, as well as by Linfield fans in Brandywell. Davy wasn't an Orangeman but he thought I would like to see the colour and spectacle of the occasion. His son, John, was serving in the army and had been stationed in Ballykelly, a few miles from Derry. His daughter, Anne, was married to a John Smith, who worked in the shipyard and was a fervent Linfield fan and offered to take me to Windsor Park any time I wanted. They lived just off the Shore Road. I was also introduced to John's parents, who lived in an area called Tiger's Bay, which was not far away from where I had been born. Thankfully, the area did not have any tigers roaming free.

One of the last memories of that summer was my mother taking me to the Odeon cinema on the Strand Road to see *The Sound of Music*. We both enjoyed it greatly and what also made it memorable for me was that it was possibly the first time that my mother arrived at a cinema on time for the start of a film. In this instance, this was due to the fact that the film was so popular that you had to queue early to ensure admission. Through my primary school days, my mother would often have asked me if I wanted to see a particular cowboy film in the Palace or City cinema and off we would go. My mother never checked on the starting time of the films, which were usually shown on a continuous loop. Often we would arrive just as the hero was slaying the villain, or the Indians, and the heroine was falling into his arms. We would then sit and watch the film roll again until it reached the part at which we had come in. My mother would then tell me it was time to go home. I remember arriving at one film, which I later discovered was *Escape from Fort Bravo*, as the Mescalero Indians are about to make their final assault on a motley group of Union and confederate soldiers. Just when all seems lost, the distant sound of the bugles of the 7th Cavalry can be heard riding to the rescue. One legacy of this has been that throughout my life, I have had no difficulty in watching the final fifteen minutes of any film, without seeing what went before. I have to confess that I take great enjoyment from watching, over and over, only the final scenes from films such as *She Wore a Yellow Ribbon, High Noon, The Searchers* and *Air Force One* to name but a few.

I readily took to musicals on the big screen. A year earlier, I had gone on my own to the Strand Cinema to see Mary *Poppins,* with its great song *Supercalifragilisticexpialidocious,* which was probably the longest word in my dictionary. A few years later, at the same cinema, I enjoyed *Chitty Chitty Bang Bang* but my favourite was *The Jungle Book,* based on Rudyard Kipling's novel and I especially identified with Baloo the Bear singing *The Bare Necessities,* which just about summed up all that was important in life;

Look for the bare necessities
The simple bare necessities
Forget about your worries and your strife

So, after my years at the Christian Brothers I passed a leisurely summer playing football on the wide spaces in Creggan and going to the cinema. It was my pride and joy to own a Manchester United jersey, round neck and long sleeves, and I swaggered around holding the cuffs, just like my hero, Denis Law. We had mini-tournaments. It is surprising what you can do with a plastic Domestos bottle to convert it into a small football cup. Firstly, cut the funnel off and remove the top screw section, followed by cutting off the middle cylindrical section which left the base for the trophy. I then glued the remaining funnel to the base and cut strips from the middle section and these became the cup's handles, which were attached to the side by making small holes at the end of the strips and the side of the 'cup' and using hair pins to secure these handles. The final act was to spray the cup with silver paint. We had no other care in the world and, on a nightly basis, we fought for the Domestos Cup and looked forward to the next part of life's journey.

Chapter Five

Becoming Politically Aware

My Confirmation day in 1962 coincided with a General Election for the Stormont Parliament in Northern Ireland. At the time, Belfast was the only centre of devolved government in the United Kingdom and the local parliament had been established in 1921. One of the polling booths was St. Mary's Secondary School, just a few hundred yards from our front door. I passed it on my way to my Aunt Bridget's house to hoover up the traditional donations from her and my cousins. Two groups of young people had taken up positions on the walls outside the school and were busy chanting for their respective favourite candidate. I was completely uninterested, although the election in the Foyle constituency was a contest between the fathers of two of my classmates at the Christians, Eddie McAteer, the leader of the Nationalist Party, and Stephen McGonigle, representing the Labour Party. I asked my parents who they were going to vote for and both replied McGonigle. I had the impression that my father had little time for either the Nationalist or Unionist parties. I remember him watching one of the first televised debates, between a Nationalist MP and Brian Faulkner, who was a Unionist cabinet minister. He was angry that Faulkner was running rings around his Nationalist opponent, who was obviously totally unprepared. The age of television politics had finally hit Northern Ireland

Years later, I researched both that television debate and the General Election fight in the Foyle constituency. The Nationalist MP on the television that night was James O'Reilly and the subject being debated was religious discrimination. O'Reilly was pathetic and failed to produce any cogent arguments. He rambled on and on with a case that was not documented. In the election campaign, McGonigle accused the Nationalists of being "a single issue party." In reading about the election, I came across the following comment by McGonigle; "the Border would not go away overnight as the real problem, basically and fundamentally remained the deep divisions among the people of the Six Counties...McAteerism and all it stood for, was time and time again, driving a wedge deeper and deeper between the people." McGonigle was ahead of his time and no wonder my father voted for him. Nationalists were taking about a united Ireland as both desirable and inevitable, without having a clue as to how it was going to be achieved or what benefits would accrue. I also discovered that twenty two of the fifty two seats in the Stormont parliament were uncontested. It did not say much for a thriving democracy and the final outcome was almost identical to what it had been for the previous forty years, with the Unionist Party winning forty of the seats. One party government would continue until Ted Heath suspended Stormont in 1972.

My first awareness of political dissent and disorder came with the Westminster Election of 1964, and reports on radio and television of rioting in Belfast. Republicans were contesting the West Belfast constituency and had established election offices in Cromac Street. In the window of their election headquarters, they placed an Irish Tricolour, the flag that had flown over the GPO, in Dublin, during the Easter Rebellion of 1916. Nowadays you see Irish Tricolours everywhere, they are even waved at Premier League soccer matches in England. However, back in 1964, the flying of the Irish Tricolour was banned by the Northern Ireland Government under the provisions of the Flags and Emblems Act. A rising star of hard-line unionism, a cleric, by the name of Ian Paisley, objected to the appearance of the Irish Tricolour and demanded that the flag be removed from the Republican election offices. At the end of the day the police forcibly removed the flag, and rioting broke out in Belfast. With elections in America and Ireland in 1964, I asked my father if the Republicans in Derry were the same as Barry Goldwater, who was challenging Lyndon Johnson for the American presidency. With hindsight I can see that Barry Goldwater would turn in his grave if he thought he was a kindred spirit of Sinn Fein!

The year 1964 was a good one for getting to know my father. He was a postman, whose daily work started in the early hours of the morning and ended at lunchtime. He had both an interest in, and time, to enjoy the political party and trade union conferences that were broadcast live on BBC and he encouraged me to take an interest in what he called real politics. Television was the conduit for my political education. One day, I sat with him watching Terence O'Neill, Northern Ireland's Unionist Prime Minister, introduce Sir Alex Douglas-Home; the then Prime Minister of the UK, at what must have been a Unionist Party conference. The meeting was held in the Ulster Hall in Belfast, the same venue in which Sir Randolph Churchill had urged unionists to oppose Home Rule, in 1886. The two of them were guffawing on stage, mouths stuffed with marbles, or so it seemed to me. O'Neill spoke with a nasal drawl, while Douglas-Home was eloquently talking about 'Alsta' and 'Aland.' It took me some time to work out that 'Alsta' was Ulster and that 'Aland' was Ireland, rather than a region of Finland at the entrance to the Gulf of Bothnia in the Baltic Sea. Creggan might as well have been in the Baltic Sea as far as the two Premiers were concerned. O'Neill presented a tie of '*Alsta*' linen to Home and, to the delight of the audience, Home proceeded to undo his own tie and replace it with his new present.

A number of years later, I read about the this event in '*The Making of the Prime Minister*,' by Anthony Howard and Richard West. The book was about the General Election of 1964 and, with reference to the Ulster Hall rally, they wrote, 'The ceremony was watched with delight that evening, by Harold Wilson, who realised that it would lose Home thousands of Roman Catholic votes in Merseyside and Clydeside.' In the General Election, the Conservatives lost four of their Liverpool seats. While he had a small majority in the House of Commons, it seemed, to me, that Wilson would continue to vent his wrath on the twelve Unionist MPs, who took the Tory whip. The background of the Unionist MPs was no different from that of their Conservative Party counterparts in Great Britain. Landed gentry, farmers, industrialists and lawyers, mostly educated at English public schools and Oxbridge, although a fair few of them had gone to Trinity College Dublin.

The Conservatives had been in power for thirteen years since 1951 and in the February General Election, they lost office, much to the delight of my father. As an ex-serviceman, he had seen the Labour landslide of 1945. However, no similar political earthquake had occurred in Northern Ireland, where the Unionist Party was not dislodged from power, in spite of the efforts of the Northern Ireland Labour Party. In Britain, Wilson was to talk excitedly about 'the white heat of technology,' but Northern Ireland seemed mired in what Winston Churchill had once called 'the dreary steeples of Fermanagh and Tyrone.' My father was dismissive of what passed for politics in Northern Ireland, with Unionists and Nationalists caught in a time warp. Elections centred exclusively on the constitutional position of Northern Ireland. This, he told me, had been settled decades ago and how right he was. I later discovered that in 1925 there was a tripartite agreement, between the governments in London, Dublin and Belfast, recognising the constitutional settlement of the six counties of Anrim, Armagh, Down, Londonderry, Fermanagh and Tyrone as being part of the United Kingdom.

However, every election since then had been dominated by the Border issue and 1964 was no different. In the Londonderry constituency, Robin Chichester-Clarke, the incumbent Unionist MP, was opposed by Paddy Gormley, who was the Nationalist MP at Stormont for Mid Londonderry and Neil Gillespie, who stood as a Republican. In the usual sectarian headcount, Chichester-Clarke outpolled Gormley by more than twelve thousand votes. There did not seem to be much appetite among the constituency's nationalist electorate for separatist, republican politics, as Gillespie polled just fewer than three thousand votes. The local election caused hardly a ripple in our house, where the overall result in Britain was eagerly followed. My only memory of the local contest was the arrival at our door, one evening, of Dr. McCabe, my doctor. My mother was surprised as I was not sick but he told her he was simply canvassing for support for Gormley. At that time, Dr. McCabe was also a Nationalist member of Londonderry Corporation. We never saw our MP canvassing in Creggan, which he probably wrote off as a lost cause and his only election communication was a post-card sized address with a picture of him against a large Union Jack, exhorting my parents to save the Union.

I think that the 1964 General Election was the first for which BBC ran late on election night and it was a cliff-hanger. When the dust had settled, Labour had 317 seats and the Conservatives 304, which included the twelve Unionist MPs from Northern Ireland. The Liberals had 9 seats. It proved to be the last General election, in which the Unionists would make a clean sweep of the Northern Ireland seats. There was some excitement as to whether the Liberals were about to make a breakthrough and build on their stunning by-election victory of March 1962, when Eric Lubbock sensationally won a by-election in the Tory stronghold of Orpington, in Kent. Alas, a net gain of three seats hardly seemed that they had broken the political mould.

I sat up late on election night and apart from the issue of who would be the overall winner, I vividly remember the big news story being the defeat of Labour's Patrick Gordon-Walker, Shadow Foreign Secretary in the Birmingham constituency of Smetwick. His Conservative opponent, Peter Griffiths had been widely reported as using the slogan 'if you want a n....r for a neighbour vote Liberal or Labour.' He won by a majority of over 1,700. The liberal Establishment went ballistic, with Harold Wilson calling on the Tory party to disown Griffiths, whilst failing to mention that the Labour clubs in the Birmingham area operated a colour bar at that time. Interestingly, it was in the West Midlands that, a few years later, Enoch Powell unleashed his 'rivers of blood,' speech for which he was dismissed from the Tory front bench by Ted Heath. As for the hapless Gordon-Walker, he had the loser tag after Smetwick and failed to win the safe Labour seat of Leyton in a by-election, in January 1965, but took the seat in the General Election of 1966.

Maybe future generations of historians will call the 1964 General Election 'The Steptoe and Son Election.' It has emerged that the famous Marcia Williams, Harold Wilson's secretary and intimate member of his 'kitchen cabinet', discovered, to her horror, that on election night, the BBC was due to broadcast Steptoe and Son. It was one of the most popular programmes of the period. Her consternation was due to the fact that it was due for airing at nine o' clock, an hour before the polls closed and at a time when the largest number of Labour supporters traditionally came out to vote. She told Wilson, who immediately telephoned Sir Hugh Greene, the BBC Director-General, and argued that the timing of the programme would reduce the turnout of both Conservative as well as Labour voters. He suggested an alternative, 'Greek drama, preferably in the original.' The BBC demurred as it did not think Wilson's suggestion was suitable for peak-time broadcasting but it did move *Steptoe*. The incident caused Wilson to say that but for Marcia, Alec Douglas Home would have remained prime minister. He believed that broadcasting *Steptoe and Son* at prime time would have cost Labour twenty seats. Whilst I enjoyed watching the Wilfred Brambell and Harry H. Corbett as father and son running their rag and bone business in Shepherd's Bush, I never imagined that the timing of the television series could have had such a profound effect on the outcome of a General Election.

Whilst I took an interest in the General election in the UK, it had been events in America that had kindled my interest in politics, with the emergence of the first global political superstar in the person of John F. Kennedy. I had been vaguely aware of the Cuban missile crisis in 1962, as the Christian Brothers had reminded us that communist Russia's nuclear missiles were probably targeted on Derry, where the Americans had the most westerly communications base in Europe. The Brothers denounced Castro and the Soviet Union as godless communists, who should be wiped off the face of the earth. Kennedy, the first Roman Catholic president in the history of the USA, was the white knight who was going to save the world from communism. He had defiantly stood in the shadow of the Berlin Wall and uttered the words, 'Ich bin ein Berliner,' made an historic visit to Ireland, the land of his ancestors and seemed destined to be the world leader throughout the 1960s.

There were many homes in Creggan, where a picture of JFK was hung beside that of the Sacred Heart and the Pope. Kennedy's re-election as President in 1964 was considered a formality. That political dream came crashing down one Friday evening in November 1963. We were sitting at home watching Michael Miles introducing his weekly game show, *Take Your Pick*, when it was interrupted for a news flash. 'The President of the United States, John F. Kennedy, has been shot in Dallas Texas,' intoned a newsreader, who continued, 'His condition is described as serious. More news later.' A few minutes into *Emergency Ward Ten* came the confirmation that Kennedy was dead. The rest of the evening's programmes on both BBC and ITV were dominated by the assassination. Sir Alec Douglas-Home, who recently succeeded Harold Macmillan as Prime Minister came on air and spoke of 'this young, brave and, gay statesman...killed in the full vigour of his manhood.' Satellite technology beamed photos, across the screens, of the motorcade, the book depository from which the fatal shots were fired, the mad rush to the hospital and the swearing in of Lyndon Johnson as Kennedy's successor on board Air Force One. History was being acted out in front of our eyes and we all had a ringside seat.

Events moved quickly, with the news that a man had been arrested as the suspected shooter. He was Lee Harvey Oswald and news reports played up the facts that he was a former Marine and had defected to the Soviet Union. Within two days of his arrest, while in police custody and being led through the basement of the Dallas Police Headquarters, he was shot dead by Jack Ruby, a nightclub operator. The shooting was caught live on television and broadcast around the world in minutes. Even as a ten year old, it was like watching a Hollywood gangster movie. I was stunned that the man suspected of killing the American President was transported through an area open to the public, which seemed an invitation for someone to try to kill him. From the earliest days, even in school, there were conspiracy theories. Was there another shooter? Was Ruby part of the conspiracy to silence Oswald? That debate still rages, in spite of the findings of the Warren Commission, appointed by President Johnson to investigate the assassination. It reported in September 1964 that Oswald had acted alone in assassinating Kennedy.

It was little consolation to the devotees of JFK that Lyndon Johnson won the 1964 Presidential Election, by a landslide, against Barry Goldwater, the Republican nominee. With the death of Kennedy, my interest in American politics waned considerably, which was a terrible pity, as Lyndon Johnson actually took up some of the causes that Kennedy had ducked, such as Civil Rights. The news programmes on BBC and ITV regularly showed reports of Civil Rights marches in America during Kennedy's Presidency. The summer of 1963 was particularly brutal with footage of police in Alabama turning fire hoses and dogs on black demonstrators. At school, someone asked why Kennedy was allowing this to happen. The question was met with stony silence. That summer, Martin Luther King, delivered his famous speech, which has simply become known as the '*I have a dream*' speech and which was widely reported on television. It was said to be one of the greatest speeches of the 20th century. At school, we had been told that the American civil war, fought a century earlier, had been about the Confederates wanting to retain and extend slavery. The Union won the war and slavery was abolished. So, I could not understand why, a century later, black people were in revolt nor just what Civil Rights meant. In the summer of 1964, Johnson secured one of the most important congressional victories in history by having the Civil Rights Act passed, against the strident opposition of Democrats from his native South. Civil Rights were to be one of main issues in America in the 1960s, surpassed only by the escalating Vietnam War.

The New Year, 1965, started with the pomp and fanfare of Winston Churchill's state funeral. Churchill had been Prime minister when I was born! What impressed me even more was that Churchill had been a Cabinet Minister when my father had been born. I sat I front of the television watching the entire event, listening to the sombre tone of Richard Dimbleby, who was the sole commentator. Brother Keane was none too keen on Churchill and blamed him for the partition of Ireland. However, I was fascinated as the BBC told his life story. As a young lieutenant, he had taken part in the cavalry charge at Battle of Omdurman, in 1898, and then had been taken prisoner in the Boer War and escaped. In World War One he was both a politician and commander on the Western Front. From 1918 onwards, he was heavily involved in British and international politics. I certainly had the feeling that he was the key leader in ensuring that Britain held its nerve and continued to oppose Hitler in the Second World War. At an early age, it wasn't just watching the life of Churchill that impressed me but the BBC's coverage of the event and all major events, which for me, ranged from the FA Cup final to *Last Night of the Proms*. Outside of such pomp and circumstance, my favourite television programme had become *Perry Mason*, a fictional American criminal defence lawyer, played by Raymond Burr, who never lost a case.

There was great excitement in Derry, at the beginning of 1965, with controversy raging over the location of a new proposed university. Every politician in Derry believed that it should be located in the city as the natural development of Magee College, which had been established in the mid nineteenth century. Brother Keane told us that this was a university that we might aspire to attend. The government appointed a committee, headed by a distinguished British academic, Sir John Lockwood, whose terms of reference were 'to review the facilities for university education in Northern Ireland and make recommendations.' The committee made recommendation for the location of new university to be in the market town of Coleraine and not Derry. To rub salt into Derry's wound, it also recommended the closure of Magee College. There was near hysterical reaction in Derry. Nationalist politicians cried that it was a sectarian decision, devoid of any academic factors. For once it seemed that both Unionist and Nationalist politicians were united, as they condemned Lockwood's decision. A University for Derry Action committee was set up under the leadership of a young teacher called John Hume. A motor cavalcade travelled to Stormont with a petition but to no avail. The government accepted the Lockwood recommendations, creating great anger and resentment, especially among the Catholic and Nationalist population. Conspiracy theorists sprang up overnight and it was the first time that I heard the expression 'the faceless men,' a term used to describe a group of Unionist politicians from Derry who were accused of lobbying against their native city and secretly supporting the location of the new university in Coleraine, an overwhelmingly Protestant town thirty miles from Derry.

There have been many commentators, who have contended that the decision of the location of the university was one of the first measures that provoked the emergence of the Civil Rights movement. This may be something of an exaggeration but the decision certainly damaged the reputation of Prime Minister, Terence O'Neill. In the eyes of many Catholics, O'Neill was making the headlines with visits to convent schools and being regularly photographed with nuns. The reverend mothers seemed to be lapping up the attention. My father said this was all 'smoke and mirrors politics.' O'Neill milked the photo opportunities but they had little impact on the real issues affecting Northern Ireland. He had grabbed the headlines a month earlier when Sean Lemass, the Prime Minister of the Republic of Ireland came to Stormont and met him. The only protest at the Lemass visit was by the young fiery clergyman, Ian Paisley, who threw snowballs at the Lemass car as it drove through the gates of Stormont. The name that was entering the political lexicon as the rising star of Ulster politics was Brian Faulkner, the Minister for Commerce. He was both an effective minister and a good communicator. My father said that Faulkner was bright and was the best Unionist performer on television. He had, of course, run rings around a senior Nationalist politician on a programme about jobs and alleged discrimination. He had all the statistics at his fingertips. They showed that he had brought more jobs to Derry in his period in office, than his predecessors had in the previous decade. However, the government's decision on the location of the new university, coupled with the closure of the Great Northern Railway line were seen as failures by O'Neill to deliver tangible benefits for Derry. However, the issue that I heard my parents complain of most was the fact that the Mater Hospital in Belfast, which had a Catholic ethos, was denied any state funding, even though it was located close to the fiercely Protestant Shankill Road, from where anyone seriously injured was rushed to its casualty department.

Chapter Six
First Year at St. Columb's

*Ducking the Yaps – Avoiding the Monk – Introductions to a La Mor, World
Cup Willie & Lundy's Day on Derry's Walls*

In preparation for my September start at St. Columb's College, there was the need
to ensure that I was suited and booted, which entailed a visit to Paddy Bannon's
Boys and Gents Outfitters in Butcher Street, the official stockist for College blazers.
It was a black blazer, with blue piping along the edges and a badge with the school
crest and emblazoned with the Latin words, *'Quaerite Primum Regnum Dei.'* This
translated into English as 'Seek Ye First the Kingdom God,' from the Gospel of
St. Matthew and which had been adopted as the College motto in 1928. Grey
shirt and school tie were also the order of the day. The first dilemma was would I
continue to wear short trousers or graduate to long trousers. I was quite stunned
to be presented with a choice and had never thought of wearing long trousers and
so I opted to continue in short grey flannel trousers with knee length grey socks
for my first year. I felt sure that Brother Keane would have been proud of me as I
stood before the large mirror in Paddy Bannon's fully, attired in College uniform.

Not all boys from my days at the Christians went on the College. The
alternative was to continue in what was known as the Christian Brothers' Tech,
situated on the same site as the primary school or go to the recently opened St.
Joseph's Secondary School, which was situated on Westway, on the periphery of
Creggan. However, there were many boys from Creggan who went with me to
the College that year, including a number of altar boys from St. Mary's, as well as
my classmates from the Christians. My first year contemporaries at the College,
from Creggan, were numerous. The names that come readily to mind are Nigel
Cooke, Brian Barr, Colm Mullan, Damien Conaghan, Gerard McLaughlin, Paddy
McGavigan, Hugh O'Donnell, Tony McLaughlin, Raymond O'Connell, Dessie
Baldrick, Gerry Doherty, Eddie Kerr, Joe Carton, John Brown, Paul Kearney,
Danny McNally, Gerry Quigley, Declan O'Donnell, Pat Thompson, Charles
Duffy, Jim Harkin, Tony McGuinness, Gerry Henderson, High Crossan and John
Hamilton.

St. Columb's was then, and to this day remains, an all boys' school, just the
same as the Christian Brothers. The school day began at quarter past nine and
ended at twenty past three. On our first morning, we were again herded into

the Senior Study to be allocated classes, teachers and time-tables. The first year intake was about one hundred and eighty, divided into six classes, bringing the number of pupils to just over one thousand, the highest in the school's history. There was streaming and the A and B classes were top ranked, based on Eleven Plus results and the entrance tests we sat before leaving the Christian Brothers. The only difference between Junior 1A and 1B was that the boys in the B class were regarded as having artistic ability, which translated as an ability to paint. I found myself in Junior IA and most of my classmates were from my Christian Brothers' days, which spoke volumes of our artistic abilities!

Of course, there were also boys from other primary schools in Derry, the travelling day boys from the direction of Strabane and Limavady, as well as about half a dozen boarders, who came from counties Derry, Tyrone and Donegal. At morning and lunch breaks on that first morning, 'Yaps,' as first years were referred to contemptuously, were subjected to an initiation ceremony known as 'ducking.' Compared to what I had read in *Tom Brown's Schooldays*, this was quite mild and simply involved having your head held under a water tap in the toilets, located behind the Senior Study. Unfortunately, some Yaps received multiple duckings and the secret to avoid this was to get on to one of the two football pitches as soon as break started rather than be seen wandering around the grounds, like a hostage waiting to be snatched.

The College had been established in 1879 on the site, on Bishop Street, of the Casino, or summer house that had once belonged to Frederick Hervey, the famous Anglican Lord Bishop of Derry. The walls surrounding the College had a coping of stones, made from the lava from Mount Vesuvius, brought back by Bishop Hervey from his many travels. Established as a diocesan seminary, its student numbers were quite small by the end of the Second World War, numbering less than three hundred at that time. To its original buildings had been added a large number of what were euphemistically called 'temporary classrooms.' These were erected to cope with the vast increase in numbers of pupils who arrived with the advent of the Education Act of 1947, which introduced the Eleven Plus and opened up grammar schools to boys like me. It had burgeoned into Derry's Catholic grammar school for boys. For five years, I had gone to primary school in the shadow of St. Columb's. It was now time to move to the next level of my education and enter the school, the back of which overlooked our primary school classrooms on the Brow of the Hill. The move represented a move to an academic, as opposed to a technical, education and we were thrown into the deep end very early in our first week as we realised that the subjects to be studied were English, Maths, French, Latin, Irish, Science, History, Geography and Religious

Knowledge. We had lessons six days a week, with half days on Wednesday and Saturday. Wednesday afternoon was reserved for either going swimming at the City Baths in William Street or playing Gaelic football, which was also an infrequent Saturday event.

On that first, day we were given the names of our teachers and spent quite some time asking about their reputations. The first thing we learned was their nicknames. I also discovered that many of the boarders and travelling dayboys also had nicknames, something that had been missing in our days in the Christian Brothers. So, in our year group, we had Charlie 'Granny' Bryson, Frank 'Turkey' McGurk, Michael 'Drake' O'Doherty, Sean 'Ching' O'Neill, Declan 'Scoots' McCotter, Gerry 'Scones' Conway and Desmond 'Chirpy' O'Donnell. One of the first questions asked of me by a second year, who had also been an altar boy in Creggan, was; 'Did you get the Monk for Latin?' When I answered in the negative, I was told that I was lucky but was intrigued as to the identity of this man with a fearsome reputation. It transpired that his name was Fr. Robert Devine. He was also the College Dean, who enforced discipline within the school.

Thankfully, it was to be some time until our paths crossed and then it was over what appeared to me to be a trivial incident concerning crumbs on a desk in his classroom. As there was no school canteen, I would daily take a packed lunch to school and each class was allocated a specific classroom in which to eat sandwiches. We drew a short straw in being allocated Fr. Devine's room. One day after lunch a prefect came into our class and told us that everyone who had been eating lunch in that classroom was to report to Fr. Devine, who put before us the charges that we had failed to clean up the room and that there were bread crusts and crumbs on a number of desks. I greatly doubted the authenticity of the charges as I felt sure that the boarders, who were always complaining that they were being starved, would have made short work of any errant crusts. However, with the Monk, there was no point in arguing, as it only meant that you were also charged with insubordination. Therefore, we pleaded guilty and were given detention, for the following Saturday, which prevented me from going to the Brandywell. The upside of detention was that it gave two hours of uninterrupted study to get most of the weekend's homework out of the way and was preferable to being walloped with a leather strap.

My next and only other confrontation with the Monk was again over food, or to be more precise, feeding the boarders. Dayboys at the College were forever being told by the boarders that the College authorities were starving them to death. We took this with a pinch of salt as we had never seen any emaciated boarders wandering the corridors or walks. One Friday, a boarder classmate asked me if I would bring him back a bag of chips from the chipper in Bishop Street, where many of us regularly went. I readily agreed and accepted his money and I did not charge a fee, which some of the more entrepreneurial dayboys did. As I was walking through the front gate, with the bag of chips in hand I was espied by the Monk, who pounced and asked if the chips were for myself or another. I naturally replied that they were for me, which he did not believe but could not prove. My starving boarder classmate looked on in anguish as the prospect of steaming hot chips, drowned in vinegar, receded. The Monk directed me to his classroom to eat the chips. I was waiting for him to follow me there, when there was a commotion at the front gate and he went off to investigate. Like a war-time spy, I quickly passed the parcel to its rightful destination and made myself scarce, keeping well out of the Monk's way for the rest of that day and probably much longer. The lesson that I learned was to conceal any fish and chips that were being brought back to school for the boarders or risk their confiscation as contraband. I also learned that fish and chips were the least of the Monk's concerns and that his real target was to catch boys smoking in the bicycle shed. Thus ended my experience with Fr. Devine until my upper sixth year, when he was our Religious Knowledge teacher for one term before he went off to become the President of St. Patrick's College, Maghera, in County Derry.

The beginning of the school year also brought the much awaited Preliminary Round of the European Cup, in which Derry City were drawn against F.K. Lyn from Oslo and not Manchester United. We lost the first away leg by 5-3. On a rainy night in the Brandywell, however, we overturned this deficit winning 5-1 and became the first Irish team to progress beyond the Preliminary Round. The dream of being drawn against Manchester United lived on. When the draw was made it paired Derry City with Anderlecht, with Derry being away for the first leg. The Belgians, formidable team, which included Belgian international, Paul Van Himst, won the first leg 9-0. There was no second leg in the Brandywell as the Irish Football Association stepped in and declared that the Brandywell was not up to European standards. A stand-off ensued and Derry City withdrew from the competition. It was another example of a growing belief that the powers that be in Northern Ireland simply had a deep-seated prejudice against the city. They would not let us have a university; they closed the railway and now they were depriving us of European football!

Within a few days of entering the College, we seemed to know our way about as if we had been there for an eternity. We also learned that there was plenty of homework and the threat of the strap if we did not perform. Having spent a few years focused on the Eleven Plus, the move to the College was a considerable step up in our learning curve and we had to adjust quickly or be left behind. There was a natural progression in each subject and if you missed out on one aspect, it was difficult to progress to the next lessons. We studied three languages, French, Latin and Irish, of which the last was the hardest. Fr. Grant was our Latin teacher and I was fortunate in that I was to have the same teacher for most of my subjects for my three Junior years. In all three languages, we learned verbs by heart. Even fifty years later I can rhyme off the present tense of the Latin verb 'amare,' to love, as though it is my party piece. '*Amo, amas, amat, amamus, amatis, amant.*' I intoned my well-learnt verbs as if I was reciting the Confiteor as an altar boy. Fr. Grant seldom used the strap and our text book, *Latin For Today Book One*, told interesting stories of ancient Rome that made me want to ensure that I understood the language was able to follow the stories. The typical Roman family seemed to consist of pater, mater, puer, puella, servus, serva (father, mother, boy, girl, male and female slaves) and of course the faithful canis (dog). The homes were elegant and life was idyllic except for that of the Sabine women. The fate of conquered tribes was to be '*sub iugum mittere,*' sent beneath the yoke, which was not part of an egg but looked more like samba dancing. These stories complimented the poetry of Lord MacAulay's *Horatius*, whose stirring exploits on the bridge kept us in awe. Faith and fatherland were obvious themes, as Horatius, the intrepid captain of the Gate posed the rhetorical question:

> *And how can man die better –*
> *Than facing fearful odds*
> *For the ashes of his fathers*
> *And the temples of his gods.*

I also have fond memories of Fr. Grant reading aloud, in a drawling American accent, extracts from Damon Runyon novels in our last class before Christmas or the end of the school year.

Mr Hughie McGeown's Irish classroom was a few doors away from Fr. Grant's classroom. For my three junior years, Big Hughie, as he was called, was my Irish teacher. We pored over *Progress in Irish* and were put through the rigours of the present, past and future tenses of the irregular verbs, all of which were examined in a '*La Mor,*' a big day. Knowledge was rewarded by being given a reprieve for when you next failed to answer all questions correctly. The penalty for failure to know each answer was usually the dreaded strap. However, if Hughie was feeling in generous mood, he would offer you the choice of 'pen or sword,' take your slaps or write out the verbs one hundred times. I once elected for the strap and received six very sore slaps before remembering that I had stored up a reprieve. I did not forget again. We did not know it at the time but Hughie was a noted Irish language scholar and an authority on Irish grammar. He had been consulted by Tomas de Bhaldraithe when he was editing his English-Irish dictionary in the 1950s.

Mr. Tom Dunbar taught us French in a classroom above the Senior Study with a panoramic view over the College walks. He encouraged us to watch the BBC television series on French that were broadcast at the weekends. One in particular sticks in my mind, which was a series called *Suivez La Piste*. While we were not pushed very hard by him, we had an enjoyable introduction to the language. Our French class taught us that nouns were masculine or feminine, while Latin had neuter nouns as well. In spite of this laissez faire style of teaching I was pleased to do well in the class test in French. Next door to our French classroom, Fr. Mc Glinchey taught us Religious Knowledge in another high-ceilinged room that had plenty of natural light and a magnificent view. Fr. Mc Glinchey was one of the gentlest, genial but firm, teachers I had in my College days. It was a pleasure to listen to him with his great sweep of knowledge on St. Luke's Gospel that we studied in first year, as well as a catechism that was definite progress on the one we learned by heart at the Holy Child Infants' School. On the other side of the corridor was the office and inner sanctum of the College President, Fr. John Farren. We were told he was the nephew of Bishop Farren and account of that fact he soon acquired the name '*The Man From Uncle*,' after the popular television series. For years in the school, his nickname had been Wee Johnny, which was not to be confused with a shop in Bishop Street, where College boys bought cigarettes that were sold singly and penny lemonade drinks. Needless to say, the shop was often raided by prefects and the puffers of cigarettes had their names taken and were reported to the Dean. One of my friends had the ignominy of being reported by his brother, who was a prefect.

The science labs were in the old and original wing of the College, not far away from the Senior Study. We had a substitute teacher for the first few months as we waited for the arrival of Mr. Kerr. The wait was worth it, as there were plenty of practicals demonstrated by Mr. Kerr as we looked on. Most of these centred on the Bunsen burner and litmus tests, a phrase I identified later in life with political choices. I was fascinated by the high-sounding term, 'the co-efficient of linear expansion', and wrote quite knowledgeably about it in an assignment. Even in first year, you could see which boys had a more natural bent for the sciences than the arts and, in spite of all the endeavours of Mr. Kerr, I leant to the latter camp.

English, as taught by Mr. J.J. Keaveney, had plenty of bounce and panache. He raved about an emerging poet called Seamus Heaney, a past pupil of the College, who produced his first work, *Death of a Natura*list, during our Junior I year. Another past pupil, Brian Friel, had his play, *Philadelphia Here I Come*, premiered on Broadway. We were introduced to *The Faber Book of Childrens' Verse*, one of the finest books of poetry, which opened up a whole new world, with poems by Yeats, Wordsworth, Frost, Byron cascading out of its pages. We had hardly done any poetry at the Christians. Seeing the book, my father posed me a riddle. 'Which poet is this' he asked, 'who sat on the bridge and whose feet touched the water?' I was completely stumped. 'Longfellow,' he replied. His favourite poem, however, was Tennyson's Charge of the Light Brigade. Maybe, it was the old soldier in him, as he fondly quoted the lines

> *"Forward, the Light Brigade!*
> *Was there a man dismayed?*
> *Not though the soldier knew*
> *Someone had blundered.*
> *Theirs not to make reply,*
> *Theirs not to reason why,*
> *Theirs but to do and die.*
> *Into the valley of Death*
> *Rode the six hundred."*

One of the first poems we studied was also about war, *Irish Airman Foresees his Death* by William Butler Yeats. It is a poem to which I have often returned to read throughout my life. My first reaction to it was that it could have been written about almost any combatant in war. However, JJ brought it to life as he explained that Yeats dedicated it to his friend, Major Robert Gregory, son of Lady Gregory of Coole Park in County Galway. Educated at Harrow and Oxford University, he joined the Connaught Rangers at the outbreak of the Great War, before transferring to the Flying Corps. He died, aged thirty six, shot down in Italy in 1918.

From our primary school days, we had been conditioned by the words of G.K. Chesteron that the great Gaels of Ireland were people that God made mad, because all their wars are merry and all their songs were sad. However 'The War Song of Dinas Vahr,' by Thomas Love Peacock, from the comic novel, *The Misfortunes of Elphin,* written almost a century and a half earlier, dealt with legends in a unconventional way. The poem had blood flowing in all directions and being celebrated by the victorious warriors of the fictional king. JJ told us that Peacock was a satirist and, in this poem, he was poking fun at the Welsh, who took to song to describe almost everything. The poem ended jauntily with the words:

> *"Ednyfed, king of Dyfed,*
> *His head was borne before us;*
> *His wine and beasts supplied our feasts,*
> *And his overthrow, our chorus."*

'R-H-Y-T-H-M,' was a phrase we soon got used to hear from JJ, as we hastened to identify the difference between rhythm and rhyme. One poem, in particular stands out in my memory, W.H. Auden's 'The *Night Mail.*' As the train sped towards Edinburgh, we were caught up in its accelerated motion with '*letter of thanks, letters from banks.*'

Whilst the study of poetry was novel to us, we had been encouraged by the Christian Brothers to read novels in our primary school days. Now, we undertook serious reading about which we would be questioned in an examination. Our first novel was *The Silver Sword* by Ian Serraillier, and JJ encouraged us all to aim at creative writing. I did a piece, *Carrickfergus Castle*, which was published in the school magazine, *The Columban* that year. It was JJ, who also introduced us to Shakespeare through *The Merchant of Venice*. While most of my classmates focused on Shylock and his desire for his pound of flesh, I was quite taken by the eloquence of Portia's speech as she pleaded for mercy:

> *"The quality of mercy is not strain'd,*
> *It droppeth as the gentle rain from heaven*
> *Upon the place beneath: it is twice blest;*
> *It blesseth him that gives and him that takes"*

One of JJ's brothers, Michael, was a priest, who taught Maths in the College and JJ seemed a very devoted Catholic. For an essay he proposed we write about our experiences of going to Mass, a subject we thought more likely to be taught in our Religious Knowledge class. JJ asked a few boys what was the highlight of the Mass and he freaked out when two of the answers were 'getting out at the end,' and 'seeing the talent,' which referred to girls. No one else in class seemed surprised by these answers but we quickly learned that the best course of action was always to give the standard, expected, answer to any such question.

We were reacquainted with Mr. McMahon, who had supervised our Saturday 'entrance' tests just after the Eleven Plus results. His nickname was Hammie, which initially I thought had something to do with him possibly looking like a hamster, which he certainly did not. I was put right on the subject, being informed of his acting abilities as Hamlet, the Shakespearean character and not the cigar as advertised on television. We were not at all surprised to discover that the core of the Maths course in first year was the algebra, geometry and trigonometry that Brother Keane had putting us through in our last six months at the Christians. I remember Mr. McMahon as a good teacher, who had a dry humour. In our first year, he announced that the mathematician's song has reached number one on the pop charts. We were somewhat perplexed until he told us that it was *We Can Work it Out*, by the Beatles. Now, he posed the question; 'what did a right angle say to an angle of 30 degrees? You're a cute angle.' He even told one of the first risqué jokes I ever heard from a teacher. At the time, the television advertisements for Smirnoff vodka usually contained a play on the words 'I thought such and such was such and such until I discovered Smirnoff.' Hammie coined his own commentary for the ad, which was, 'I thought wan king was a province of China until I discovered Smirnoff.' It took a lot of boys in the class some time to work out the hidden meaning!

The cultural highlight of my Junior 1 year was the school production of *The Mikado*, and being introduced to the light operas of Gilbert and Sullivan. It was very funny to see three boys dressed up as the *Three Little Maids From School*. A future Chief Justice of Northern Ireland, Declan Morgan, appeared as Katishaan, an elderly lady of the royal court, in love with the Mikado's son, Nanki-Poo. Our weekly cultural experience was a singing class in the Junior Study, taken by Mr. Raymond Gallagher. There we sang our tiny hearts out and almost yodelled to the lyrics and chorus of *Emmental*;

> "There is no place in the wide world
> Half so fair as Emmental
> And the maidens ofthe valley
> Love the men of Emmental."
>
> Hol-di-ri-di-a ri- ho
> Hol-di-ri-di-a ri- ho
> Hol-di-ri-di-a ri- ho
> Hol-di-ri-di-a ho."

We went from the heights of yodelling to the Robert Burns poem '*Ca' the Yowes to the Knowes*,' with its awful Scottish lyrics. How I longed nostalgically for the good old days at the Christians, singing along to the BBC schools' programmes. The closest we got to those good old days was one morning when JJ started on the poem, '*The Oak and the Ash*,' which we had enthusiastically sung a few short years earlier. Beyond this, my most precious memory was learning the lyrics of *The Battle Hymn of the Republic,* written by Harriet Beecher Stowe, a wonderful song derived from *John Brown's Body.* It still sends goose bumps down my neck. Whilst I enjoyed singing, I developed an intense dislike of our singing classes after we discovered Mr Gallagher's way of dealing with boys whose singing was not up the high standards that he demanded. He would drag boys out of desks by the cheeks. I think it was called 'lugging.'

Most of our classes were in the huts spread around the College grounds and after second lesson each morning there was a ten minute break. I was amazed to discover that there were little or no facilities for the teachers in break time and generally they congregated around the toilets indulging in smoking cigarettes. You could hear the guffawing as palls of tobacco smoke rose into the Derry air. It was a poor example to set for students as well as a sad indictment of the facilities for the teaching staff. The Maths and English classrooms were located in what was called the 'Top huts,' temporary structures dating back to the late 1940s. A few rooms away from Hammie's class we had our history class, where we were taught by Mr. John Hume.

My father told me that Mr. Hume had been one of the leaders in the campaign to have the second university located in Derry and that he would not be surprised if this young man didn't end up in politics. The Prime Minister, Captain Terence O'Neill called a snap General Election for the Stormont parliament to be held in November 1965. There was much speculation that Mr. Hume, seemingly basking in the publicity of his public exposure on the university issue, would challenge the Attorney General, Teddy Jones, who was the sitting MP for the Londonderry City constituency. One day in class, someone had the temerity to ask Mr. Hume if he would be back in school the week following the election and received a withering look. Mr. Hume kept his political powder dry and did not run, leaving it to Claude Wilton to make an unsuccessful challenge as a Liberal candidate. Overall, it was hardly an exciting campaign and did not register any interest with me. Twenty of the fifty two seats were uncontested. This included the four seats in the Queen's University constituency that had been contested in the previous General Election. Johnny Mc Quade, in whose house on the Shankill Road I had sat the previous summer, was elected as MP for the constituency of Woodvale.

This was to be the last General Election to the Stormont Parliament in which any seats were uncontested. Much was to change before the next General Election in February 1969.

Meanwhile, back in Mr Hume's history class, the core of first year syllabus consisted of Britain in Roman times. Our first exercise was to make a list of as many military centres as we could that had been established by the Romans. We had a few clues from our text book, which mentioned Chester and to which we added Colchester, Cirencester, Winchester, Leicester and Gloucester as well as a host of other towns, none of which were in Scotland or Ireland. We also had an introduction to Irish history through J.C. Beckett's *Short History of Ireland,* which cost me fifteen shillings and which I still have. It was so unlike the highly partisan account of history doled out at the Christians. The highlight of the period of study was the victory of Brian Boru over the Norsemen at the Battle of Clontarf, on the outskirts of Dublin, in 1014. Mr. Hume was quick to point out that, in this battle, the Irish of Leinster actually fought on the side of the Danes and against Brian Boru, as they resented his attempts to destroy their independence. The Norman conquest of Ireland, a century later, was somewhat glossed over and we were spared the gory details of 'the rape of Dervorgilla.' We learned that she was the wife of the brutal Tiernan O'Rourke, king of Breifne. In 1152, she was abducted, along with many cattle, by Dermot Mac Murrough, king of Leinster. This was part of an ongoing power struggle, over the high kingship that had gone to Turlough O'Connor, king of Connacht. Poor Dervorgilla has been blamed by many for the Norman invasion of Ireland, which led to centuries of English domination. As Mr. Hume was quick to remind us; it wasn't the English who invaded Ireland more than eight hundred years ago but the Normans!

It was one thing to study history but as William Faulkner, the American novelist, once wrote '*the past is never dead. It's not even past.*' Lord MacAulay, who wrote of the Siege of Derry, put it more tersely with his comment that '*to write about Ireland to tread on a volcano whose lava was still glowing.*' After class, one afternoon in later December in our first year at the College, we came face to face with the truth of these words. We stumbled upon a commemoration of an important event in the city's history about which Macauley had eloquently written. It took place inside the walled city. Annually, on the 18th December, the Apprentice Boys of Derry commemorated the shutting of the gates of the city, in 1688. In late afternoon, they burned a large effigy of Governor Lundy, known as Lundy the Traitor, as he allegedly wanted to surrender the city to the advancing Jacobite soldiers. The huge frame of Lundy was hoisted up Walker's Pillar, overlooking the area that has become known as the Bogside, and set alight. As we walked along Bishop Street Within, as the part of the street inside the city's walls is known, a few of us went along to see this ceremony. We buttoned our riancoats over our college blazers as we walked along Society Street, which was a throng of mainly middle-aged men in crimson sashes and bowler hats waiting for the burning to begin. There was much on-street drinking and alcohol flowed freely from W.G. O Doherty's pub at the corner of Bishop Street as he did a roaring trade to match the canon, Roaring Meg. One of my classmates, Con Bradley, whose family had been heavily involved in the pub trade, told me that the days of such commemorations, which included July 12 (the Battle of the Boyne,) and August 12 (the Relief of Derry,) were some of the best trading days for local pubs, which were mainly owned by Catholics.

Geography was taught on one of the 'Lower huts', that overlooked the Brandywell area and our teacher was a Kerryman, Mr. Sean Moynihan, whose accent was difficult to understand, at first. He took us through our paces learning the counties, rivers and mountain ranges of Ireland as well as reminding us that Kerry should simply be referred to as 'the Kingdom,' on account of its beauty, mountains, lakes and supremacy at Gaelic football. We giggled as he spoke of 'Mc Gillycuddy's Reeks,' a mountain range near the Lakes of Killarney. With his thick accent, we initially thought he was talking about a rather smelly, unwashed person and were tempted to reply, 'We'll take your word for it, Sir,' but discretion was the better form of valour and Mucker Moynihan was not a man to be provoked, especially about his native Kerry.

Gaelic football, not soccer, was the game played at the College, and at which the school excelled. At the end of the 1964/65 school year, the College had won the All-Ireland Colleges' Football trophy. The school also provided the backbone of the County Derry team that beat Kerry to win the All-Ireland minor title at Croke Park, just a few weeks after we had started the College. The reason I remember that victory so well was that we got a free day to mark the victory. The College's football teams were dominated by the boarder contingent from county Derry and included Martin O'Neill from Kilrea, who was a pupil until his family moved to a few years later to Belfast and he transferred to St. Malachy's College. A few years later, Martin would score two goals for Distillery, in an Irish Cup final victory over Derry City. While the College was highly successful in Ulster Colleges' Gaelic football competitions, this passed over the heads of most of the city-based day boys in our first year, for whom Derry City, and soccer in the Brandywell, remained the number one attraction, on Saturday afternoon, after classes.

Not everyone in our class participated in playing football but we were still able to field a full fifteen for our weekly Gaelic football jousts in the class league, which was played on the pitches in the school. Mr. Tom Dunbar, our French teacher, encouraged the non-playing members of the class to come along to the games and support their classmates. *'Il faut avoir esprit de corps,'* was his rallying cry and his words must have made an impression as I remember Gerard Quinn, Con Bradley, David Doherty and Michael J. O'Doherty regularly standing on the side lines or behind the goals offering their support. Another phrase of Mr. Dunbar that has stuck with me was, *'Parlez Anglais, parlez Français, mais ne pas parlez Derryois,'* which was a clear instruction to speak in a manner that would ensure that outsiders understood us. The boarders smirked and felt that this was directed solely at the Derry boys. The smirk was quickly knocked off the face of Michael J. O'Doherty, when Mr Dunbar reminded him, quite erroneously, that the name O'Doherty was ever remembered in Irish history as that of the clan who stole cattle from the Doherty clan!

As we were Junior 1A we seemed to think that we had a divine right to be champs but were quickly disabused of such arrogance as 1C established itself as the best team in our year, winning the league and beating us in the cup final. Mark McFeely, who later played rugby for Ulster as well as Gaelic football for the senior Derry county team, was their stalwart, both in goal and outfield. Mid way through the year, each class team was given a mentor, one of the senior boys who were good footballers in their own right. Colm P. Mullan, a boarder from Ballerin in County Derry, was the Head Prefect and became our mentor. He was a great motivator and it was due to his efforts that we reached the cup final, which we narrowly lost. Colm went on to Maynooth to study for the priesthood. Unfortunately, he was involved in a serious car accident while at Maynooth and was forced to give up his studies.

The weekly visit to the William Street swimming baths, on Wednesday afternoons, appeared chaotic with dozens of boys from the three junior years all milling around the pool. The good swimmers were given pride of place and the rest of us were pitched into the junior pool that had been added at the Baths in the early Sixties and it was here we were taught to swim. Our only sojourn in the main swimming arena was as spectators at the annual school gala. The best swimmer in the College was Liam Ball from Creggan, who represented Ireland at the 1968 Olympic Games in Mexico City. Four years later he was again competing at the Olympic Games in Munich, where he was joined by three other Derry men, Neil McLaughlin and Charlie Nash in boxing and Terry Watt in judo.

Having mastered Pythagoras's theorem, Roman settlements in Britain, Euclidean geometry, irregular verbs, and knowledge of Ireland's counties and read a host of poems, I returned to the College after Christmas and became immersed in an interesting history project. Mr. Hume directed that, in groups, we should do an historical project and to our group he assigned the 1916 Easter Rising, the 50th anniversary of which was due to be celebrated at the beginning of April. It proved an enjoyable exercise. One of our group obtained a few copies of the Christian Brothers' periodical, *Our Boys,* which published a special supplement on the 1916 Rising and we were able to use many of the photographs of Dublin in rubble and the short biographies of the Rising's leaders, many of whom had been educated by the Brothers. The focal points of our project were the reading of the proclamation by Patrick Pearse on the steps of the General Post Office on Easter Monday and the executions of the leaders of the Rising.

The narrative of *Our Boys* was more hagiography than any of the history in Beckett's *Short History of Ireland*. It was interesting to compare the hero worship of the former with the realism of the latter. Beckett wrote, 'The insurrection of 1916 was not the result of intolerable oppression, nor did it begin with any reasonable prospect of success.' Within years of the Rising, Ireland was partitioned and again, I was impressed with the clinical commentary of Beckett, who wrote that the partition of Ireland did not depend upon a physical boundary that could be removed by political action but on the more important differences in outlook between two groups of people, unionists and nationalists. Our project on the Easter Rising was the first time that I was confronted with the clear juxtaposition of religion and republican politics. The Rising's leader, Patrick Pearse, painted the rising in religious terms of the blood sacrifice of Christ, even to the point of symbolically timing it with Easter. In later years I realised that it was no wonder that Republicans identified Easter with insurrection rather than Resurrection!

When we were going through the wording of the Proclamation, read aloud by Patrick Pearse on the steps of the GPO, in Dublin, on Easter Monday 1916, I asked Mr. Hume who were the 'gallant allies in Europe' who had rendered assistance to the rebels. Without batting an eyelid or giving any form of explanation, he replied, 'the Kaiser's Germany.' I was a bit perplexed, as my grandfather had been fighting against the Kaiser's Germany in the First World War and had been wounded for his troubles. So, Patrick Pearse and the rebels were in league with the enemy, which greatly coloured my view of the Rising. At home, I mentioned this to my father, who reminded me that there had been a lot of significant events in 1916, in addition to the Easter Rising in Dublin. He then proceeded to tell me about the Battle of the Somme about which there had been no mention in school. Across the Border, things seemed to be heating up, as the Easter approached. Nelson's Pillar was blown up in the centre of Dublin and it was said that the IRA had been involved in this.

At school, the most important assignment after Easter was called the Bishop's Exam. This was an examination on our religious knowledge and we had been told that failure in this exam meant expulsion from St. Columb's. To be expelled from the College for failing a test in religious knowledge would have been the biggest disgrace. Everyone in the school did the exams on the same day, with the questions based on the class work studied in the year. As it transpired, no one was expelled and I have yet to meet any pupil, who failed the exam. Fr. Mc Glinchey was very focused on ensuring that not only did we pass the exam but passed with flying colours. In the middle of the preparations, however, he was also delirious with joy at the news report that the Pope had met Michael Ramsey, the Anglican Archbishop of Canterbury in Rome. This was hailed in the press, on radio and television as a breakthrough in relations between the Churches. Meanwhile, there was also widespread coverage of two Free Presbyterian ministers from Belfast, who objected so strongly that they flew out to Rome to stage a protest there, only to be summarily despatched, by Roman police, on the next plane home. Of course, one of them just had to be Rev. Ian Paisley, Moderator of the Free Presbyterian Church. He was someone we were increasingly seeing on our television screens, protesting against ecumenism and a perceived republican threat to Northern Ireland.

The commemoration of the 1916 Easter Rising took place only a few weeks after the General Election in the United Kingdom, which I followed mainly through BBC programmes such as *Panorama* and *Tonight*. I always enjoyed the subtle play on words that the presenter, Cliff Michelmore, used to sign off the latter programme; «That's all for tonight, the next 'Tonight' will be tomorrow night. Until then, good night!» These current affairs programmes opened up the wider world beyond Derry and highlighted two emerging stories that would continue to grow. Firstly, the name, 'Vietnam,' seemed to be coming more into prominence, with increasing numbers of American soldiers being sent there to fight. Secondly, we were somewhat vaguely aware of the break-up of the British Empire, with many of its African colonies gaining independence. Late night news reports showed the Union Jack being lowered in a formal ceremony and flags that reminded me of my mother's multi-coloured curtains being raised in its place. Years later, I came across the wounding comment of Dean Acheson, an American Secretary of State, that Britain had lost an empire but had failed to find a role in the world.

The seamless transfer of power in the colonies was halted abruptly when it came to what had been Southern Rhodesia. This presented increasing difficulties for Harold Wilson, the Prime Minister, who had a slender majority from the

General election of 1964 and whose authority was further undermined by a series of by-election defeats. The term, UDI, Unilateral Declaration of Independence, entered the political vocabulary. I learned, from the television reports that it appeared that Wilson lacked the power to stop Ian Smith, the leader of the white Rhodesians, from declaring UDI, in November 1965, effectively telling the British government to take a hike. It also appeared that Smith had many supporters back in Britain, who wanted white minority rule in Rhodesia to continue. A few months later, Wilson secured an increased majority of almost one hundred in a snap General Election but his problems in Rhodesia only intensified. The highlight of that election in Northern Ireland was that the Unionist Party lost West Belfast to a new political face, Gerry Fitt, who had been a Republican Labour councillor on Belfast City Council.

The political climate in Northern Ireland took a turn for the worse as I progressed through my first year at the College. Republicans organised marches to commemorate the 1916 Rising, which drew a hostile reaction from within the Unionist community. A number of commentators highlighted *John Bull's Political Slum*, an article on Northern Ireland that appeared in the Sunday Times on July 3, 1966. "When the flags and bunting are hauled down after the Royal visit," it began, "Mr. Wilson's government will still be confronted with a sharp alternative; whether to use reserve powers to bring elementary social justice to Ulster or simply allow Britain's most isolated province to work out its own bizarre destiny. During the forty five years since partition the latter has often been negligently adopted with what looks like disastrous results." The article went on to document political gerrymandering and high levels of Catholic unemployment and emigration. However, Derry was, by and large, a sleepy slum most of the time, with the potential to explode. I remember my father saying that the Labour government should be more concerned with Northern Ireland as it was a part of the United Kingdom and he hoped that the election of Gerry Fitt would encourage a change in government policy. Maybe, however, Edmund Burke was a better reader of British government intentions towards Ireland when, in the 18th century, he wrote that the desire of all British governments was to hear as little of Ireland and its concerns as possible!

The drift towards violence culminated, in June 1966, in what became known as the 'Malvern Street killing,' in Belfast, carried out by a new loyalist organization calling itself the Ulster Volunteer Force, the UVF. It took its name after the force raised a half century earlier by Edward Carson to oppose Home Rule. Members of the group shot dead a Catholic barman, Peter Ward, and wounded two of his colleagues as they left a public house. Terence O'Neill, the Prime Minister, cut short his holidays and returned to Northern Ireland and immediately outlawed the Ulster Volunteer Force under the Special Powers Act. In October, its leader, Gusty Spence, and two other men were sentenced to life imprisonment for the murder. The three were members of the Prince Albert Loyal Orange Lodge No. 1892. The following July, in the course of the 12th parades, the lodge, which included Johnny Mc Quade in whose living room I had sat as a guest, passed the Crumlin Road jail, where the three convicted killers were being held. The parade paused to pay its respects to its incarcerated brether.

By the end of the summer of 1966, press interest in Northern Ireland, which had been momentarily aroused, evaporated as winter fell. At around this time, however, there were the first stirrings of interest in Northern Ireland by Labour MPs at Westminster. Paul Rose, a young MP, who had been elected for a Manchester constituency in the 1964 General Election, came to public notice. He became the first chairman of an organization called Campaign for Democracy in Ulster and I remember seeing him on a number of current affairs programmes.

I recently carried out some research on Paul Rose and his efforts to get Westminster interested in the internal workings of the Northern Ireland government. I discovered that his political leader, Harold Wilson, obviously had enough fish to fry with the Rhodesia issue and, to the delight of Unionist MPs, slapped down Mr. Rose in the House of Commons. Rose had the audacity to call on the Westminster government 'to set up a committee of enquiry into the working of the government of Northern Ireland. Wilson replied that he was 'not aware of any issue in which an enquiry was needed.' As a back up to the Prime Minister, the Speaker of the House of Commons ruled any discussion out of order, which followed a Westminster convention, dating back to the 1920s, that the Westminster parliament was not the appropriate forum to discuss matters that had been devolved to Stormont. Rose challenged this and, in the ensuing years, there was a posse of Labour MPs visiting Derry, being photographed on the Walls and telling reporters of their deep concerns about the workings of the government of Northern Ireland. By this time, of course, Harold Wilson was secure with a majority of almost 100 seats in the House of Commons. His previous ire at the Unionist MPs, who made his tenure of office uncomfortable for almost two years, seemed to have subsided. Wilson disappointed my father with regard to Northern Ireland, as he seemed to draw his guidance from the saying of one of his predecessors, Sir Robert Walpole; 'let sleeping dogs lie.'

My first year at the College passed quickly and uneventfully as I kept my head down and got on with ensuring that I would do sufficiently well in class tests to ensure that I would remain in the A stream in Junior 2. I exceeded my targets and expectations and got glowing reports after both the Christmas and Summer tests. The school year ended with the Beatles again topping the charts with *Paper Back Writer*. A few months earlier, Fr. Mc Glinchey, our Religious Knowledge teacher, had despaired when John Lennon announced that the Beatles were more popular than Jesus Christ. As lessons ended, our excited focus was on the World Cup that was being played in England in July, with all the games broadcast live on television. The draw had been made in January and England was in the same group as France, Mexico and Uruguay. It was the first World Cup with its own mascot and major marketing. World Cup Willie emerged as the mascot, a lion wearing a Union Jack jersey, with the words World Cup. I bought a world Cup Willie badge and pinned it on my college blazer, only for JJ to confiscate it. There was even an official World Cup song released, which was sung by Lonny Donegan, whose previous hits had included *My Old Man's a Dustman* and *Does Your Chewing Gum Lose Its Flavour on the Bedpost Overnight?* This time round, he was singing the World Cup Willie song, the England team's anthem, whose chorus was:

Dressed in red white and blue
He's World Cup Willie
We all love him too
World Cup Willie
He's tough as a lion and never will give up
That's why Willie is favourite for the Cup

In March, in the run-up to the World Cup, the trophy was stolen, only to be recovered a week later. It was wrapped in newspaper and the official story was that a dog, Pickles, had sniffed it out under some bushes. The tournament was a solid month of soccer, with the hosts bidding to become only the third country to win the Jules Rimet Trophy on home soil. It was a tall ask for England, given the presence of Brazil, the reigning world champions, who had won the cup in both 1958 and 1962. With all the usual fanfare, the tournament was officially opened by the Queen, ahead of the first game at Wembley between the hosts and Uruguay. After the game, she quickly nipped over to Northern Ireland for a state visit in Belfast. For many years, the IRA had shown its stern disapproval of such royal visits by blowing up inoffensive customs posts, cutting down telegraph poles in remote areas, or daubing public monuments. This time round, a large breeze block was dropped from the top of a building onto the bonnet of her car by a young, seventeen year old teenager, named John Morgan, who claimed he was acting alone. For the Queen, this must have been greater excitement than she experienced at the opening game of the World Cup, at Wembley, which was something of an anti-climax. Putting it bluntly, it was a damp squib and ended in a goalless draw, which seemed to please the visitors more than the hosts. England redeemed themselves in the subsequent games, defeating both France and Mexico to top the group and ensure a continued stay at Wembley for the quarter final showdown with Argentina. Bobby Charlton, one of my Manchester United heroes, scored twice in the victory over Mexico.

Elsewhere, West Germany topped the second group, thus avoiding England in the quarter finals. The real excitement was in Group Three, played at Old Trafford, in Manchester, and Goodison Park, in Liverpool. Sensationally, the defending champions, Brazil, were knocked out as Hungary and Portugal, making their World Cup debut, qualified. An even greater surprise was the results from Group Four in the North-East, where North Korea beat Italy, one of the pre-tournament favourites and qualified alongside the Soviet Union. The stage was set for interesting quarter finals. At Wembley, England beat Argentina, in an ill-tempered game, thanks to a late strike by Geoff Hurst. Up until the goal, the most exciting passage of play had been the dismissal of Argentina's captain, Rattin. Uruguay, another South American team, had two players sent off as they crashed 4-0 to West Germany. The Soviet Union, captained by the legendary goalkeeper Lev Yashin, beat Hungary 2-1 and the other quarter final at Goodison Park, between North Korea and Portugal was a cracker. The minnows raced in to a three nil lead within twenty minutes and looked to be heading for a massive upset. Then, just like in the Roy of the Rovers stories from the comic magazines, in stepped a hero, in the person of Benfica's Eusebio. He scored four goals as Portugal ran out 5-3 winners and booked a semi-final place against England. People were now speaking of Eusebio with the same veneration as they had for the talents of Brazil's Pelé.

The semi-finals were both mid week games, with England beating Portugal 2-1, with goals from Bobby Charlton and West Germany triumphing over the Soviet Union by the same score. The story of the final is often shrouded in the debate as to whether the ball fully crossed the line to give England a 3-2 lead in extra time. There was the famous outburst of match commentator, Kenneth Wolstenholme; 'Some people are on the pitch. They think it's all over. It is now,' as Geoff Hurst rifled a fourth, giving him a world Cup final hat trick. My memory is the more humorous satire of Johnny Speight in his television script, 'Till Death Us Do Part,' where Alf Garnett, played by Warren Mitchell, claimed that it was Harold Wilson, the Labour Prime Minister, who forced England to wear red shirts as this would reflect well on socialism if they won. The World Cup ended at Wembley, where it had started and the Queen's final task was to present the cup to Bobby Moore, the England captain.

The World Cup final marked the end of what had been for me a disappointing football season. Derry City surrendered the Irish League Championship to Linfield, where Tommy Leishman, a former Liverpool player, had taken over as player-manager and where Sammy Pavis was a sensational centre forward, regularly being the top marksman in the Irish League. Many Linfield fans simply called him, 'Sammy Save Us', Manchester United suffered a similar fate to Derry City, finishing four points behind Burnley in the English first division. The real disappointment, however, was United's failure to win the European Cup, after they had soundly thrashed Benfica in the quarter finals. United had a slender 3-2 lead from the first leg, at Old Trafford, but took Lisbon by storm winning the return game 5-1. As the game was late in the evening, I listened to it on my transistor radio under the blankets for fear of my mother catching me. I whooped for joy as George Best scored two goals within the first quarter of an hour. The next morning the press was singing the praises of El Beatle, as he was instantly dubbed, and the road to the final looked easy to me, as Partisan Belgrade were the opponents in the semi-final. However, United stumbled and crashed out, losing the first leg 2-0 in Belgrade and only winning the return 1-0. The dream final against Real Madrid thus never materialised. To win the cup, the Spanish champions had to come from a goal down to beat the Yugoslav champions 2-1 in the final.

In August, with the World Cup over, my parents took me to Butlin's Holiday Camp in Mosney, County Meath, for a week's holidays. On a Saturday morning, there was special bus that went direct from Derry to the camp and I was quite excited about the holiday. The holiday camp was situated on the coast, about thirty miles north of Dublin and offered a full week's accommodation, entertainment, sporting facilities and food and drink all within one compound area. I had a very carefree week, having enrolled as a Butlin's Beaver at the outset but apart from participating with my fellow beavers in a rowing boat race, I tended to stick to myself. I played pitch and putt with my father, and one of the redcoats, Auntie Anne, as we called her, taught me table tennis and how to jive.

One day, I must have had the head staggers as, unknown to my parents, I entered the junior talent competition and appeared on stage to sing a song that had been in the pop charts, 'Almost Persuaded'. I didn't really have a clue about its meaning but here I was, a thirteen year old singing about being in a bar room with a woman 'with ruby red lips and coal black hair and eyes that would tempt any man.' This was certainly not the genre we learned in singing classes. My greatest surprise was that I won my way through to the final, to sing before a full house in the Butlin's music hall. I plucked up the courage to tell my parents and they complimented me on my achievement. I left out the minor detail of the lyrics of the song. Alas, my hopes of stardom were dashed in the final, as the judges awarded the crown to an Irish dancer, Patrick Farrington, who seemed to have come to Butlin's with the sole intention of participating in the junior talent competition. He came prepared with his full Irish dancing outfit, which was something I thought any normal boy would not otherwise have brought on holiday!

I quickly got over any disappointment that I may have harboured, especially when I came across a broken slot machine that paid out sixpence at every turn. I was quietly pocketing such rich pickings until one of the staff caught on and unplugged the machine. I was 'almost persuaded,' to quote from my song in the talent competition, to leave it at that, but returned the next day, and, when no one a looking, I nimbly plugged the machine back on and continued on my winning ways. It must have been the only time when a slot machine was rigged in favour of the punter!

Chapter Seven
Preparing for the Junior Certificate and the End of the Age of Innocence

A 'Magical Mystery tour' to Old Trafford as we were taught to speak properly and watching Gary Sobers hit six sixes in one over

I had the distinct feelings of both pleasure and achievement as I made my way back to St. Columb's College, in September of 1966, to begin my second year. I had graduated to wearing long trousers, which distinguished me from the Yaps, none of whom I was inclined to duck for their initiation. Some of my classmates, like George McGowan, were now, in words from the hit by the Kinks, 'dedicated followers of fashion' and were wearing trousers called 'hipsters.' Based on exam results of the previous year, I was now in Junior 2A. We embarked on the first year of two that would end with sitting the next public examination, the Junior Certificate. I retained most of my first year teachers. The major casualties were our previous Science teacher, Mr. Kerr and our History teacher, Mr. Hume. The latter left the teaching profession and became the manager in a local salmon processing factory. It was widely said that this career change was simply to pave the way for a political career, as he could not stand for public office while remaining a teacher. There were also changes in the composition of our class. Damien Conaghan, with whom I had been at the Christians, left the College as his family moved to England, while David Doherty's family moved to Ballymena. Some boys dropped into other streams and were replaced. The most noticeable aspect of these changes was that we had a better football team than in first year and looked forward to challenging for top spot in both the class league and cup competitions.

Just a few days before term began, the big news story was about an English yachtsman, Francis Chichester, who left Plymouth in his ketch, Gypsy Moth IV, to attempt to circumnavigate the globe. In the course of the next year we studied previous voyages of explorers such as Vasco Da Gama, Ferdinand Magellan and Christopher Columbus in our history syllabus. However, the name of Francis Chichester was always to the fore as JJ Keaveney put up a large Sunday Times map showing the proposed voyage of this modern explorer. We were excited when a few weeks before the end of the academic year, the intrepid yachtsman returned after an epic voyage of 226 days. I recall the television pictures of thousands of small boats accompanying Gypsy Moth IV into the Plymouth Sound, letting off hooters and sirens. Fire boats sprayed what we were told was red, white and blue water. A few months later, he was knighted. For the ceremony, the Queen used the same sword used by her predecessor and namesake in 1581 to knight Sir Francis Drake, who was the first Englishman to complete a circumnavigation of the globe. As we had also learned, Drake was a privateer and slaver, as well as being a navigator and that voyages of exploration had a heavy commercial design.

Our new History teacher was Mr. Dennis Ruddle, from Limerick, with a thick Munster accent. He was quickly given the nickname, Barney Rubble, a character from the *Flintstones*, an animated American television series that was very popular. Fr. Regan, better known as Busty, became our Science teacher. The first choice we had to make was between History and Geography, and I plumped for the former. Farewell to Mucker Moynihan and tales of Kerry's greatness. Having oscillated between Roman Britain and the Easer Rising under Mr. Hume's tutelage, we were now focused on Elizabethan Ireland, the Spanish Armada, the Great Fire of London, the English Civil War, the Plantation of Ulster and the Williamite Wars. It was interesting to learn that it was the Tudor monarchs who established the county division of Ireland, so beloved to that most nationalist organisation, the Gaelic Athletic Association. We also learned that Irish chieftains were eager to embrace the policy of 'surrender and regrant,' that allowed them to pass on their new titles, and more importantly their lands, to their oldest son. This enabled them to dispense with the Brehon property laws that had been in place for centuries and under which the lands reverted to the clan on the chief's death and the clan then determined the successor.

For once, history was not simply about battles, as Mr. Ruddle taught us quite a lot about the legal nature of the administration of Ireland from 'Poynings' Law' of 1494 onwards. It was a more intense programme of the study of history than we had been used to in first year, and this applied across all our subjects. Beckett's *Short History of Ireland* was of great assistance in studying Irish history, especially as we had to mark on maps the position of principal places referred to in our answers and Beckett provided good maps. Mr Ruddle often reminded us that our fate in the exams lay in our own hands. His favourite sentence was, 'It's your baby when it comes,' which was a bit of an enigma, as most of us were somewhat ignorant of this fusion of the study of history with biology. Having Irish history taught by someone who was not from Northern Ireland was a novelty and while Mr Ruddle may have had strong views on the seventeenth century 'Broken Treaty of Limerick,' he was highly objective in teaching our curriculum.

Our study of Elizabethan Ireland, as taught by Mr. Ruddle, was augmented by a visit to the Strand Cinema to see the Walt Disney production of *The Fighting Prince of Donegal*, loosely based on the life and times of Red Hugh O'Donnell. It began with an old woman in the fields uttering that the prophecy had come to pass, that 'Ireland shall be free,' as Hugh had succeeded Hugh as Prince of Donegal. The English had obviously heard of the same prophecy, as they quickly took Hugh captive and lodged him in Dublin Castle. A daring escape ensued, accompanied by the song '*O' Donnell Abu* that had everyone in the cinema stamping their feet. The lyrics, written by Michael Joseph McCann in 1843, were stirring but would hardly have made anyone in the audience want to rise up in revolt:

> *"Proudly the note of the trumpet is sounding;*
> *Loudly the war cries arise on the gale;*
> *Fleetly the steed by Lough Swilly is bounding,*
> *To join the thick squadrons on Saimear's green vale.*
> *On, ev'ry mountaineer,*
> *Strangers to flight or fear,*
> *Rush to the standard of dauntless Red Hugh.*
> *Bonnaught and Gallowglass,*
> *Throng from each mountain pass.*
> *On for old Erin, "O'Donnell Abú!"*

As we anticipated a great battle, the scenes of courtship between Hugh and Kathleen Mc Sweeney, daughter of another Irish chieftain, were, for us, unnecessary interludes. In class, we were forced to confront historical facts. O' Donnell won a victory over the English, at the battle of the Yellow Ford, in 1598 but four years later, his forces were defeated at Kinsale and he left Ireland and sailed into exile.

While we enjoyed our new History teacher, our new Science teacher, Fr. (Busty) Regan, was another matter. It was the opinion of many of our class, myself included, that he was highly obnoxious and was a useless teacher, to boot. Coming from the rolling hills of County Derry, he appeared to look down his nose at boys from Derry City and hankered for the good old days, before the 1947 Education Act, when the College was the preserve of sturdy boarders and well-heeled city dwellers. He spent most of his time in class reading *The Irish News* and we were shocked that the President, the Board of Governors and the Department of Education's inspectors tolerated such poor teaching standards. One day, someone produced a Polaroid camera and took a picture of Busty as he was sitting reading the newspaper and the picture was pinned on the College notice board. Busty never knew which class had taken the picture as he read the paper in every class. I passed my Junior Science exam, with no input from him. However, I learned quite a lot from his failure to teach, which was that if you wanted something, you went and got it yourself, without having to rely on others. I passed Junior Science, in spite of rather than because of, Busty Regan and felt very proud of this achievement.

Our progress in learning the Irish language, under Hughie McGeown, progressed from remembering the irregular verbs to a study of *Rotha Mor an Tsaoil*, literally translated into English as the *Big Wheel of the World*. It was an autobiography by Mici Mac Gabhann. A translation of the book into English, by Valentin Iremonger, had appeared in 1962 under the title *The Hard Road to the Klondike*. I remember Willlie McGoldrick, a boarder from Castelderg, having the English translation and using it for translation of the Irish text. Hughie caught him out rather quickly and gave him six of the best from his famous leather strap. Willie was also branded a 'cute hoor,' which was the first time I had ever heard the phrase and had the feeling that it was not one of praise.

Apart from my memory of Willie McGoldrick, trying unsuccessfully to get the better of Big Hughie, my abiding memory of the book is Mac Gabhann writing about his life from abject poverty in West Donegal to living in Scotland and going on to America, where he joined the great gold chase in the Yukon. I was stunned to learn from the first few chapters that Mac Gabhann wrote of his going to a hiring fair in Letterkenny, when he was nine years old, which would have been around 1874. For the princely sum of thirty shillings for a six month period, one pound fifty pence in modern money, he was hired as a cow herder to a farmer in Glenveagh, County Donegal. We were not studying any social history at that time and the autobiography seared into my memory the reality of poverty in rural Ireland and its effects, less than a century before I was born.

First year at the College had been a transition from primary to secondary school and had been navigated with some ease. Now, we were stepping up another gear. For English, we still had J.J. Keaveney and we moved on to *Henry V* as our Shakespearean play for study. The alternative was *A Midsummer Night's Dream*. One of my personal achievements was to learn by heart the speech of Henry before the walls of Harfleur; 'Once more unto the breach dear friends, once more. ' In our history class, Mr Ruddle had told us that in medieval warfare the first troops into a breach in a besieged city's walls were usually slaughtered. No wonder Henry had to summon up all his inspiring words to persuade men to charge to impending death. The other speech that I learned by heart was his address to his troops before the battle of Agincourt; 'This day is called the feast of Crispian.' It was therefore fortuitous that the question on the Junior Certificate paper was 'imagine you have seen a stage performance of Henry V. Describe, as vividly as you can to someone who has not seen it, the scene in the English camp immediately before the battle of Agincourt is joined...' In the play, there were a number of scenes just before the battle from which to choose but the scene that I wrote about was Henry's stirring address to his soldiers.

Taking us to the cinema had been a novel way of preparing us for Confirmation at the Christian Brothers but the cinema had also opened up a new educational milieu for us. In our secondary school years at the College, films on the big screen would be an important adjunct of our education. *Henry V* was better understood and more fully appreciated by seeing the film, starring Laurence Olivier as the king. It is hard to believe that the film was released in 1944. I recently saw it again after a gap of many years and thought it very wooden, compared to the Kenneth Branagh version, made more than four decades later. When we were studying the life and times of Henry VIII, we were taken to see Robert Bolt's, *A Man For All Seasons*, which had a host of leading actors, Paul Scofield, Robert Shaw, Orson Wells, Leo Mc Kern and John Hurt. It was a magnificent film, highly educational and with wonderful scenery. It also marked out Sir Thomas More, played by Paul Schofield, as one of my schoolboy heroes.

The Faber Book of Childrens' Verse was replaced by *Poems of Spirit and Action*. The novels for the exam were as diverse as *Jane Eyre*, *Moonfleet* and *Shane*. The biggest change in any syllabus was in Maths. We still had Mr McMahon, who took delight in telling us that we were to be the guinea pigs for what was called Modern Maths and that we would have two subjects on our Junior Certificate, Maths A and Maths B. We were introduced to bar graphs, Venn diagrams, pie charts, theories of probability and we each acquired a Slide Rule. One of our first bar graphs was based on the number of siblings each member of the class had. I discovered that I was the only boy with no siblings and Hammie nicknamed me the Lone Ranger. At the other end of the spectrum there were boys who had up to thirteen brothers and sisters.

With Fr. Grant, we progressed to *Latin for Today Books 2 & 3*, and learned some Roman history such as Pompey's wars in the East and the career of Gaius Gracchus. One Tuesday morning, I was walking along the corridor that joined the senior and junior studies, when Fr. Grant called me and asked me two questions. The first was whether I had a free class at this time and the second was whether I had ever been an altar boy. When I gave a positive response to both questions, his eyes lit up and he asked me if would clerk his Mass every week during my free period. How could I say no and hope to survive? I readily agreed and was immediately brought into the College Chapel and I served my first Mass in almost three years. I was surprised how quickly the Latin responses returned and I was somewhat pleased with the apparent avalanche of Latin that trooped from my lips. Fr. Grant never showed the least favoritism to me for being his personal altar boy every Tuesday morning.

A revolutionary development for us was that at the start of second year in the College, in the Junior Study, we had one class per week, called Elocution and our new teacher was a woman, Miss Bridget Keenan. Talking properly had never been an issue in our education and, initially, we were somewhat taken aback to learn that this was now a subject. For the next two years, she endeavoured to teach us 'voice production, breath control, the placing of vowels, the clarity of consonants and the natural and lively flow of speech,' to quote from our text book, *Speech in Practice*. After some reservations, we looked forward to each class and I remember her imploring us to keep our lips clear of our teeth as we uttered the words:

We have a speaker in Leek
Reads a speech to us once every week.
This evening his niece
Had to read out his piece
As he's broken his teeth and can't speak!

One day, I went home and repeated to my mother a line that we had spent quite a lot of time practicing in class; 'Yeast, black treacle and wheat meal are rich in Vitamin B.' my mother looked at me and asked if the College was now teaching us to bake! It was a terrible pity that they did not teach us what was called Domestic Science at Thornhill Girls' Grammar School. Miss Keenan was forever telling us about a school, attended by her nephew, where the names of the pupils were put down at birth for entry eleven years later. From her pronunciation, we thought the school was called Guarantor. I only found out years later that it was called Garron Tower and was in the Glens of Antrim. It was funny when boys from the Creggan and Bogside would stand in front of class and recite the following lines, which were regarded as 'excellent for limbering the jaw;'

Father's car is a Jaguar
And Pa drives rather fast;
Castles, farms and draughty barns
We go charging past.

Arthur's cart is far less smart
And can't go half so far,
But I'd rather ride in Arthur's cart
Than my papa's fast car.

Away from the classrooms, the highlight of our lives was that we won the class football league and cup, in both Junior Two and Junior Three, exacting revenge for our defeats in first year. We played all of our games in second year on pitches in the school grounds, which was a godsend, as the changing rooms in the College pitch, beside Celtic Park, were more like a cattle byre.

Soccer had always been a greater attraction and during free classes in school, it was soccer that was universally played by all years, from Junior 1 upwards. Back in Creggan, soccer, and only soccer, was played. We often used to go over to the Bishop' field, which was on the other side of St. Mary's Church, to play as it was grassy and often cut, thus providing a fine playing surface. One Wednesday afternoon, when we were free from Gaelic football and attendance at the City Baths, we were having a game. Mickey Devine, who had been at the Holy Childs' with me, emerged from the grounds of St. Mary's Church, on his way home from St. Joseph's Secondary School. The day stands out in my memory, because Mickey was wearing a Glasgow Rangers' football scarf, something you did not see in Creggan. He threw down his school bag and joined in our match, at the end of which I asked him did he support Rangers. He replied; 'No way,' but said he was wearing the scarf simply not to conform to the herd mentality that all Catholics were automatically Celtic supporters. Mickey certainly was not a conformist and became a left-wing radical, progressing from the Labour Party, through the Republican Clubs, to join the Irish National Liberation Army. In 1981, he was the tenth and last republican to die in the Hunger Strike, in the Maze Prison, just outside Belfast. I regarded his death as another tragic loss of a young life.

In my second year, the most I joined was St. Eugene's Boys Club, which was housed in the bowels of St. Columb's Hall. Its great attraction was the opportunity to play a soccer game, every Sunday morning, in the Brandywell Showgrounds, which had changing rooms with showers. The boys' club had teams competing at every junior level competition in Northern Ireland but I was quite happy simply to play in an internal league, where I won a medal playing at left half, rather than at my favourite position as a left winger. A number of years later, one of my contemporaries told me that it was only in playing football that I had ever been a left winger! The club leader in St. Eugene's was Tony O' Donnell and he organised trips to English football matches, for which you had to be over fourteen years of age. My second year had seen Manchester United win the English First division championship. I was excited when, at start of my third year, Tony put up a notice asking for interest in a trip to Old Trafford, in March 1968, for a game against Nottingham Forest. The total cost was £5, for which we would have a return train journey to Belfast, two overnight stays on the boat, crossing to and from Liverpool, train journey to Manchester and back, ticket for the game, lunch and dinner. I started saving pocket money and put my name down for the trip.

On a Friday afternoon, about thirty of us, with an age range of 14 to 18, gathered at Waterside train station on Duke Street, the same spot where eighteen months later, the Civil Rights marchers were to assemble on 5th October for their ill-fated march to the Guildhall. For our gathering, there was no ban from the Minister of Home Affairs. There was, however, a slight element of illegality. Larry Doherty, photographer from *The Derry Journal*, was there to capture the moment but there was only one snag. About a third of us were College boys. We had school on Saturday mornings and had not sought permission from the College to miss class and we were thus mitching school and were about to be photographed in the act. The simple solution was that 'for security reasons,' we avoided the photo opportunity, much to the mirth of the rest of the group. With tongue in cheek, Larry suggested that he take a separate photo of the College boys and send it to the College President!

Our Odyssey began and when the train stopped at Coleraine, we started shouting 'Derry, Derry' at bewildered bystanders, who didn't have a clue where these schoolboys, bedecked in red and white football scarves and bob hats, were going. From York Street train station in Belfast, it was a short walk to the boat, which sailed about nine o'clock. We were divided into groups of four and allocated a cabin. I could not really sleep with excitement. With dawn breaking I went on deck as the boat began the final leg of its journey on the river Mersey. The city looked so big and it seemed to take hours before we berthed. The next leg of the journey was the train journey from Lime Street station to Manchester, passing canals that were no longer used. And then we had our first glimpse of Old Trafford rising against the skyline. It seemed as if I was in a dream. Rather than sitting in class in Bishop Street in Derry, I was close to the centre of Manchester.

With duffle bags on our backs we marched through Manchester city centre, heading toward a cafe to have lunch. A group of Manchester City supporters, about the same age as us, appeared en route to the train station, for an away game to Everton. We looked to be in the lions' den and there was the usual exchange of cat-calling when suddenly one of them grabbed a United scarf that one of our group as wearing. We were heading into a cafe before any other spoils were lost. I remember an adult in a City scarf then entering the cafe with the United scarf in hand and apologising for the behaviour of one of his group, which was re-assuring. Having tucked into a fish supper, which could not hold a candle to Brennan's, we caught a double decker bus from the city centre to Old Trafford. I felt my pulse racing as the stadium came into view. We had reached the Promised Land, the hallowed turf on which I would see George Best and Bobby Charlton. Alas, Denis Law was injured and would not be playing.

Outside the ground, I looked, in awe, at the thousands who were arriving for the game. My experiences had been mainly limited to a few thousand at the Brandywell to see Derry City. The hard nuts were heading for the Stretford end and, to my surprise, were wearing the football scarves of other first division clubs, tied together so that they went all the way to their ankles. It transpired that these were trophies; battle honours won in what I concluded were fights with opposing fans. It was a time when English football had a reputation for hooliganism on a grand scale and each club had its own 'firm.' United's 'firm' was simply known as *The Red Army.* By contrast, West Ham's firm had the grandiose name of *The Inner City Firm*, the *ICF.* Tony quickly moved us away from any possible confrontation and gave us our match tickets. Our seats were in the new Cantilever Stand. The price of the ticket was seven shillings and sixpence, or thirty seven and a half pence in decimal currency. How times have changed for the worse, in terms of fans being fleeced by outrageous ticket prices. From the comfort of the stand I watched the swaying masses in the Stretford End, in an era before grounds were all-seaters, and before what Roy Keane famously called 'the prawn sandwich brigade,' had arrived.

The United team, that day, was almost identical to that which played in the European Cup final a few months later, with Alex Stepney in goals, having signed from Chelsea a few years earlier. Forty years later, I took my son to Old Trafford and we met Alex and I told him that I had first seen him, in my first visit those decades ago. The game itself saw United race into a three goal lead, as David Herd netted early and there were further goals from an unlikely source, the full backs, Francis Burns and Shay Brennan. The goals were scored at the Stretford End, which was bouncing. The second half was marking time and there were no further goals. Whenever George Best even touched the ball, the young girls around us almost swooned. He was their hero and icon.

For the long return journey home we were in cloud cuckoo land. That night, I slept soundly on the Belfast boat, from Liverpool, and when we arrived at York Street railway station I bought my mother a box of Milk Tray chocolates. I had marked off one of those things that you promise yourself you will do before you die and the season ended on a high. Although United lost their league title, on the last day of the season, to Manchester City, this paled into insignificance, as Matt Busby finally got his hands on the European Cup after a 4-1 victory over Benfica, at Wembley. I had watched the game at home with my father and it was end-to-end stuff. Bobby Charlton gave United the lead, only for Benfica to equalise late in the second half. Alex Stepney made a point blank save to deny Eusebio a winner and the game went into extra time. A piece of individual magic from George Best restored United's lead, which was extended when Brian Kidd headed a third on his nineteenth birthday. To round off the evening, Bobby Charlton, a survivor of the Munich air disaster, headed a fourth and celebrations began. I think there was almost universal delight for Matt Busby, the man who had pioneered British clubs participating in European competitions and who had almost died at Munich. The unfinished business had been completed.

By contrast, on the local scene, Derry City failed to build on their successes of the previous years and failed to win either the league or cup. We still went to the Brandywell, on a Saturday afternoon, but bemoaned that Ronnie Wood, one of our star players, had been transferred to Linfield. Local derby games against Coleraine seemed to have an extra edge as City fans would shout, 'get stuck into the university thieves,' an obvious reference to the decision to locate Northern Ireland's second university in Coleraine rather than Derry. As a sign of my growing up a bit, my parents allowed me to go to Coleraine, on Boxing Day, for a derby game and a few of us went on the midday train. It was the first time that I appreciated the beauty of the coastline around Castlerock and Benone strand. Not surprisingly, a few years later, in his programme series, *Great Train Journeys*, Michael Palin, described the Derry to Coleraine train journey as one of the most beautiful in the world. As the train approached a tunnel, I could just see Bishop Hervey's Mussenden Temple standing majestically on the cliff top.

Back in the College, Mr. Ruddle's history classes opened up a new vista about the historic significance of Derry and a few of us decided to explore its past in a little greater detail. Having witnessed the burning of the effigy of Governor Lundy, we felt that the next logical step in our education was to pay a visit to St. Columb's Cathedral. Situated within the city's walls, the cathedral dated back to the early seventeenth century and was the first cathedral built after the Reformation. Like the City Walls and many other buildings within the walled city, the Cathedral had been built by The Honourable the Irish Society. This was a London based organisation, created by a Royal Charter of King James I, in 1613, to undertake the Plantation in the North West of Ulster. Just inside the porch is the foundation stone, part of which is originally from the 12th Century Templemore Monastery and is inscribed with the following words:

'If stones could speake
then London's prayse
should sound who
built this church and
cittie from the ground.'

Quite close to the inscription is the Bomb Font, a cannon ball and many other artefacts from the siege of 1688/89. Visiting the Cathedral took us on to a part of the walls, with which we were unfamiliar. Our usual walk along the walls had taken us in the opposite direction. Many a day, after school, we would head up Bishop Street and enter the walled city through Bishop's Gate. We would then turn sharp left at the Elephant Bar and climb the steps on to the Walls. Our normal walk was towards the Grand Parade, a promenade in the 19th century that overlooked the Bogside. On Grand Parade, there were thirteen sycamore trees, planted to commemorate the thirteen apprentices who shut the gates against the advancing Jacobites in 1688. Governor Walker's monument towered above Nailor's Row, a twisted terrace of houses, far removed from the elegance of St. Augustine's Church and the Masonic Hall that used to be the residence of the Church of Ireland Bishop of Derry. The imposing building on the corner of Society Street was the Memorial Hall, the headquarters of the Apprentice Boys. My mother told me that when she was a young woman, she would regularly sneak off to dances in the Mem, without telling her parents. This was most common during Lent, when dance halls in Catholic areas were closed. The last part of our walk took us to the bottom of Magazine Street, just beside the Creggan bus stop. The final bastion was called Cowards' Bastion, so named because, during the siege, it was seldom attacked by the Jacobites and became a refuge for the shirkers within the besieged city.

Of course, we did not have to go even outside the grounds of the College to find connections to the Siege. Just behind the Senior Study was one of Derry's most historic monuments, a windmill, around which some of the fiercest fighting had occurred. In the later part of the 18th century, the windmill was incorporated into Earl Bishop Frederick Hervey's summer estate, during which time it was modified to function as a pigeon house. Our research discovered that during the Siege, King James II rode up to Bishop's Gate, through which we passed almost daily, and demanded that he and his army be admitted to the city. He was refused admission and the battle cry, 'No Surrender' was hurled in defiance at him.

Facing the walled city, King James may well have stood on ground that, a century later, became the site of Derry Gaol in Bishop Street. We later learned that the United Irish leader, Wolfe Tone, was incarcerated in Derry Gaol in 1798, having been arrested at Buncrana, in County Donegal. The history of the gaol was itself, interesting. The first gaol had been built within the walled city and dated to 1791. The final gaol was built in the 1820s and was in use until 1953, the year I was born. Derry republicans had been interned there during the Second World War.

As our interest in the history intensified, we learned that the 1609 Regional Plan for Ulster created twenty three new towns and Derry's walled city was the first piece of true urban planning on the island of Ireland. Of the twenty three towns, Derry was the only one whose streets were laid out in a formal grid, just like ancient Roman settlements. That design remains to the present day. The four main streets inside the walled city, Bishop Street, Shipqauy St., Ferryquay St. and Butcher St. intersected at the Diamond, once known as King William Square, where the War Memorial is now located. However, the Diamond was dominated by the five stories of Austins department store, which was established in 1830 and was the world's oldest independent department store. We often went to its third floor café and a particular alcove that afforded a magnificent view down the river to Lough Foyle. It was the view that the beleaguered defenders on the ramparts of the city's cathedral would have had, in 1689. They would have seen ships, further out in the Lough that had been sent to raise the siege. There was a bronze plaque on the walls in Shipquay Place, just beside the Creggan bus stop, commemorating Michael Browning, Master of *The Mountjoy*, which broke the boom and raised the siege. It read; 'He died by the most enviable of all deaths in sight of the city which was his birth place which was his home and which had just been saved by bravery and self-devotion from the most frightful form of destruction.' The plaque marked the spot where his body was found. His name was seldom, if ever, mentioned in Catholic Derry, while his heroics were highly regarded only by Protestants; all of which I found to be both a sad and terrible shame.

Learning about the city's history was a pleasant interlude to the history syllabus. However, for the two years leading up to the Junior Certificate examinations, my focus was almost exclusively in maintaining high marks in school tests and enjoying both the playing and watching of football. There was more to life than study as it was also as period when the musical revolution caught my ear, in an era dominated by the Beatles. Second year had started with *We all Live in a Yellow Submarine,* and throughout those years *Penny Lane, Hello Goodbye and The Magical Mystery Tour* were hits that bring back fond memories. They were not the only ones to make a mark as the Monkees, the Kinks, Procul Harem and many others challenged. The Dubliners even made it to the charts with *Seven Drunken Nights*. There was a bit of excitement at the start of third year, when the Prime Minister, Harold Wilson, announced that he was suing a pop group called The Move over a postcard that they had published as an advertising feature for their single, *Flowers in the Rain*. I thought that Wilson would have more important matters to attend to, until I discovered the postcard was a cartoon that depicted him naked in bed with a woman, who many believed was supposed to be Marcia Williams, his secretary. Wilson was successful in his lawsuit but Marcia kept her powder dry for a few decades until 2007, when she successfully sued the BBC for libel.

Looking back, however, the piece of music that epitomised those times was Scott Mc Kenzie's *San Francisco*, the music of flower power; 'If you're going to San Francisco, / Be sure to wear some flowers in your hair.' Somehow, I could not see the inhabitants of the 'dreary steeples' of Northern Ireland walking around with flowers in their hair

I was, however, becoming gradually aware of events in the wider world, some of which eventually impacted on Derry. There was, however, no sign of 'flower power.' By contrast, there have been a number of books written with lurid titles such as '*Countdown to Disaster*,' by Frank Curran, a former editor of the Derry Journal. He has suggested that, from the mid-1960s onwards, Northern Ireland was on a slippery slope to inevitable chaos and that Derry would be the catalyst for this volcanic eruption. At the time, it did not seem that way to me. By contrast, *The Columban* magazine published in the College, at the end of my second year, in 1967, carried a half page advertisement for careers in the Royal Ulster Constabulary. 'Outstanding opportunities,' it read, 'to young men of good character and physique, aged 18-27, who have received a grammar school education. Starting pay £700 per annum plus allowances.' One of my neighbours in Fanad Drive, joined the RUC but within a few years was forced to move out of Creggan as his life was in danger from the IRA.

In the years prior to the eruption of violence in Derry, on 5th October 1968, I was more aware of global events, mainly through the medium of television. However, on occasions, when standing at the Creggan bus stop in Guildhall Square, I was aware of on-going protests about housing and unemployment, outside the Guildhall. However, these seemed to be confined to a small group of members of the Derry Labour Party and two new bodies, called the Derry Housing Action Committee and the Derry Unemployed Action Committee. The membership of these new groupings seemed to be drawn from the same source, young militant republicans and socialists. Politically, there was a ripple of excitement when, for the first time in many years, the election to the Corporation, in 1967, was actually contested, with the Labour Party putting up candidates against both Unionist and Nationalist sitting councillors. The electorate remained true to its sectarian roots and no Labour candidates were elected, although, in some wards, the party received 30% of the votes cast.

While the Nationalist Party, in Derry, continued to hold the political allegiance of most Catholics, it was clear that its grip was slipping. This was against a background of continuing job losses at the BSR in Creggan. The closure of the Derry/Glasgow boat in October 1966 added to a general feeling of impending doom, building on such incidents as railway closures, the university debacle and the government's decision to build a new city of Craigavon in County Armagh, rather than develop Derry. My walk from school to the Guildhall took me past the massive red-brick building in Bishop Street, the Labour Exchange, which was a grim reminder of the lack of job opportunities if we did not excel in our studies. However, my walk was also often punctuated by visits to the APCK and Derry Journal bookshops, on Shipquay Street, where I enjoyed browsing. Con Bradley took the title of a Beatles' hit, *Back in the USSR*, and created the alternative, *Back in the APCK*.

In June 1967, as I was completing my second year at the College, there was the first war to be broadcast on television, with wall to wall commentary on the conflict between Israel and its Arab neighbours, which became known as the Six Day War. Yitzhak Rabin was the Israeli chief of staff, who masterminded the military master plan that destroyed an overwhelmingly superior force in a matter of days. The public front of the Israeli war machine was Mosche Dayan, the one-eyed Defence Minister, who regularly appeared on our screens. Before I went to school each morning, I would watch the early morning news, which broadcast up to the minute details of the advances of the Israeli forces. The Israelis were portrayed as the good guys, fighting for their survival in a David versus Goliath struggle. With breath-taking speed, television crews captured, on film, the blitzkrieg that captured Jerusalem, Bethlehem, the West Bank, the Golan Heights and the Suez Canal. All was changed, with television now bringing into our homes vivid, and almost instantly available, footage of important global events. A few years earlier, the film, *Exodus*, based on the novel, by Leon Uris, of the same name, was the cinema's depiction of the founding of the state of Israel. The film had been made in 1960 and Paul Newman was the star. A few years later there was another film with a cast of top actors, starring Frank Sinatra, *Cast a Giant Shadow*, which portrayed the founding of the state of Israel in a very favourable light.

While we were watching our first war on television, there was little attention given to events in Nigeria that would for the next two and a half years occupy a central spot on television news reports across the globe. In May, Colonel Emaka Ojukwu, the Oxford educated governor of Eastern Nigeria, unilaterally declared the independent Republic of Biafra. Interest in Britain stemmed from the fact that Nigeria had, until a few years earlier, been a British colony and the Labour government refused to recognise the secessionist republic. Britain, together with the Soviet Union became the main providers of arms to the Lagos government to help it crush the rebellion. Within a year of hostilities being commenced, we witnessed, for the first time on television, starvation and images of emaciated children, close to death. Harold Wilson's government, which was supporting the Lagos regime, seemed indifferent to this human suffering and appeared more interested in getting cheap oil. Wilson was quite prepared to profit from misery by trading arms for oil with the government in Lagos. The option to stop all arms supplies and promote some peace initiative was not on the agenda of the government. As a result, over the two and a half years of the conflict more than a million civilians died in fighting and from famine. A question that many were asking was 'Why is the world standing idly by?' There was no satisfactory response forthcoming from government and the episode was a salutary lesson in learning that self-interest took precedence over humanitarian relief.

The year 1968 is oft regarded as the year of global protest, although there were few protests about the civil war in Biafra. I could not help but become caught up following the unfolding stories. While we were having a free day from school, to celebrate St. Patrick's Day on 17th March, London was rocked with a full scale riot outside the American Embassy, in Grosvenor Square, in protest against the Vietnam War. Little did the world then know of a terrible atrocity committed by American soldiers, the previous day in Vietnam, in a village called My Lai. Between 347 and more than 500 unarmed civilians were killed, including women, children and infants. The news of the massacre only emerged twenty months later. In May, France erupted in violence and seemed close to revolution, just as my attention was on the European Cup final. The television brought to the fore a new revolutionary leader, who sprang to world-wide prominence in a matter of days, Daniel Cohn-Bendit, better known in the media as Danny the Red. Television also taught me one of Newton's laws of physics; that to every action there is an equal and opposite reaction. Revolution in France was thwarted as almost one million De Gaulle supporters marched along the Champs Elysées, waving the French Tricolour and singing *La Marseilleise* rather than the Marxist *Internationale*.

I was growing up in an age of new uncertainties. The most frightening images on our television screens were of the Revolutionary Guards of Chairman Mao, brandishing their Little Red Books and threatening world revolution. Given the size of China, it was not unimaginable that its millions of Revolutionary Guards would descend on Europe, as had Genghis Khan eight hundred years earlier. A new term entered the political lexicon, Maoists, with marches of students also brandishing their own Little Red Books. I discovered that the Little Red Book was a collection of quotations. There were plenty of people in Ireland, who, whilst deploring the communism of Chairman Mao, were very soon to be very much in tune with one of his sayings, 'political power grows out of the barrel of a gun.'

As we approached the end of third year, there was political uproar in Britain when Enoch Powell, a leading conservative politician, made what became known as, '*the rivers of blood*' speech. He was talking about the issue of immigration and used very colourful language. "As I look ahead," he intoned, "I am filled with foreboding. Like the Roman, I seem to see the River Tiber foaming with much blood. That tragic and intractable phenomenon, which we watch with horror on the other side of the Atlantic but which there is interwoven with the history and existence of the States itself, is coming upon us here by our own volition and our own neglect." He was promptly sacked from the shadow cabinet by Ted Heath, the Tory party leader. However, although judging from the television news, Powell had massive public support. Our MP at Stormont, Eddie McAteer, waded into the controversy. He did not criticise Powell but wrote an open letter to Ted Heath, pointing out that his Tory allies in the Unionist Party were Grand Masters of discrimination and equally deserving the weight of his disapproval. In school, Fr. Grant raised the speech in class, not to discuss immigration into Britain, but to welcome a return to classical references in modern political speech-making. He pointed out to us the original text to which Powell was referring. It was an allusion to Virgil's *Aeneid* in which the Sibyl prophesises *Bella, horrida bella, Et Thybrim multo spumantem sanguine,* which translated in to English as 'Wars, terrible wars, and the Tiber foaming with much blood.' He also reminded us that Powell had been a professor of Classics.

The year 1968, however, was remembered mostly for two assassinations. In April, in Memphis, Tennessee, Martin Luther King, the American Civil Rights leader, was shot dead. There were major riots in more than one hundred American cities in response to his killing. Two months later, while campaigning in California for the Democratic nomination for the American presidency, Robert Kennedy was killed by a twenty four year old Palestinian, Shiran Shiran. That summer, Dick Holler wrote *Abraham, Martin and John*, which was initially recorded by Dion, and was a tribute to the memory of assassinated American leaders, Abraham Lincoln, Martin Luther King, John F. Kennedy.

I was in the seaside town of Portstewart on holiday, in August, when the news broke of the Soviet invasion of Czechoslovakia. On television, we saw Russian tanks rumble through the streets of Prague, as a reminder that the Cold War had not thawed. The invasion force numbered over three quarter of a million soldiers and six and a half thousand tanks. The reformist Czech Communistic leader, Alexander Dubcek, was removed from his post and the country reverted to being a puppet of the Soviet Union. Life on the Portstewart promenade was unaffected by these global events, which appeared to be multiplying by the week. For me, the most important matter were my grades in the Junior, which were more than pleasing, and the prospect of returning to the College to begin studying for my O levels. My Junior 2 & 3 years had passed somewhat uneventfully and, apart from going to Old Trafford to see Manchester United, the most daring feats were to gain admission to the Palace cinema to see *Rasputin the Mad Monk,* played by Christopher Lee, and *Bonnie and Clyde*, which starred Warren Beatty and Fay Dunaway. Both films had been rated X certificate by the censors, meaning that they were to be viewed only by persons over eighteen years old.

While the world was watching events from the Middle East to Paris and the Soviet Union's invasion of Czechoslovakia, there were a few incidents closer to home, in Northern Ireland, that received only local media coverage and did not seem to threaten peace and stability. Politics seemed marginal to most people's lives. The sleepy village of Caledon, in County Tyrone, was an unlikely place for the Civil Rights banner to be raised. By 1968, all over the world, people with causes, were working to copy the Civil Rights movement in America. They even adopted its anthem, Pete Seeger's *We Shall Overcome*. Originally, this was a folk song, turned labour song that Seeger had turned into a Civil Rights song when sit-ins began in 1960. Austin Currie, a Nationalist MP at Stormont, squatted in, and was forcibly evicted from, a house in Caledon. He was protesting at the decision of the local council to allocate the house to a nineteen year old unmarried Protestant girl, who was secretary to a local Unionist politician.

There was hardly any public interest, in Derry, when an organisation called the Northern Ireland Civil Rights Association announced that it was organising a march from Coalisland to Dungannon in the wilds of County Tyrone, at the end of August, just before we were due to return to school. The objective of the march was to protest against the housing policy of the local Unionist council. Anyone, with knowledge of Irish history, should have known that the ancient quarrel between nationalism and unionism wasn't far beneath the surface in rural Ulster.

Two years earlier, in Coalisland, over twenty thousand people had attended republican celebrations commemorating the 50th anniversary of the Easter Rising of 1916. We had just spent a lot of time in studying the period of confiscation and plantation in Ulster and the revolts by the native clans to reclaim their lands and power. It was therefore no surprise to learn that the bands accompanying the Civil Rights march played music such as *Who Fears to Speak of '98*, commemorating the United Irish rebellion of 1798 and *Faith of Our Fathers*, a Catholic hymn. At the end of the march, the crowd sang a nationalist anthem, *A Nation Once Again*, rather than *We Shall Overcome*, which was only later adopted as a Civil Rights anthem. The first Civil Rights March, from Coalisland to Dungannon took a course that would become familiar in future, with the marchers being prevented from reaching their planned destination due to Loyalist protests led by Rev. Ian Paisley. On this occasion, violence was avoided but there were indications that more marches were planned for the autumn.

The squatting incident, organised by Austin Currie, was broadcast on the BBC evening television news and was probably the first time that many people in Britain had ever heard of allegations of religious discrimination in Northern Ireland. In Derry, a high-profile act by the Derry Housing Action Committee consisted of placing a caravan cross the Lecky Road to highlight the poor quality of housing. Neither the squatting in a house in Tyrone, nor the sight of a caravan across a busy street in Derry was likely to register alongside global events in terms of television viewing. It seemed that both incidents would quickly drift into the margins of the news. Harold Wilson seemed too preoccupied with Rhodesia to pay much attention to his backbenchers, such as Paul Rose, who were increasingly popping up on our television screens and talking about Northern Ireland. To the outside world and to most people in Northern Ireland, it seemed that some progress was being achieved. Terence O'Neill and the Irish Taoiseach, Sean Lemass, had helped a thaw in relations between the two jurisdictions. Staunchly Unionist Ballymena had become twinned with Castlebar in County Mayo. The Nationalist Party, under the leadership of Eddie McAteer, the MP for the Foyle constituency in Derry, had agreed to become the official opposition in the Stormont parliament. There were no indications that before the end of the year the international media would be camped in Derry or that the balloon was about to go up.

As the summer holidays ended, the focus of my attention was not on Churchill's 'dreary steeples of Fermanagh and Tyrone,' but had returned to America and Democratic Party's convention in Chicago, which degenerated into a police riot outside the convention centre. The Democrats chose Hubert Humphrey, President Johnson's Vice-President as their candidate for the Presidency to oppose Richard

Nixon, whom the Republicans had chosen earlier in the month. It was a dull and anti-climactic end to a year of campaigning in which the late Bobby Kennedy and Senator George McGovern had electrified audiences across America in their quest of the Democratic nomination. Humphrey, whatever his political virtues may have been, simply looked like a loser.

My final memory of the summer of 1968 is of Gary Sobers, the West Indian cricketer, scoring six sixes in one over, in a county championship match, when he was playing for Nottinghamshire. Throughout the Sixties I had watched Test cricket on television and enjoyed the Ashes series between England and Australia. There were great batsmen in both sides, Ritchie Benaud and Bobby Simpson, Aussie captains and Geoffrey Boycott and John Edrich, the English openers. Sobers was, however, a star attraction, an all-rounder with both bat and ball, and it was fitting that the end of what I would describe as 'the age of innocence' was marked by that one over in his long, illustrious career. His six sixes brought down the curtain on that leisurely summer in which I played cricket on a green on Westway, just opposite St. Joseph's Secondary School. Many of the players were friends from the College or my years as an altar boy, Kevin Coyle, Joe and Dessie Carton, Danny McNally, Mickey McKinney, to name but a few. In addition to playing cricket on the green, I watched the Ashes series on television. Thus, the summer of 1968 came to an end. Looking back it seems to have been a marking point is as the end of an age of innocence in Northern Ireland.

My mother, Mary, in the mid-1930s.

Daddy, extreme left. Taken in Alexandria in 1943,
after his service in Malta and en route to Greece.

Ready for the Tour de France.

With the Thornton sisters, outside Carrickreagh Gardens,
in Creggan, in the late 1950s.

Primary One at the Holy Child School, 1959.

Confirmation Day at St Eugene's Cathedral, Ascension Thursday, 1962.

One of the Christian Brothers choirs at Feis Doire Cholmcille,
outside the Guildhall. I am in the front row, extreme left.

My CBS year group that won the Rice Cup, without my efforts.

115

Daddy, the postman, on Strand Road, in the late 1950s.

With Mammy at Butlin's Mosney in the mid-1960s.

St Mary's Church, Creggan.

My days as an altar boy in St. Mary's, in the early 1960s.

Mammy and Daddy at an ordination celebration, in the early 1970s.

Junior 2 English class at St. Columb's, taken by our teacher, J.J. Keaveney. As ever, I am in the front row, second from the right.

St Columb's College, Bishop Street, Derry.

Junior 3A - St Columb's College, 1968.

Front Row: Willie McGoldrick, Declan McCotter, Frank Diggin, Fr Regan, George McGowan, Denis Ferry and Desmond O'Donnell

Second Row: Kevin Doherty, Mario Hegarty, Gerry Murray, Eamon Barr, Peter McGranaghan, Martin Tucker, Gerard Quinn and Peter Jackson.

Third Row: Brendan Doherty, Seamus Murphy, George Chambers, Harry McDaid, Neil McCafferty, Mark McFeely and Terry Duddy.

Back Row: Michael J O'Doherty, Paul Kearney, Jim Harkin, Maurice Brennan, Nigel Cooke, Pearse Doherty and Eddie Brady.

Summer in London, 1972, awaiting A Level results.

PART TWO
WAR

Chapter Eight
First Term as a College Senior before the Dike Burst

From 'Hey Jude' and 'The Auld Triangle' and 'Arma Virum Cano.' Music hall Jingoism as – Gladstone chops down trees while Bismarck replants them, while Henry IV questions his legitimacy to be king.

As I prepared to return for my senior years at the College, I was blissfully unaware that life in Northern Ireland was destined soon to be changed, irrevocably. London, Paris and Prague had been the focal points for the world's media in the first half of the year. Little did I think that before the year was over their focus would turn to Northern Ireland. Before every explosion there is a period of calm and so it was for me before the tsunami hit. On the surface, all seemed quiet and free of any strain of revolutionary activity. Life continued as before, uneventfully.

As I commenced my senior years in the College, *Hey Jude*, by the Beatles, ruled supreme in the pop charts and 1968 was a good year for the group, with other hits such as *Lady Madonna* and *Hello Goodbye*. Unlike most of the followers of the Beatles, I was well aware that St. Jude was the patron saint of hopeless cases. There were not too many boys in Derry named after him. Apart from me, the only other person I knew with the name Jude was one of my contemporaries at the College, Jude Coyle, from Rosemount. I wondered if it would become a more popular name after the publicity given to it by the Beatles.

The B side of that pop hit was called *Revolution,* which seemed to chime with the events of that summer across Europe. However, Lennon and McCartney ducked any mention of the events that had occurred in Paris and beyond that summer. There was only one direct reference to any specific country or political creed as we were advised that "… *if you carrying pictures of Chairman Mao/You ain't going to make it with anyone anyhow.'* The Beatles were unlikely to get an invitation to play a live concert in Peking, as Westerners still called the capital.

There was no reason to believe that, on the global stage, the mayhem of the early months of the year would dissipate once that a new academic year had begun. On the eve of the Olympic Games in Mexico City, in October, up to three hundred student protestors were killed by police and military in a massacre in one of the city's main squares. As I returned to the College, in September, it was more in anticipation of a new era in my academic development than in anticipating further events on the global stage. Peace and order had been restored in Western Europe. The Soviet occupation of Czechoslovakia had ended that country's government dabbling in liberalisation. The Vietnam War remained the major issue, provoking protest both in America and the wider world and there looked no prospect of the war being concluded. The major headache for Harold Wilson, apart from the state of the British economy, was Rhodesia, with its white minority government having unilaterally declared independence.

Sport was back in the news but not for the reasons that had brought Gary Sobers to the front page. Now, it was the heady cocktail of sport and politics. Marylebone Cricket Club, the MCC, cancelled a proposed tour of South Africa, when its government refused to accept the presence of Basil D'Oliveira in the side. D'Oliveira, a regular in England's cricket team, was a Cape Coloured. Earlier that summer, there had been rumblings in the press that the South African government had interfered with the initial selection of the team, when D'Oliveira was omitted from the squad. His later inclusion was due to the injury of one of the players selected ahead of him. That summer, on television, my father and I had watched the Ashes series between England and their Australian visitors and D'Oliveira had been one of the few stars for the home team with both bat and ball.

The football season in England had started in early August and after reaching the dizzy heights in winning the European Cup a few months earlier, my beloved Manchester United started poorly, losing three of their first seven games. September was not much better with a win, draw and a loss in three games played. With football in the doldrums, my focus was on the return to school and a course of study that would result in obtaining what used to be called the Senior Certificate, and which was now called O levels and was the second rung on the ladder of academic qualifications. There was some excitement in having graduated from being a Junior to now commencing senior years and I had managed to stay in the A stream. Rather than being herded into the Senior Study to be allocated our teachers and timetable, we were in the more expansive Concert Hall. It seemed much more civilised and we were actually consulted about our subject choices in the few of the subjects where there was a choice. No more Hammie roaring at us but the first signs that we were being treated like responsible teenagers.

For the majority of subjects in my junior years I had been taught by the same men. It was, therefore, a new experience to learn that we would be leaving most of them behind. Hughie Mc Geown, our Irish teacher, was the last survivor and we were somewhat relieved as the other teachers in that department had an awesome reputation. It was said, only half in jest, that the method of teaching Irish was the partitionist one. Initially, I thought this had something to do with the political partitioning of Ireland in the 1920s, only to discover that its true meaning was that boys had their heads bounced of the partition at the back of class for inability to give correct answers. We also quickly discovered that teachers in the Irish department, including Hughie, were still to the fore in liberally using their leather straps, a procedure that appeared to be on the wane for senior boys but had not entirely disappeared. These two years with Hughie were by no means dominated by his strap and my vivid memory is the novel, *Mo Bhealach Fhein, My Own Way,* by Seosamh Mac Grianna. Born in Hughie's beloved Ranafast in 1900, Mac Grianna had been a student at the College for a few years. Hughie must have had a thing about epic autobiographical novels in our years under his tutelage.

We were introduced to a new array of teachers; Jimmy Sharkey for History, Frank O'Kane for French, Peter Mullan for English, Brian Duffy for Maths, Fr. Seamus Farrelly for Latin, Gerry McLaughlin for Physics and Fr. Willie McElhinney for Religious Knowledge. With the exception of Peter Mullan, who hailed from Newry, all the other teachers were past pupils of the College. One of Peter's first pieces of advice to us was to read *The Sunday Times* in order to broaden our understanding of world events. It was sound advice and every Sunday morning I picked up a copy in McCool's paper shop. The subject areas for the Senior Level Certificate were well defined in each subject. In each of the three languages there were plenty of translations both from English and into English with orals in Irish and French that accounted for 30% of the total marks.

The O Level English syllabus was divided into two subjects, Language and Literature. In the latter, we moved on to Shakespeare's *Henry IV Part 1* and Goldsmith's *She Stoops to Conquer.* Poetry came from the *Albatross Book of Verse.* In our first English Literature class with Peter Mullan, he had us underline poems by Wordsworth, Coleridge, Keats, Tennyson, Hardy, Hopkins, Yeats, Frost and Owen, which were to be our staple diet. One of our first poems for study was Coleridge's *Kubla Khan.* The only other time I had ever heard of 'the black barren land of Xanadu' was the pop hit, *The Legend of Xanadu,* by a group called Dave Dee, Dozy, Beaky Mick and Tich. I was sorry that we had parted company with J.J. Keaveney as our English teacher but was very impressed by Peter Mullan. We quickly moved from Auden's poems such as *The Night Mail* to a more interesting and thought-provoking elegy, *In Memory of W.B. Yeats,* in which Auden made the observation that 'mad Ireland' drove Yeats to write some of his poetry. However, he then added that 'poetry makes nothing happen.' I thought Yeats would have certainly disagreed with such sentiments as we read. In his old age, Yeats wrote 'The Man and the Echo,' in which he reflected on the 1916 Rising and a one act play he had written in 1902, *Cathleen Ni Houlihan.* He posed the question as follows:

I lie awake night after night
And never get the answers right
Did that play of mine send out
Certain men the English shot?

I greatly regretted that we had not been introduced to the poetry of Yeats when we were doing our project in first year on the Easter Rising. Peter Mullan also encouraged us to read widely from a vast field of novels by Orwell, Salinger, Huxley and Joyce to the extent that I can't really recall which of these novels were on the syllabus and which ones we read for enjoyment.

Peter was a radical socialist and a graduate of Queen's University in Belfast. He opened our eyes to a brave new world. One of the novels we studied was Alan Paton's *Cry the Beloved Country*, a story about South Africa, published a few months before the imposition of the apartheid laws. Paton told a story through the experiences of a black clergyman, Kumalo, who goes to Johannesburg to help his sister, a prostitute, and search for his son, Absolam. Through his eye we saw the vast economic and social divisions in South Africa, which made the divisions in Northern Ireland seem minor. I will always remember the lines from the novel; "Cry the beloved country for the unborn child that's the inheritor of our fear." Paton was the eldest son of English settlers and not an Afrikaner. He was charged with treason against the state in 1960, by which time he had become a founder member and Vice President of the Liberal Party. *The Sunday Times* magazine ran a detailed piece on him and the Liberal Party of which he was a co-founder, as well as reports on South Africa under apartheid. We were studying the novel just as a Civil Rights movement was emerging in Northern Ireland and many Nationalists identified their position with that of the blacks in South Africa and the USA. What struck me was that the position of Northern Irish Catholics was not remotely akin to the plight of black South Africans or blacks living in the former Confederate states of the USA.

As the top stream, we had two Maths subjects, Ordinary and Additional. After the experimentation on modern Maths we reverted to more traditional methods. The Maths department in the College had a reputation of good teaching and exam success and Brian Duffy continued this tradition. Under his tutelage, we mastered differentiation, quadratic equations and moved into the realm of physics with momentum, acceleration and gravity. Apart from teaching us, Brian, together with another Maths teacher, Fr. Eamon Tierney, was responsible for preparing the entire time table for the school, at the start of each year. In an age before computers, they always got it right and explained that their success was due to mathematical training. Brian left teaching a few years later and became a chartered accountant.

Fr. Tierney, better known by his nickname 'the Bird,' was the greatest enigma in the Maths department. He was a brilliant mathematician and the story doing the rounds was that he ended up in the College, having been passed over for a lecturership at Maynooth University. He was also quite an eccentric. His devotion to the drama of Brendan Behan, and not geometry, meant that pupils, all of whom he addressed as 'friend,' were asked, 'What does the auld triangle do, friend?' The correct answer to give, based on lines from Behan's *The Quare Fellow* was, 'the Auld Triangle goes Jingle Jangle.' Failure to give the correct answer resulted in slaps from the dreaded strap. None of his students went through life without a knowledge and appreciation of Behan's Auld Triangle. I never had Fr Tierney as a teacher in any of my five years studying Maths, which I regret. One of my friends, who went on to do a PhD in Maths, was taught by Fr Tierney, for A Level, and years later he told me that the Bird was a superior mathematician to anyone who lectured him after his College years. When he retired from teaching, Fr. Tierney became a curate in a rural parish and spent his final years living back in his native Derry. I had the pleasure of driving him to a parish function in Moville in County Donegal and it was an enjoyable and informative journey. I asked him if he had missed teaching when he left the College and he replied, 'Not at all. I still had friends who had problems that had to be solved mathematically.' I was a bit puzzled and asked him for an example. 'Well,' he replied, 'One Saturday evening, after Mass, a friend came to me and told me he had a problem. He had a wife and a girlfriend. I told him that he had two problems!'

Fr. Seamus Farrelly's Latin classes were a big step up for us as we now had Livy and Vergil to study. The history of Rome featured in the former, while the latter told the legendary story of Aeneas who left the shores of Troy to found Rome. '*Arma virum cano*,' it began; 'I sing of arms and the man.' Of course, it also featured a woman, Dido, a queen of Carthage who fell in love with Aeneas and committed suicide when he sailed away in quest of his destiny to found Rome. Fr. Farrelly was uninterested in portraying the Aeneid as an ancient version of a Mills and Boon novel. He focused us on the scansion of the lines and the alteration of rhythm through long and short syllables.

I was looking forward to the History syllabus, as it was modern Britain, Europe and Ireland, 1865 to 1945, and I was not disappointed with either the courses or the teacher. Jim Sharkey was a young teacher and a history graduate of University College Dublin. He was, in the words of a Leonard Cohen song, 'only passing through.' He had the radicalism of his generation and within a week we had been thrust into the Paris Commune. Our study of 19th century Europe also enlightened us to the fact that there was massive anti-Semiticism long before Hitler came to power in Germany in the 1930s. It seemed as though Jews, from all parts of the spectrum, from Trotsky and Rosa Luxemburg on the left to the Rothschilds of high finance, were being blamed for all the woes of the world. The Tsarist regimes were forever persecuting their Jewish subjects and we studied the Dreyfus affair in France, which had anti Semiticism at its core. We became great admirers of Emile Zola and his famous letter, *J'Accuse*, which opened up a hornet's nest in the French Establishment; although the vindication of Dreyfus was only accomplished after another few decades. We also learned that there were anti Semitic riots in the Irish city of Limerick at the beginning of the 20th century, encouraged by the Catholic hierarchy.

I asked my father if there had been a Jewish community in Derry and he remembered them living around Bishop Street and the Fountain and that there had been a synagogue in Kennedy Place. There was the story of a Jewish peddler, who went from door to door selling framed pictures. He carefully assessed the religion of the householder and potential customer and produced a picture of either the Sacred Heart or King Billy. The only Jewish people that I had any contact with were Mr and Mrs Pollock, who owned a grocery and confectionery shop at thee top of Beechwood Avenue and who lived next door to the shop. They were very quiet and kept themselves very much to themselves. They were very courteous to their customers and. I used to wonder if they had escaped from Nazi Germany and settled in Derry.

Ireland and the Balkans were the issues that greatly concerned successive British governments in the late 19th century and would, with remarkable frequency, dominate events in succeeding decades right up to the 21st century. We learned that Disraeli's Conservative government was concerned about Russia extending its power into the Balkans and wished to support the Ottoman Empire (as had been the case in the Crimean campaign). There was plenty of gunboat diplomacy and in early 1878, British battleships were sent to protect Constantinople (Istanbul) from Russian occupation. History was not just about prime ministers and we were interested in an individual, Gilbert Hastings MacDermott, the son of Irish working-class parents, who became one of the biggest stars of the music halls, and was billed as the "Great Macdermott." It was quite an irony that it was an Irishman, who sent audiences into imperialist raptures as he sang,

We don't want to fight but by Jingo if we do,
We've got the ships, we've got the men, we've got the money too,

We've fought the Bear before, and while we're Britons true,
The Russians shall not have Constantinople.

The enthusiastic singing of this song resulted in the word "jingoism" being added to the English language. The song was so influential that it merited a leader in *The Times* and was quoted in the House of Commons. For any politician, even in the modern age, the song showed the power of a good tune with catchy lyrics. Music hall was also a reminder that a fight with the Russians was not universally acclaimed and Herbert Campbell parodied MacDermott with an alternative chorus;

I don't want to fight, I'll be slaughtered if I do,
I'll change my togs, I'll sell my kit and pop my rifle too,
I don't like the war, I ain't a Briton true,
And I'll let the Russians have Constantinople.

The age of the music hall had long passed but we did have a glimpse of it in a BBC programme, *The Good Old Days*, performed in the Leeds City Varieties, attempted to re-create an authentic atmosphere of the Victorian/Edwardian heyday of the genre. The audience was dressed in period costume and Leonard Sachs was master of ceremonies. John Major, whose father was a music hall entertainer, has written that the show captured the rapport between artiste and audience, especially in rousing sing-along moments. However, he also pointed out that it lacked the drinking and heckling that was present in the era of the Great MacDermott and any innuendo was sanitised.

My father told me that the nearest that Derry ever had to a music hall was the Opera House on Carlisle Road, before it was converted to a cinema in 1938. He remembered the artists staying in boarding houses on Orchard Street, especially a troupe of dwarfs who gave him three pence for reaching to the knocker of the front door for them. As we studied British History, I remember Jimmy Sharkey explaining that the brewing industry became major financial backers of the Conservatives, when the Liberals introduced a measure to forbid the addition of salt to beer, which made the drinkers thirstier. The titanic struggles between Gladstone and Disraeli were taught in a way that these characters seemed more real than Harold Wilson and Ted Heath. We learned that Gladstone was chopping down trees on his estate when news arrived that he had won the 1868 General Election. He reputedly paused and said, 'My mission is to pacify Ireland,' before resuming his tree felling. By complete contrast, the passion of Otto Von

Bismarck, the Prussian Chancellor, was planting trees. When it came to Ireland, nothing was simple and clear cut, as Jim Sharkey pointed out. While Home Rule aspirations were tied firmly to Gladstone's Liberals, the Catholic hierarchy found the Conservatives more appealing in educational policies. Jim, a future diplomat, also taught us that the Conservatives were generally the pragmatists in matters of policy, a useful insight in the light of what would follow in the politics of Northern Ireland.

To me, this was a fascinating period of British politics, as I observed Gladstone and Disraeli slug it out in successive elections. Queen Victoria was none too keen on Gladstone but seemed a great fan of Disraeli. I was particularly impressed by Gladstone's Midlothian Campaign, as he toured the constituency in what was the first ever pre-planned campaign of public orations. His grand tour was a comprehensive attack on the Conservative government's policies and I was quite stunned to read that Gladstone even calculated that the total audience who heard him was 86,930!

The history we were studying was that of a period in which party politics was developing in Great Britain and electoral contests were between Conservatives and Liberals. It was also the period of the emergence of the Labour Party. All of this made us appreciate that while Northern Ireland was an integral part of the United Kingdom; its politics had not developed on similar lines. At Westminster, governments came and went, whereas at Stormont, the seat of the Northern Ireland parliament, the Unionist Party had remained in power since the establishment of the state, in 1921. Local politics was not based on social and economic divisions but on the constitutional future of the region. It all came down to supporting the link with Britain or supporting a united Ireland.

At the beginning of the 1968 school year, I was sure that Harold Wilson, Gladstone's successor, had few thoughts on either Ireland or chopping down trees. With regard to the former, this situation was to change very rapidly, even before the end of our first term. The Ireland that Gladstone sought to pacify had just emerged from attempts by republican separatists to achieve a break of the Act of Union by physical force. The Fenian Rising of 1867, which had seen dynamiting in English cities, was a complete shambles and ended in the widow O' Brien's cabbage patch, in Ballingarry, County Tipperary. Gladstone's reaction had been to embark upon land reform measures and the dis-establishment of the Anglican Church. A measure to repeal the Act of Union, in the form of a Home Rule bill, only emerged in the mid 1880s. By 1968, his successor, Harold Wilson, who had ultimate responsibility only for six of the thirty two counties of Ireland, probably regarded any involvement in Irish issues as something to be avoided.

James Callaghan, his Home Secretary wrote in his memoirs that the advice from all sides was on no account to get sucked into the Irish bog. However, as events were to transpire, this is precisely what did transpire and Wilson's days in his first government administration ended with physical force Irish republicanism returning to the stage. Within the Catholic community, I was to witness a struggle between constitutional nationalism and physical force republicanism for the allegiance of my generation.

Chapter Nine
The Civil Rights Era Begins

'Don't trust anyone over thirty'-'civil rights for boarders' as marching mania gets into full swing

My senior years in the College were to coincide with the beginning of greatest upheavals in Northern Ireland since the foundation of the state. Within a year of returning to the College, there would be more reform measures announced than had happened in the previous half century. Terence O'Neill, the Prime Minister, would depart the political stage and be gone, as would Eddie McAteer, the Nationalist Party leader, and the British Army would be deployed on the streets. However, that September Northern Ireland seemed a sea of tranquillity before the Troubles erupted.

No one living in Derry or Londonderry could have failed to have been aware of allegations by Nationalists of discrimination in housing and employment by Unionism. There was the added discontent that the electoral areas in the Corporation had been gerrymandered to ensure that the nine thousand Unionist electors returned twelve members to the Corporation, while the fifteen thousand Nationalist electors returned only eight. There had not been a Nationalist Mayor of Derry since 1923. In the Reference Room of the Brooke Park Library, I did some research on this term 'gerrymander' and discovered that its origins were American and dated back to the early decades of the nineteenth century, in Massachusetts. Its originator was a politician called Eldridge Gerry and even before him, one of the Founding Fathers, Patrick Henry, had been trying to rig electoral areas in Virginia. Gerrymandering and electoral malpractice seemed to have been rife, even with America's Founding Fathers, which taught me that no grouping wants voluntarily to surrender power. In Derry, the Unionists had the system refined to perfection for election to the Corporation, to such an extent that there were no electoral contests for seats in the Corporation. It seemed there was tacit agreement from the Nationalist Party as the Unionists only put up candidates in the two wards where they had an electoral majority and the Nationalists only put up candidates in the south ward. There were usually no other candidates from any other party, which ensured that the twenty members of the Corporation were returned unopposed. Derry politics was, to borrow a phrase from Wordsworth, 'a fen of stagnant waters.'

Nationalist discontent had been bubbling over ever since the establishment of the Northern Ireland state. The Nationalist Party continued to call the Dublin government 'our government.' Until the mid-1960s, the party was a part-time opposition at Stormont. In Derry, it resented Unionist hegemony but had no effective way to challenge it. There had been sporadic attempts by republican separatists in the Irish Republican Army, the IRA, to launch campaigns of violence in the vain hope of securing a united Ireland. The most recent failure had begun in 1956 and had petered out six years later, without achieving any tangible support from the Nationalist population in Northern Ireland. Republicans had not made any electoral breakthroughs in elections after that and the Nationalist Party had even become the official opposition at Stormont. However, republicans had not gone away and by the late 1960s had re-emerged, under a new Marxist oriented leadership, supporting campaigns on issues such as housing. In Derry, as elsewhere, there was the old guard, men like Sean Keenan and Neil Gillepsie. They appeared to be more at home with the traditional republican rhetoric and tactics than the newly-found attachment to Marxist political involvement. There was also a younger generation that joined the James Connolly Republican Clubs and became involved in social agitation. Eamon Melaugh, Finbarrr O'Doherty and Johnny White were the leading members of this grouping.

After the Civil Rights march in Dungannon in August, it seemed only a matter of time before a similar march would be planned for Derry. Likewise, it was no surprise that Eamon Melaugh emerged as one of the organisers of the march that was planned for Saturday 5th October 1968. Prospects for the march did not seem bright, especially as its local organisers did not really carry great weight within the Catholic community. The march was ostensibly under the auspices of the Northern Ireland Civil Rights Association (NICRA), which had been established in Belfast, in February 1967. Few people in Derry had ever heard of it and it had no leading members on the ground and it had no branch in the city. It was a remote organisation, chaired by Betty Sinclair, a well-known Communist, whose political affiliation would have made it highly suspect to the Nationalist Party leaders and clerics in Derry.

Though nominally under the auspices of NICRA, the detailed organisation of the proposed march fell to an ad hoc committee, consisting of what would have appeared to government as the usual left-wing and republican suspects. Eamon Melaugh, Finbarrr O' Doherty and Johnny White were joined by two well-known leftist members of the local Labour Party, Dermie McClenaghan and Brendan Hinds. In reality, the ad hoc committee did not function and the driving force for the march became Melaugh and Eamonn McCann, a firebrand in the local Labour

Party. In his memoir, *War And An Irish Town,* McCann has written extensively about the march and the days leading up to it. The organisers apparently tried to get well known figures and respected figures in the Catholic community, to sign the papers notifying the police of the proposed march. They approached James Doherty, a local businessman and Nationalist Councillor on the Corporation, and our former History teacher, John Hume, but they both refused. More significantly, McCann has written that the date for the march was selected by the organisers in the mistaken belief that Derry City would be playing away from home. If they could not organise a march, how did they expect to organise a revolution?

On Saturday 5th October, Derry City were to play in the Brandywell against Distillery, while Manchester United were trying to kick start their season with a home game against Arsenal. While the outcomes of those games are but footnotes in sporting history the real question is: was the day the Troubles started in Northern Ireland? There had been some of talk in the College about the march, which was viewed with little anticipation, until it was banned. For a few of us, the agonising choice was the march or the Brandywell. I usually went to the Brandywell, so why should I change my habits for the 5th October? I finally decided that, just maybe, the march was a chance to see history in the making. After all, the game in Brandywell was only against Distillery, not a real match like having Linfield or Glentoran, or even those university thieves from Coleraine. Mr. Sharkey, our History teacher, helped me to make up my mind when he said this march could be an historic event. There would be plenty of other games to watch in the Brandywell. After school that Saturday, I went home and said I was going along to watch the proposed march and was told to watch myself.

Even without the gift of hindsight it was clear, at the time, that the proposed route of the march was designed to provoke controversy. A commission of enquiry, headed by a Scottish judge, Lord Cameron concluded that 'a section of extremists actively wished to provoke violence or, at least a confrontation with the police without regard to consequences.' The march was scheduled to begin at the railway station in the predominantly Protestant Waterside, a place we simply called the Gorbals. It was to procced to the War Memorial in the Diamond, passing through the Walled City, which was traditionally the preserve of the Orange Order and Apprentice Boys. It was unheard of for a non-Unionist procession to enter the walled city. The last time it had been attempted was in the 1950s when a parade attempted to march down Shipquay Street, with the Irish Tricolour at its head, only to be batonned off the street by Northern Ireland's police force, the Royal Ulster Constabulary (RUC). In those days, there were no television crews hanging around, awaiting a 'scoop.'

In the days leading up to 5th October, the inevitable happened as William Craig, the Minister for Home Affairs, banned the march's proposed route, which only added interest. In fairness to him, he let it be known that the march could take place anywhere else in the city but the organisers were intent on their chosen route. It was also widely rumoured that the police were under strict instructions to ensure that the Minister's ban would be upheld and that additional police units, known as 'the riot squad,' would be deployed in Derry for the march. Neither of my parents was going to the march and my father viewed the organisers with some suspicion In addition, given that the march was banned, my parents had little interest in defying the rule of law, irrespective as to whether they agreed with the ban or not.

With a couple of my classmates, I made my way to the Waterside and soon discovered that the march organisers had been forced, at the last minute, to change the proposed route. In their attempt to reach Craigavon Bridge, they were now set on proceeding via Duke Street. We took up a vantage position on Duke Street, about twenty yards in front of a police cordon that had been hastily assembled in front of police tenders. The building, which afforded us a good vantage point, had barred windows and a ledge that allowed us to stand up to get a better view of proceedings. We were quite close to what was to become the police line. The policemen were not clad in riot helmets but their ordinary caps. They wore a grim determination to ensure that the Minister's ban was enforced. In the distance we could see a relatively small crowd that had gathered at the railway station to march. The organisers may have hoped that four thousand would attend but the number was closer to four hundred. There are three certainties in life; death, taxes and protest marches never starting on time. Derry's first Civil Rights' march was due to start at 3.30 p.m. but that time came and went with the motley crew still hanging around the railway station. From my vantage point, there appeared to be more onlookers than marchers and by the time the march reached the police lines. I was beginning to think that I should have gone to the Brandywell.

As the marchers approached the police lines I noticed that there were no revolutionaries in the vanguard. The front row consisted, in the main, of middle-aged men in their best Sunday suits, white shirts, all highly respectable citizens. I could see the tall and imposing figure of Eddie McAteer, MP for Foyle in the Stormont Parliament and leader of the Opposition. Close to him stood Gerry Fitt, also a Stormont MP as well as being a Westminster MP. I heard a number of people say that there were Labour MPs from Westminster also in attendance as 'observers.' As Cameron reported, 'The precise sequence of events during the afternoon is to some extent confused and not easy to ascertain, but in general outline is reasonably clear.' The march stopped in front of the police lines and no one seemed to know what to do next. The first police batons were drawn and the first casualties were Gerry Fitt and Eddie McAteer. The former was led away with blood running from a nasty head wound. It seemed unreal that a Westminster MP and the leader of the official Opposition at Stormont would be batonned by the police.

However, order was quickly restored. The organisers of the march had clearly been told that they would not be allowed to progress any further and a standoff developed. After the unprovoked attack on Fitt and McAteer, things seemed to have settled down a bit and there was a stand-off between the marchers and the police. There was, as yet, no sign of the NICRA chairperson, Mrs Sinclair, who arrived late and the police provided her with a chair and a loud speaker to address the marchers, which was hardly a sign of actions of a police state. She certainly was no Rosa Luxemburg and her speech was boring. Initially there was no trouble, just a scratching of heads and the question 'What now?' Betty certainly wasn't for inciting revolution and her words to the marchers were ones of great congratulation on their turnout and then she told them to go home for their tea. Austin Currie and Eamonn McCann upped the temperature with their remarks, most of which were inaudible to us.

It was beginning to look like a dull, scoreless draw when another group of late comers, the Young Socialists from Belfast, arrived and entered the fray. Now, here were the kindred spirits of the student revolutionaries on the streets of Paris that we had seen on our television screens earlier that year. They wasted no time in making their presence felt in a predictable manner. I could clearly see as they pushed their way forward towards the police line and placards and stones were thrown. It seemed to me that they were trying to provoke a reaction. Then came the fateful moment when the order was given to the policemen to draw their batons which they did and as Cameron concluded, used 'them indiscriminately on the crowd.' Cameron was correct to conclude that 'the police handling of the situation in the Waterside was ill-co-ordinated and ill-conducted.' In one case, the assailant was a senior commander, wielding his Hawthorne stick.

As events deteriorated, my personal safety became of prime importance and I decided that it was time to find a safer vantage point. Safer ground consisted of moving behind the marchers and then walking up a steep brae towards Spencer Road, which ran parallel with Duke Street. From Spencer Road, I could just see the appearance of a new formidable weapon in the police's armoury against protestors, the water cannon. Its driver must have been having field day as he proceeded up Duke Street and on to Craigavon Bridge spraying everyone in sight, marcher and non-marcher alike. I stayed well ahead of its line of fire and stopped only to ask a man, wearing a Derry City scarf, coming along the Bridge in the direction of the Waterside, how Derry City had done. He duly informed me that City had come from behind to win a thriller by three goals to two, with Danny Hale scoring the winner. I was beginning to think that I should have gone to Brandywell. My mother had asked me to call into Wellworth's Supermarket, in Waterloo Place on the way home and had given me a small list of her grocery requirements. By tea time, however, there were running battles between stone throwers and the police in the city centre and some shop windows had been broken.

On the evening of Sunday 6th October there was further rioting in the city centre, as crowds of young men invaded the Diamond from the Bogside, through Butcher Gate. They broke windows and looted shops in the Diamond before being repulsed by the police. The mob had entered the fray and their first targets were Protestant owned shops. Within a month, there was an unofficial boycott of Protestant owned shops. The rioting and looting was fast becoming a rerun of what had happened in American cities in the summer months. The first modern-day riot had occurred in Derry and the first barricades were erected at the bottom of Fahan Street. Stones and petrol bombs were thrown at the police. Confrontations quickly assumed what was to be a predictable scenario, with the police driving the Catholic rioters back from the city centre and into the area that was to be named 'the Bogside' by a commission established to enquire into riots in the city in 1868. A century later, riots and confrontation were taking place on traditional spots. I had only been familiar with the name Bogside as a single street of terraced houses, which ran off Rossville Street. I remember the name because the Ward twins, who had been in my class at the Christian Brothers, lived in Bogside. But the name stuck and all subsequent rioting was said to be taking place in the Bogside.

Almost overnight, Derry was on the news. I remember William Hardcastle's BBC Radio programme, *The World This Weekend*, talking about police brutality in a place he seemed to call 'Londondry.' In the coming weeks and months, English broadcasters would have great difficulty in getting their tongues around the quaint names of Ulster towns. The events in Derry also put the Unionist government on the defensive. Over the next few weeks, cabinet ministers regularly appeared on television to label the Civil rights march as a republican and communist conspiracy, defend the ban and voice support for the police actions on the day of the march. The international press corps, having tired of reporting riots in London, Paris and Prague now descended on the Maiden City and was holed up in the City Hotel, from where they sent lurid accounts of the street violence to readers and listeners across the globe.

For Catholics, the Unionist bête noire was William Craig, the Minister of Home Affairs, who had banned the proposed 5th October march route. He vigorously defended the decision to ban the march and the police actions in enforcing the ban. I remember my father having some sympathy for Craig at the time. He thought he had been a progressive Minister for Development and had talked about a master plan for the development of the North West. He thought that Craig was in a 'no win' situation regarding the ban which was inevitable given the route selected. Craig's standing in my father's eyes was also improved by the fact that he had been a sergeant in the RAF during the War and had flown as a gunner in many combat operations. My father often spoke disparagingly about politicians, who in his word 'had never seen an angry German.' I think that my father would have agreed with Craig that the local organisers of the 5th October march were republican and communist trouble makers. Maybe, he was reflecting the general mood in Catholic Derry, when the simple fact was that only four hundred turned up for that march!

The indiscriminate use of batons by the police was caught on camera by a film crew from Radio Telefis Eireann (RTE), the Republic of Ireland's state broadcasting authority. The film had to be taken back to Dublin and it was only on the following day, or maybe even the Monday that RTE broadcast the film of what was termed 'police brutality.' The images on our television screens were more akin to those from the anti-Vietnam demonstrations outside the American Embassy, in London, and the Democratic Convention in Chicago. Soon, October 5th in Derry would enter the lexicon of scenes of police brutality. The images from Duke Street, on that Saturday afternoon, would reverberate around the world. What had unfolded before my eyes on the streets of Derry seemed surreal. The genie was out of the bottle and I wondered if I had just witnessed a turning point in the politics of Northern Ireland.

The afternoon may have eventually been more exciting than watching a football match in Brandywell. However, it was difficult to realise that we had just witnessed the opening scene in a drama that was set to run for almost three decades. With hindsight, it is safe to say that the events in Derry on Saturday 5th October 1968 had opened Pandora's Box in Northern Ireland. Political life would never be the same again. Derry was now on the map with all those European cities that were seen as hotbeds of political radicalism, or so it seemed. The following Monday, in our History lesson in St. Columb's, Jim Sharkey told us that we had witnessed one of the defining moments of political life in modern Ireland. We almost convinced ourselves that being at the march was something akin to having been in the General Post Office, in Dublin, in the 1916 Rising.

That summer, I had watched, on television, the crass stupidity of various baton wielding police forces, in London and America, lay in to demonstrators. I was now left with the distinct impression that there had been a lack of strategic thinking, on the part of the RUC, for the Civil Rights march, in Derry. Obviously, senior commanders had not read Dale Carnegie's classic, *How to Win Friends and Influence People*. The police placed a cordon behind the marchers, as well as in front of it, which left the marchers with no escape route except through police lines. I had often heard my father say that it was prudent to give even a cornered rat an escape route, unless you were going to kill it. Now, I did not think that the police were going to kill any marchers, even if they did believed them to be rats and should therefore have left them a safety escape route. There had been plenty of examples when non-violent police reaction had been the best tactic, even in face of provocation. With hindsight, I am surprised that the police had made no effort to impound the RTE film reel as the footage was being shot. Without that film clip, the police behaviour on Duke Street and Craigavon Bridge would not have achieved any publicity. Who was advising the authorities?

With the actions of one afternoon in Derry, the RUC were presented overnight as very partisan and had used excessive force against civilians. The police over-reaction to the antics of the Young Socialists was a catalyst for a general descent into anarchy. Terence O'Neill called for moderation and restraint. I arrived home that afternoon to discover that Manchester United had played out a drab scoreless draw against Arsenal. How Terence O'Neill must have wished that a similar result had emerged from the confrontation on the streets of Derry, rather than the RUC score quite a few own goals.

There were similarities between the action of government in France and Northern Ireland, and lessons from the streets of Paris had not been learned at Stormont. As Daniel Cohn-Bendit, the left wing leader of the modern Paris Commune, later said, 'If the government had not thought they had to crush the movement, we would never have reached this part of a fight for liberation. There would have been a few demonstrations and that would have been that.' Had the government from the beginning simply ignored the enragés, France might well have avoided its summer uprising. I often wonder what the history of the 1970s in Northern Ireland would have been if the 5th October march in Derry had been allowed to proceed unbanned. However, allowing the march to proceed over its proposed route would have represented a major U-turn in the Unionist psyche. It would have been unheard of for the Stormont government to allow any Nationalist or Republican parade to breach the sacred walled city.

When we returned to school on the Monday morning, the weekend demo and ensuing riots were widely discussed. Mr. Sharkey predicted a fundamental shift in the way Northern Ireland would be governed from now on. It was the beginning of the end of one-party Unionist rule but there was great uncertainty as to what was going to emerge. The immediate reaction of the two communities to the events in Derry over the weekend of the 5th and 6th October could not have been more different and polarised. Catholic Derry focused on the action of the police in Duke Street during the Civil Rights march, while the Protestant community highlighted the ensuing violence. *The Londonderry Sentinel*, under the headline '*Worst Disturbances in City for 50 years,*' reported that forty business premises had been smashed and windows broken in the Apprentice Boys' Memorial Hall and First Derry Presbyterian Church. The Unionist MP for Londonderry, Robin Chichester-Clark felt so incensed by the reporting of the BBC that he sent a telegram to the chairman, Lord Hill, complaining of 'unbalanced and irresponsible and inaccurate version of the situation in Londonderry,' a view shared by the Sentinel's editorial. Each side saw what it wanted to see in the weekend's events and ignored what did not suit its political outlook.

A book with the title *1968 – The Year that Rocked the World*, written by Mark Kurlansky, appeared in 2005. It made no mention of events in Northern Ireland but I believe that the events that I witnessed in Duke Street on that Saturday afternoon in October of 1968, meant that, in the words of W.B. Yeats, 'All changed, changed utterly.' Little did we know the following line of the poem would soon be acted out before our eyes, 'A terrible beauty is born.' The genie was out of the bottle. The weekend rioting had created a political vacuum in Catholic Derry, which, within a week, was filled, as one of our former teachers, John Hume, emerged as one of the leading Civil Rights leaders and spokesmen. The left-wing ad hoc committee that had botched the finer organisational details for the 5th October march was quickly brushed aside with and replaced by the Derry Citizens' Action Committee, DCAC. It was something of a right wing, Catholic Social Action, coup and was perfectly executed by Hume and his supporters. It was derided by the left wing socialist leader in the city, Eamonn McCann, as 'middle aged, middle class and middle of the road.' His comment reminded me of the advice given by Charlton Heston to the young, rebellious chimpanzees in the film, *Planet of the Apes;* 'Don't trust anyone over thirty.'

Republicans and communists may have been the founders of the Civil Rights movement but, in Derry, its new leadership and its foot soldiers, were people with moderate views and for whom it was right, just and reasonable to demand fair treatment within the Northern Ireland state. Thousands of Catholics, like my father, had fought in the World War and were demanding British rights for

British citizens. Of course, this approach was not helped by comments from the Dublin government. The first reaction to the events of October 5th from Prime Minister, Jack Lynch, was a knee-jerk statement that the first and foremost root cause of the problem was Partition. Talk about handing a PR victory to the hard line Unionists, who were busy saying the Civil Rights movement was nothing but a front to overthrow the state of Northern Ireland. Not for the first time did politicians in the Republic behave like dinosaurs.

This Derry Citizens' Action Committee organisation quickly became the tool of John Hume and Ivan Cooper, a local shirt factory manager, and sought to ensure that it controlled the situation, rather than have the militants in charge. The DCAC called a public meeting in the Guildhall for the Wednesday following the October 5th march. Such was the turnout that it spilled over to Guildhall Square, to which proceedings were relayed on a Tannoy system. Inside the building the leaders were clearly enjoying their new-found status and promising to return to the streets and complete the route of the banned march. The only voice dissenting from the calls for 'one man, one vote' was that of veteran republican, Sean Keenan, who also addressed the meeting. He took the issue back exclusively to the issue of the partition of Ireland, rather than demands for 'British rights for British citizens.' He even quoted words from the poem, 'The Rebel', by Patrick Pearse, a leader of the 1916 rising:

"And I say to me people's masters: Beware
Beware of the thing that is coming, beware of the risen people
Who shall take what you would not give."

Summonses were served on the organisers of the 5th October march and when they appeared in court, at Bishop Street, there were large crowds there to support them. It was also the first time that I heard the crowd shout 'SS RUC' at the policemen on duty outside the courthouse and give them the Nazi salute. A growing number of summonses were served and court proceedings changed radically, in Derry. My father had often told me that in the previous years it was not uncommon for there to be no criminal cases to be heard and the Presiding Magistrate was presented with a pair of white gloves, a tradition that went back a few centuries. After 5th October there were no other such occasions at the Magistrate's Court in Bishop Street. Meanwhile, in Belfast, a left-wing new student based organisation calling itself the People's Democracy emerged calling for, 'Tories out North and South.' It was to influence future events in a way viewed as negative by many and some of its actions were deemed to be fomenting further violence. It sought 'calculated martyrdom,' a phrase used by Lord Cameron. There was a general feeling that Harold Wilson would now be forced to take a direct interest in the governing of Northern Ireland.

For years, the months of July and August, in Northern Ireland, were known as 'the marching season,' with a proliferation of parades by the Orange Order, Apprentice Boys of Derry and the Royal Black Preceptory. Parades by Catholic organisations such as the Ancient Order of Hibernians seemed restricted to 15th August, the feast day of the Our Lady. October 5th 1968 had unleashed a new phenomenon, a Catholic marching season. Marching became the safety valve through which was released all the pent-up frustrations of the North's Catholics. In the aftermath of the 5th October Civil Rights march, the newly formed DCAC felt that it had to keep up some momentum by action on the streets. There was a sit down protest in Guildhall Square organised, and this attracted about 5,000, people on a Saturday afternoon. It was a bit of a damp squib, both literally and metaphorically, and the crowd went home, a tad disappointed. The risen people needed more excitement than John Hume telling them that the Civil rights demands were simply for a crash programme of housing and a fair points system for house allocation. I well remember Finbarr O'Doherty proclaiming 'We are the Negroes of Derry.' The elephant in the corner at that sit down demonstration was the issue that the Unionist minority controlled Londonderry Corporation. That day, the issue was not mentioned in any of the speeches. However, within a month a headline in the Derry Journal was proclaiming, 'Minority Rule-the Fundamental Evil.' The Maiden City was the jewel in the crown of Unionism but also its Achilles Heel.

William Craig announced a one month ban on all marches within the Walled City and the reaction was instant. With one stroke of a ministerial pen, he generated wild public protests and excitement and created a festival of marching. Almost overnight, the Catholic community became highly radicalised and addicted to the concept of marching, which grew to epidemic proportions with a desire to break the ban on a daily basis. In Derry, there were marches organised for dockers, factory girls etc., which were intent on showing that the government's writ did not run. In truth, the police did not try to enforce the ban, which left the government open to ridicule from both its supporters and opponents.

I remember my mother saying that the marches by the Catholic factory girls opened up a rift within the shirt factories, which employed both Catholic and Protestant women, who generally worked harmoniously side by side. Between the two, there was a laissez-faire relationship and tensions only soared around the 12th of July and August when the Protestant women would fly Union Jack bunting around their sewing machines. The marches by Catholic factory girls upped the temperature considerably. Catholic factory girls were attacked leaving the Ben Sherman factory at the bottom of Wapping Lane, a staunchly loyalist area of the Fountain.

Relationships were not helped by the fact that one of the Civil Rights leaders in Derry, Ivan Cooper, was also a manager in a local shirt factory. As he was a Protestant, Loyalists regarded him as a turncoat, a modern day Lundy, supporting papist causes and were quick to claim that he had, in fact, been expelled from the Young Unionists. I first saw him in Brendan Duddy's fish and chip shop at the top of Beechwood Avenue. Sporting his sheepskin coat, he looked so out of place.

The Derry Citizens' Action Committee organised a march over the same route as that banned on 5th October and an estimated 20,000 participated. The march fell under the ban imposed by Bill Craig and there was great consternation about the potential outcome. A delegation from the Derry Churches Industrial Council sought a meeting with the Home Affairs minister to urge him to lift the ban. Ominously, an organisation called 'The Loyal Citizens of Ulster,' issued a statement, warning 'No placard-carrying Fenian will be allowed to pass through Derry's walls.' Forty eight teachers from the College sent a telegram to Terence O'Neill, the Prime minister, calling for the ban to be rescinded.

As tension mounted, all-night prayers were held in the two cathedrals. Bishops Farren and Peacocke were doing their level best to keep the lid on a tense city. There was genuine fear that all hell would break loose. And yet, there was a pious hope that Derry would show the way in non-violent protest. Almost literally, the eyes of the world were on Derry. This time, my father and mother went on that march but forbade me from going. The day ended with the marchers eventually reaching the Diamond, by a circuitous route, having made a token gesture in defying the ban on the proposed route of the march. Thankfully, there was minimal violence as the march was well stewarded. One character, in particular emerged, Vinny Coyle. Towering over six foot tall, with his fedora hat and Zapata moustache, he was the self-styled chief march steward and coined a few phrases that went into Derry folklore. He would tell marchers 'don't corrugate around the lamp-posts.' In his desire to ensure that a march seemed bigger than it actually was, he would encourage marchers to stay on the road with the words, 'don't pedestrate the pavement.' He became John Hume's unofficial bodyguard for all marches.

A week after the momentous events on the streets of Derry, the Olympic Games started in Mexico City. My main sporting memory of the Games is of the American athlete, Dick Fosbury, who won the high jump with a new and unconventional technique. Rather than relying on the straddle technique, Fosbury went backwards over the bar to land safely in a soft bed of deep foam matting. The

Fosbury Flop had arrived as the standard technique for high jumping. Aside from the sporting prowess that saw George Foreman win the heavyweight boxing gold medal, the games were blighted by controversy. African countries, supported by the Eastern European countries of the Soviet bloc, had threatened a boycott if South Africa was allowed to participate. The International Olympic Committee beat a hasty retreat, under these threats. It withdrew its invitation to South Africa six months before the games were due to take place. Our television screens bombarded us with footage of two black American sprinters, Tommy Smith and John Carlos, the gold and bronze medallists in the men's 200 metre sprint. They took their places on the winners' podium and as the Star Spangled Banner was played, they bowed their heads and each raised a black-gloved fist salute. The black glove was the symbol of the Black Panther movement in America, which was way to the left of the Civil Rights' leader, Martin Luther King.

Sitting in Creggan and watching the ceremony, it seemed as though the American Civil Rights movement, looking for equality in the states of the old Confederacy, had died with Martin Luther King. The movement had turned northwards and groups like the Black Panthers and Black power were emerging as its leading spokesmen. Would the same fate befall the Northern Ireland Civil Rights Association?

Our schooling was being played out against a backdrop of intense political activity and it was important to keep our feet on the ground and get on with our studies. There was one almost farcical incident when, on a Friday afternoon, there was a protest outside the front gate of the College, with a number of the left-wing republican leadership, such as Finbarrr O'Doherty, carrying placards demanding Civil Rights for boarders. 'College President marches for Civil Rights but denies them to boarders,' one of the placards read, which was all very Monty Pythonesque. Fr. Farrelly, our Latin teacher commented that the whole thing was 'reductio ad absurdum.' The main organisers, and supporters of the establishment of a Students' Representative Council, had been three upper sixth day boy pupils, all of whom were expelled. The President's statement had classical undertones, as it said the expulsions were 'sine die.' We asked Fr. Farrelly the exact meaning of these words, which literally translated as 'without day,' and he told us that it meant there was no right of appeal, as no further day for re-consideration of the matter had been established. We thought the punishment was draconian and would have done Bill Craig justice.

The protest made the front page of the *Belfast Telegraph* but the College authorities obviously persuaded *The Derry Journal* to suppress the story. The whole incident could have been dismissed as a student prank but reached proportions that would have fitted into a Gilbert and Sullivan operetta. The President, Fr. Farren, aka Wee Johnnie, toured the classrooms flanked by a Praetorian Guard of prefects appealing for our loyalty to the College. We were in Mr. Mullan's English class when he arrived and he was heard in stony silence. 'Your College needs you,' he exhorted in tones of Lord Kitchener. The expulsions had ensured that no one was going to break ranks publicly but equally we could not be expelled for our silent reaction to the President's exhortations. The brave thing to do would have been to call for the expulsions to be lifted but there was no leadership among senior pupils and none of the staff was going to break ranks and make such a dramatic move. The expulsions were never rescinded. The school did not have the world media circus descend on it in the coming days, for which I am sure the President was relieved. While Wee Johnnie toured the classrooms looking for support, Northern Ireland's Prime Minister, Terence O'Neill was touring the country drumming up support for his reform measures.

At Stormont, Terence O'Neill was in a greater predicament than Fr. Farren had been in the College. There appeared a liberal wing to O'Neill's administration that wanted to meet the Civil Rights demands head-on before far more unpalatable concessions were imposed by the Labour government at Westminster. On the other hand, there quickly emerged a strong grouping that opposed any concession and branded the Civil Rights movement simply as a republican front, determined to smash what was called the 'constitutional settlement.' In our History class, we listened to words of wisdom from Jimmy Sharkey. He reminded us of the comment of Alexis De Tocqueville, a 19th century French historian and political commentator, that experience teaches that the most critical moment for bad governments is the one which witnesses their first steps toward reform.

It was a fact of political life that the Treasury in London was making an annual subsidy of millions of pounds to sustain the workings of government in Northern Ireland. He who paid the piper was now calling the tune. On our television screens, we became used to a regular sight of the Northern Ireland Prime Minister and cabinet colleagues being summoned to Downing Street to be instructed as to what measures were required to be introduced. This would continue with frequent regularity over the next few years.

The first meetings between Terence O' Neill and Harold Wilson resulted in a five point reform programme being announced in late November. A new points system for the allocation of houses by local authorities was to be established, an ombudsman was to be appointed to investigate complaints, the Special Powers Act was to be abolished as soon as it was safe to do so and the company vote in local authority elections was to be abolished. It appeared as though the Civil

Rights demands were being conceded and one wondered whether the movement had any remaining raison d'etre. It was the high water mark for the Civil Rights Movement, but few appreciated this at the time. Less than two months after the 5th October march, the vast majority of the demands of the movement had been met, in principle, but were yet to be implemented.

The biggest cheer that went up in Catholic Derry was to greet the announcement that the Corporation and Rural Council were to be disbanded immediately and replaced by a Development Commission. It was a terrible pity that this Commission had not been established five years earlier to address the housing problems. With one stroke of a ministerial pen, the Corporation was gone and the Development Commission was to become a major success, building four thousand houses in four years and establishing an industrial training centre. Housing, or the lack of it, had been one of the main grievances across the city and the Development Commission moved quickly in building new homes for Protestants and Catholics alike. One of my first summer time jobs was with Reggie Ryan, who owned a carpet shop in Ferryquay Street and my duties initially consisted of leaflet drops on new Protestant housing estates in the Waterside and Catholic housing estates in Shantallow.

Initially, with the package of reforms announced in November, many people seemed to believe that the Civil Rights movement had achieved its objectives and would simply fade from the scene. For most of the Civil Rights demands to come to fruition would necessarily take a number of years. Some pointed to the fact that One Man One Vote had not yet been conceded by the Unionist government. This demand only applied to council elections and these had been postponed until a re-organisation of local government was to take place. The momentum of reform would surely, in due course also incorporate this demand, which was what transpired. The problem for the Civil rights leadership was that there were calls on the streets for immediate and radical solutions. As my father told me; it is difficult to teach a dog to unbark once you have taught it to bark. Having brought thousands of people on to the streets in the previous month, the Civil Rights leaders were in a bit of a quandary. Their salvation lay in the fact that, apart from the immediate abolition of Londonderry Corporation, all the other measures were promised at some undetermined date in the future and there was no mention of the Civil Rights demand for 'one man one vote,' in local authority elections. So, the bottom line was that the package of measures did not mollify the Civil Rights leaders but, at the same time, inflamed unionists who saw them as too many concessions. O'Neill was between a rock and a hard place and took to the airwaves in an attempt to use the television media, which had landed him in such a mess, to his advantage.

On 9th December, nearly everyone was gathered around a television set as O'Neill made his 'Ulster is at the Crossroads' address. In his opening remarks he said, 'In Londonderry and other places, a minority of agitators determined to subvert lawful authority played a part in setting light to highly inflammable material. But the tinder for that fire in the form of grievances real or imaginary had been piling up for years.' To Unionists, he spelt out the hard fact that failure to face up to problems could see Westminster intervene. To Civil Rights demonstrators, he said that he was committed to reform and asked them to call off street demonstrations. He ruled out the calling of snap General Elections as 'utterly reprehensible against a background of bitterness and strife.' The next day, the full speech was carried by the *Derry Journal* on its front page and Eddie McAteer, the Nationalist Party leader and MP for Foyle said the speech was 'quite an impressive performance.'

It struck me that O'Neill had formed the view that there was a 'silent majority,' as opposed to what he called 'noisy minorities' that he could mobilise to support him. He immediately followed up the broadcast by sacking Bill Craig as Minister for Home Affairs. His efforts seemed to pay some immediate rewards as the Civil Rights leaders announced a moratorium on marches for one month. The *Belfast Telegraph* launched an 'I Back O'Neill' campaign, with coupons on its editions to be cut out and sent in support of the Premier and there were 150,000 coupons and telegrams of support. A Dublin based newspaper voted O'Neill man of the year. Over Christmas, he and Eddie McAteer appeared together on television and read passages from the Bible. There were grounds for being optimistic that the worst had passed in a relatively short period of three months and a new dawn beckoned.

In the excitement of those months, I went along with a few of my more politically committed school friends to meetings of the Labour Party Young Socialists. It was not affiliated to the Derry Labour Party but was more akin to a Trotskyite organisation. There were meetings in Magazine Street and we avidly read the party publication, *Keep Left*, which sounded more like a traffic sign than an inspiring political slogan. The new dawning of a Workers' Republic was all the rage, with novels like James Plunkett's *Strumpet City* and the plays of Sean O' Casey being a must read. Uniting the working class in Northern Ireland on social and economic policies was a noble dream. Looking back on my brief flirtation with Trotskyism that was over within a few months, I am reminded of the words of Winston Churchill; 'If a man is not a socialist by the time he is twenty, he has no heart. If he is not a conservative by the time he is forty, he has no brain.'

We had our first class tests just before the Christmas break and I was pleased to see that the heady excitement on the streets had not detracted from my studies.

In a strange way, it might have accelerated my development. The downside was that Manchester United were going from bad to worse and their only victory in December had been a one nil victory over Liverpool at Old Trafford. Poor Derry City suffered a massive reduction in attendances at the Brandywell when games coincided with Civil Rights marches.

It was about this time that I had my first glimpse of Rev Ian Richard Kyle Paisley, as he led a march along Ferryquay Street one Saturday afternoon. The crowd roared as it entered the Walled City, until recently, the preserve of Unionism. Even at that early stage in his career, he was known as 'the Big Man.' Malcolm Muggeridge had described him as 'a strange mixture of bigotry and revivalist evangelism,' and, for good measure added, 'he might have been one of Cromwell's men.' Virulent anti-Catholicism and strident Unionism were his trademarks and he spewed out both on a regular basis. Wearing a red, white and blue sash, like a French Mayor, Paisley was a tall man, full of self-confidence and beaming from ear to ear as he headed a demonstration of an organisation called the Ulster Protestant Volunteers. He was leading his Union Jack waving followers for a rally in the Diamond and appeared in high spirits.

At this time, he held no elected office but he had both charisma and momentum and it looked to me as if he was the coming man of Unionism. He was the populist leader of militant Unionism that knew what it was against but had little idea of what it was for. His supporters marched along singing a parody the Civil Rights anthem as they bellowed out, 'Paisley is our leader; we shall not be moved.' He was to the fore in counter-demonstrations in many towns across Ulster, opposing Civil Rights' marches and eventually he received a six months jail sentence for involvement in a demonstration in Armagh. His sentence was handed down by Judge Rory Conaghan, a Derryman and past pupil of St. Columb's, who was later murdered by the Provisional IRA, in 1974. At the outbreak of the Troubles, Paisley was a peripheral figure in the Protestant and Unionist community. The Church of Ireland Bishop of Derry and Raphoe, Dr. Tyndall, attacked Paisleyites as 'battalions of bigots' and asserted that moderates should follow the course adopted by Terence O'Neill in the fight against bigotry. Somehow, on that Saturday afternoon, I felt that it was Paisley, not the Bishop, who was more in tune with the views of a growing number of Protestants in Northern Ireland.

Chapter Ten
From Marching to Voting

Burntollet to Free Derry Corner – Claude, the Fenian Prod in Ulster at the Crossroads Election as John Hume ousts Eddie McAteer in Foyle.

The November package of reforms and the overwhelming positive reaction to Terence O'Neill's 'Ulster at the Crossroads' television broadcast brought a positive response from the Civil Rights leadership and an announcement was made of a truce with no marches in Northern Ireland until the end of January. Reforms had been proposed but had to be implemented. There was visible opposition to these reforms from a substantial element of O'Neill's Unionist parliamentary party and the wider unionist community. The prudent position was to create a bit of space for O'Neill to deliver on the reform package that he had agreed with Harold Wilson, the Labour Prime Minister, and which had been also endorsed by the Conservative Opposition at Westminster. The clear inference was that if Stormont delayed in the implementation of the promised reforms, the London government would intervene. The only divergence from such an outcome was in the analysis of the attitude of Harold Wilson. A century earlier, his predecessor, William Ewart Gladstone, had been hands-on on passing radical measures such as the disestablishment of the Anglican Church and Land Acts. By contrast, his successor, Wilson, seemed to be governed by a pragmatic school of thinking, which was to have the minimum involvement in Northern Ireland.

As we were completing our pre-Christmas in-house exams in the College, the agreed moratorium on Civil Rights marches received a setback when the radical left-wing student organisation, the People's Democracy, announced that it was going to have a four day protest march form Belfast to Derry, starting on New Year's Day. The march was a real slap in the teeth for the Civil Rights leaders who had supported a moratorium on marches. However, the positions was so fluid that one could readily identify just who were the leaders of the movement, assuming it had any regional leaders as opposed to local spokespersons.

I was a tad surprised to read that the march was not banned by the government. I remember my father favouring a ban of the march and he was not alone. The organisers stated clearly that the proposed march was modelled on the American Civil Rights march from Selma to Montgomery, in Alabama, in 1966, which had been met with violence and which was seen as forcing the President Lyndon

Johnson to accelerate Civil Rights reforms. Looking back, this was a march that could easily have been banned and the decision of government to allow it to proceed was clearly a mistake. A ban may not have been publicly welcomed by the wider Catholic community but it would not have been openly opposed. I still cannot understand why the government did not impose a ban. It was another example of a lack of clear thinking at the heart of government.

The decision to march divided Catholic Derry into three distinct groupings, those who, either quietly or vociferously, opposed the march, those who supported the march and those who simply sat on the fence. For many people, the decision of the People's Democracy to stage their proposed march seemed an act of madness that would bring confrontation with Unionists along the eighty mile route. 'The students are asking for trouble and they are sure to get it,' was a comment that I heard more than once. The letters pages of the Derry Journal contained many Nationalist advocates of extending the moratorium beyond January. My father had often been hostile to the Nationalist Party but, on this occasion, he was in agreement with the sentiments expressed by Eddie McAteer, 'That was not good marching weather in more senses than one,' McAteer was solely to the fore in openly voicing criticism of the proposed march. In the opposing corner was the Derry Labour Party, which was increasingly militant and seeking further confrontation with the state. It was no surprise to read that the Labour Party supported the proposed march. However, the march was neither supported not opposed or condemned by other Civil Rights leaders in Derry who seemed somewhat ambivalent. It was often said that some Catholics should keep their heads lower than that of a Catholic in Larne and in this instance, the Civil Rights leaders, who had recently come to prominence, showed no leadership. The most that the Citizens' Action Committee did was to place an advertisement in the *Derry Journal* calling 'Fellow citizens to join us in warmly welcoming the arrival of the People's Democracy group at the conclusion of their march.'

Eddie McAteer soared in my estimation. He was very magnanimous towards O'Neill and was prepared give the reform programme a chance. He realised that it did not concede all the demands of the Civil Rights movement. He made the comment, 'it's half a loaf.' At about that time, I increasingly heard Labour Party members deride Eddie McAteer for his comment and refer to him as 'Eddie Half a Loaf.' To a starving people this would indeed have been manna, but in the political cauldron of 1969, the phrase was used against McAteer. I think that it was Eamon McCann who mischievously suggested that McAteer's solution to Derry's unemployment crisis would be to build half a bakery!

Those four days in January of march and counter-protest set Northern Ireland spiralling downwards and were the nightmare that need not have happened. From the outset, there was confrontation as the students set off from Belfast's City Hall. One of Rev. Ian Paisley's henchmen, Major Ronald Bunting, had organised a counter-protest and, as the students were beginning their march, it swung in front of them and stayed there until the march reached Belfast Zoo on the Antrim Road. Some observers noted that this was a most appropriate point of departure. The march was making news because of the growing Protestant opposition to it. As the student march meandered through the roads of counties Antrim and Londonderry, it met further loyalist protests and the police had to ferry marchers around Antrim town and Randalstown, where roads were blocked by protestors.

On the Friday night, I had gone to the Palace Cinema, in Shipquay Street, to see the hypnotist, Edwin Heath, play to a full house. At the end of the show, we were walking through Guildhall Square. Inside the Guildhall, Ian Paisley was holding a rally. Outside, there was more street theatre as the building was surrounded by large groups of angry young Catholics. As if in a trance, brought on by Edwin Heath, they were voicing disapproval of Paisley by singing their own version of *The Drunken Sailor*:

> *"What shall we do with Ian Paisley?*
> *What shall we do with Ian Paisley?*
> *What shall we do with Ian Paisley, early in the morning?*

> *Burn, burn, burn the b......!*
> *Burn, burn, burn the b......!*
> *Burn, burn, burn the b......, early in the morning."*

The Festive Season of Goodwill had certainly evaporated. From the raucous singing, the mood grew more menacing as the crowd then started throwing stones and breaking windows of the Guildhall. They could not carry out their intent to burn Paisley but satisfied their desire by burning a car, belonging to Major Bunting, his trusty lieutenant. It was a massively negative photo advertisement for Derry as the car was burned out in Guildhall Square under the large Christmas tree. Attempts by some of the Civil Rights leaders in the city to get the Catholic mob to disperse failed miserably. As I stood at the Creggan bus stop, I witnessed an ugly, sectarian confrontation. I also had the nagging feeling that the leaders were losing control of the younger and more vocal elements of their erstwhile supporters. The Paisleyites emerged from the Guildhall brandishing chairs and banisters that had been broken up to make clubs. It did not augur well for the next day, which was due to see the students' march arrive in Derry on the last leg of their march.

The events of the next day have become known in folklore simply as Burntollet, named after the bridge a few miles from Derry, where the marchers were ambushed and severely beaten. Some of the attackers were allegedly off-duty members of the B specials and some of the marchers were later to allege that the police deliberately led them into a pre-arranged ambush. There were further attacks as the students passed the mainly Protestant Irish Street housing estate. Many battered, bruised and bleeding students finally arrived in Guildhall Square to end their ill-fated march. Having been at best lukewarm towards the plans for the march, the Derry Civil Rights leaders turned out, en masse, to fete the students, who had become heroes overnight. The action was far from over, as large numbers of the Burntollet attackers also made their way to the centre of Derry and the police herded them into Shipquay Street, whose gate was blocked by police tenders. Stones and bottles rained down from within the walls on the Civil Rights people in Guildhall Square. Mayhem ensued, with riot clad policemen attacking Civil Rights supporters with their batons.

Overnight, there was an attack, by policemen, on homes in the Bogside. Police had massed at Butcher Gate, just inside the walled city, and staged several charges down Fahan Street, some of them under the protection of a water canon and other police vehicles. It was alleged that the police ran amok, smashing windows and doors and hurling sectarian abuse at the residents in St. Columb's Wells. Few realised it at the time, but police reform was to become a major demand in Catholic areas of Derry. Eddie McAteer aptly summed up the feelings of residents when he said, 'I am beginning to think that the greatest civil right we need is an impartial police force' The RUC were now seen, by many Catholics in Northern Ireland, as being almost identical to Mayor Daley's Chicago police, who had batonned demonstrators at the Democratic Party convention six months earlier. Any hope of building trust and goodwill, on the back of the widely welcomed truce on marches, was washed away in a few days of madness. The first makeshift barricades were erected in the Bogside to attempt to keep the police out. That day, after the events at Burntollet, there was a menacing air in Derry. I remember that on the Sunday afternoon there was a large gathering of teenagers, intent on marching on the police barracks. To the tune of *Irish Soldier Laddie* they were singing out their own lyrics:

"Will you stand in the band like a true Irish man,
And go and fight the forces of the crown?
Will ye march with McCann to the barracks down the Strand?
For tonight we go to free old Derry town!"

I think that it was Eamon McCann, the much sung about would–be leader, who dissuaded them from heading to the barracks. Out of that weekend, however, there emerged something that became very enduring. The slogan '*You are Now Entering Free Derry*,' was painted on a gable-end wall at Lecky Road. In the days that followed, Derry recoiled from the brink and, surprisingly, settled down to normal. There was a general, if somewhat misplaced, feeling that it was outsiders, whether they were students, Paisleyites or policemen, had fomented the disturbances. However, a fuse had been lit and within weeks a Civil Rights march in Newry had ended in violence, with attacks on the police and property. Stewards were unable or unwilling to control the march and police vehicles were overturned and burned and police Land Rovers were pushed in to the canal. There was another indication of the street violence seeping into other towns beyond Derry and that the leaders of the Civil Rights movement had lost control to the mob.

There was an ever-widening chasm developing between the Catholic and Protestant communities in their analysis of the previous three months. Sir Basil McFarland, former wartime Royal Artillery commander and former Mayor of the city and a highly respected public figure, articulated the views of the Protestant business community. His address to the AGM of the Port and Harbour Board, of which he was also a former chairman, was printed in the Derry Journal. He blamed newspapers and television for being more or less 'a forging ground for a minority of individuals, who working from the back of the crowd or the sidelines, achieved results out of all proportion to the opinions of reasonable, decent people, the majority in the present era of protest.' The clear inference was that the Civil Rights movement was a collection of trouble makers who spoke for no one but themselves. What was not in dispute was that violence was attracted to the camera as the camera was attracted to violence.

At a football match, I was to gain a clear view of the growing divide. At the end of January, I was at the Brandywell for the visit of Linfield. I was greatly looking forward to the game. Derry City and the Belfast Blues were neck and neck at the top of the Irish League. Games against Linfield were always awaited with great excitement, mainly because the Blues were the yardstick against which every team was measured, and they always gave a good account of themselves. For my generation, they had a star striker in Sammy Pavis, who had signed for them from their Belfast rivals, Glentoran and who had played against Derry in the 1965 cup final. On the left wing there was Billy Ferguson who had been capped for Northern Ireland. His duels against Billy Cathcart, a burly policeman from Ballymena, were one of the highlight of these encounters. Derry versus Linfield rivalry was not a new phenomenon in local football. It went back generations. I remember my father telling me a story of a game and a famous Derry character, 'Hawker' Lynch. Hawker went on to the greyhound track that surrounded the Brandywell and took up a position facing the visiting Linfield supporters. He roared out the battle cry of Ulster loyalism: 'Derry, Aughrim, Enniskillen and the Boyne.' With the name of each place of victory in the Williamite Wars of the seventeenth century there were cheers from the Bluemen. As the cheers subsided, Hawker drew the attention of the travelling Belfast visitors to a stark reality that their little town had not even got a mention!

Unfortunately, the game that Saturday became remembered, neither for the score nor the quality of the football, but for crowd trouble between opposing fans. The game became something akin to a Celtic/Rangers game in Glasgow with sectarian songs being sung by supporters of both clubs. 'Riotous scenes of tension at boiling point,' was how *The Londonderry Sentinel* described the game. Sadly, politics had entered sport. It was the first time at Brandywell, that I had ever seen Derry City supporters waving Irish tricolors and singing rebel songs as well as the Civil Rights anthem, *We Shall Overcome*. The trouble started when Linfield fans burned a Glasgow Celtic jersey. A large group of home fans charged the Linfield supporters when Derry scored just before half time. For the record, Derry won 2-1, but the game was overshadowed by the accompanying violence. Our old friend Johnny McQuaid, was in the Brandywell that day as the chairman of the Shankill Road Linfield Supporters' Club. He told *The Sentinel* that he was greatly disturbed at the events of that day as he had always regarded the Maiden City as a paragon of virtue where politics and sport never were mixed in such a heady cocktail. How right he was.

Derry City had long enjoyed a reputation of being above politics in a bitterly divided city. Although the Brandywell ground was deep in the heart of a Catholic area, the club had many Protestant players and supporters. At half-time the police evacuated Belfast fans from the ground. In the aftermath, Linfield stated that they would no longer travel to Brandywell on security grounds and the game of 25th January was to be the last game played at the Brandywell between Linfield and Derry in the Irish League.

With regard to sport without politics, January was marked by the announcement that Sir Matt Busby would be retiring at the end of the season, having managed

Manchester United for twenty four years. On the music scene, within, a fortnight, the Beatles played their last live performance on the roof of the Apple building in London. The impromptu performance lasted almost three quarters of an hour and included *Danny Boy* as well as hits such as *Get Back, Don't let Me Down* and *I Want You*. Six weeks later, John Lennon married Yoko Ono and they made worldwide news by staging a week long love-in for peace in their bedroom in the Amsterdam Hilton. On a very sombre note, in Wenceslas Square in Prague, a student, Jan Palach, set himself on fire and died in a protest against the Soviet occupation of Czechoslovakia.

There was no love-in going on in the Northern Irish political scene. Brian Faulkner, the Minister of Commerce, resigned from the cabinet. Less than a week later, twelve backbench Unionist MPs, including Albert Anderson, the MP for Londonderry, called for O'Neill's removal as leader in the interests of party unity. O'Neill's response was that they wanted, not a change of leadership but a change of policy. I was not at all surprised when he decided to try to clear the air by calling a snap General Election for 24th February and seek a fresh mandate. This was a U-turn on his previous announcement that it would be reprehensible to call an election and how his critics in the Unionist Party rounded on him for this volte-face. It was a calculated risk and the omens seemed stacked against him. The Protestant/Unionist population was almost irrevocably split and O'Neill seemed to have as many critics within his parliamentary party as he had supporters. Outside the Unionist Party there was growing support for the hard-line stance being advocated by Ian Paisley, who was even further to the right of O'Neill's critics within the party.

In Derry, the General Election was one of two completely separate and contrasting contests. Each was to prove bitter and acrimonious. In the Foyle constituency, where I lived, the incumbent MP, Eddie McAteer declared that he would again contest the seat, just two days after announcing that he would be retiring. My old History teacher, John Hume, dropped a bombshell by announcing that he would oppose Eddie McAteer, who had held the seat since 1953. A number of my friends were the sons of local Nationalist politicians and were soon putting around the story that Hume had been a card-carrying member of the Nationalist Party and now he was stabbing Eddie McAteer in the back, having initially agreed to support him.

We had also heard rumours that our English teacher, Peter Mullan, was in the frame to be the Labour Party's candidate in the constituency. The City Hotel was the hub of all political activity and virtually anyone could gain access to whatever political meeting was taking place there. Undaunted, a few of us went along to the Labour Party meeting to select a candidate. Everyone in the hall called each other 'comrade' and Comrade Mullan was duly proposed. He stood up and gave the shortest speech, which was a 'thank you but no thank you' response. In the end, Eamonn McCann was selected as the Labour Party candidate.

Initially, I was only slightly interested in the outcome of the fight in Foyle. My overall belief was that it was simply a contest, resulting from a personal fall-out within the Nationalist Party. However, it proved to be much more than this and represented a major turning point in anti-unionist politics in the city and beyond. John Hume quickly established a new and slick election organisation. He had been active in the Credit Union movement and had a strong nucleus of supporters within that organisation. His election agent, Michael Canavan moved quickly to secure election headquarters in the Rossville Hall, and Hume adopted the black and white colours of the Civil Rights movement as his election colours. Even in the early days of the campaign, John Hume gained the upper hand by clearly articulating a four-point declaration, which called for the establishment of a 'Just Society,' a phrase that had significant meaning in the Ireland of the 1960s having been pioneered by Fine Gael's Declan Costello.

Hume was literally running for parliament as he declared that would aim to knock on the door of every house in the constituency to seek support. From the off, my father and mother said they would be voting Hume and, on my way to school, I noticed that there were many Hume posters on display on front room windows, with very few for McAteer. A few of the teachers at the College arrived at school, sporting Hume posters on their cars. One of them was our History teacher, Frank O'Kane. In our class was Tucker Doherty, whose father, James, was chairman of the Nationalist Party and who was a leading campaigner for McAteer. Tucker arrogantly dismissed Hume as the Young Pretender, who could not possibly offer serious opposition to the Nationalist Party's stranglehold over Derry Catholic electors.

The Hume manifesto was a commitment to work for the formation of a new political movement based on social democratic principles. He vowed to provide a strong energetic opposition to the incumbent Unionist government and pursue radical social and economic policies. Of considerable interest was his declaration that the future constitutional position of Northern Ireland should be decided by its people, and no change in its constitution accepted except by the consent of the people. The principle of consent had been introduced into the political vocabulary. This was radical politics and given what happened in succeeding years, it is important to recognise that Hume's first sojourn into democratic politics introduced the principle of consent in relation to the constitutional position of Northern Ireland.

Eamonn McCann dubbed Hume's manifesto as 'soggy mild and blurred' and he attacked Eddie Mc Ateer as representing a party 'paralysed by the past. As the campaign progressed, Mc Cann's supporters accused the Hume canvassers of 'using the Red smear' and the Derry Labour Party was forced to issue a statement to the effect that Eamon Mc Cann was not and never had been a member of the Communist Party. In spite of these denials the damage had been done.

The Labour Party also selected Ivan Cooper, another prominent Civil Rights leader, as its candidate in the adjoining, rural, constituency of Mid Derry. That seat was also held by the Nationalist Party. Cooper was duly nominated as the Labour Party's candidate. However, when nominations were handed in, it transpired that he was going to fight the as an Independent candidate. It was an astute move. Like many others, I assumed that Cooper and his supporters, having weighed up the odds, concluded that he would have a better chance of being elected as an independent rather than as an official Labour Party candidate in a rural constituency. I didn't think there was a Labour Party or even a Socialist in Mid Derry.

There was also considerable interest in contest in the City of Londonderry constituency. Albert Anderson was the incumbent Unionist MP and former Mayor of the city. He strongly opposed O'Neill's reform programme and was selected as the official Unionist Party candidate by the local Unionist party. His rallying call, 'We are the People,' resonated with traditional Unionism. He denounced the Civil rights movement as a conspiracy of revolutionary socialists, communists and republicans and boasted that Derry had been enjoying improved community relations before the Civil Rights movement took to the streets. Peter Campbell, a retired naval commander threw his hat into the ring as a pro-O'Neill Unionist and was endorsed by the Prime Minister, even though he was opposing the official party nominee. The constituency had a substantial Catholic electorate and Claude Wilton again stood as a Liberal Party candidate. 'Vote for Claude, the Fenian Prod,' was a comment of both support and derision, which depended upon which side you were taking. Claude, with the full support of the Civil Rights leadership, was opposing two retired Royal Navy commanders who were the pro and anti O'Neill Unionist candidates. I decided to campaign for Claude. It wasn't because of my admiration for Gladstonian Liberalism, but a simple suggestion by my friend Diarmuid MacDermott. His father, Dr. Donal, was a leading supporter of Claude. It turned out to be an enjoyable and enlightening contest.

Election campaigns are built on doing the routine as opposed to grand gestures. We were the equivalent of cannon fodder, turning up at Claude's election HQ in Castle Street and addressing election communications to the voters and then being allowed out to canvass. Claude was so relaxed that I had the impression that he really did not care if he won or lost. He enjoyed being out and about meeting people, with whom he had an easy-going manner, even when they were died-in-the-wool opponents. I was with him canvassing a rural part of the constituency when an awkward voter remarked; 'Sure, what would a city solicitor, like you, know about agriculture? How many toes does a pig have, Mr. Wilton?' Quick as a flash came Claude's caustic reply; 'If you take off your shoes and socks, I'll help you count them.' The flashpoint ended in uproarious laughter.

Claude's best hopes of winning the seat had nothing to do with Gladstone's conversion to Home Rule but on an almost even split in the Unionist vote between Anderson and Campbell. The pro-O'Neill candidate made a strong pitch for Catholic votes and O'Neill toured parts of the Waterside in support of his candidate. A number of well educated, middle class Catholic professionals threw in their lot with Campbell. They even appeared on the platform with him in the Guildhall, which was a first time in my memory that Catholics had appeared on a Unionist platform. In fairness to O'Neill, he was trying to create a pluralist Unionism, which would attract Roman Catholics to support his vision of a progressive Northern Ireland. In Derry, the Catholics who supported his nominee, Campbell, were subjected to insult and vilification in the Catholic community. One of them was the father of one of the boys in our year with whom I regularly played football. At his final election in the Guildhall, Campbell predicted that he would win the seat with a majority of around two thousand. When the election was over, the family emigrated to Canada. As the campaign entered its final days, Lord Brookeborough, who had been Prime Minister for twenty years before Terence O' Neill, appeared on the platform at Anderson's rally in the Apprentice Boys' Memorial Hall and accused his successor of 'incompetence.' In the final shake-out, Anderson, as the official Unionist Party candidate, received the support of the majority of unionist voters and he retained the seat. Claude received just fewer than six thousand votes, which was 1,800 fewer than he had polled in the previous General election in 1965. These voters had switched their allegiance to Campbell, who came last, polling just over four thousand votes. O'Neill' Terence O'Neill's charm offensive campaign had failed to deliver.

In the Foyle seat, it transpired that the poster count that I had made from the windows of houses as I walked to the College translated into votes. Hume won easily, thus beginning a long political career. The truth was that the Nationalist Party simply missed the boat on the civil rights issues and paid the price. Tucker Doherty had to return to class where Frank O'Kane invited him to eat humble pie, rather than the Doherty's sausages for which the family business was famous. In Mid Ulster, Ivan Cooper deposed the Nationalist incumbent. To quote from President John F. Kennedy's Inaugural Address; 'The torch had passed to another generation.' In defeat, McAteer was very philosophical and quoted Tennyson:

> *"The old order changeth, yielding place to new,*
> *And god fulfils himself in many ways."*

The election had not solved any problems for O'Neill. His party remained irrevocably split but he should have taken comfort from the fact that, of the thirty nine Unionist MPs returned, twenty seven of them nominally supported him, giving him a clear majority within the parliamentary party. He had, however, committed a cardinal error for a Unionist leader, in endorsing candidates who stood against official party candidates. O'Neill, himself, only narrowly defeated Paisley in the Bannside seat that he had held since 1949. In five previous General Elections, he had been returned MP, unopposed by any opponent, which said a lot about politics in Northern Ireland! Across the floor, the Nationalist Party had lost seats to emerging Civil Rights leaders. The election left large unanswered questions for both sides. For the Unionist government, the question was whether O'Neill's parliamentary majority would speed up the reform process. For those on the opposition benches, including the new MPs elected under a Civil Rights banner, the question was whether they would now be more amenable to progress their demands through parliamentary action rather than through demonstrations on the streets.

Chapter Eleven
More Street Protests as Armageddon Looms

'Death of the Civil Rights Movement' – visit to the College of the Holy and Undivided Trinity of Queen Elizabeth, near Dublin and 'If we are forced to fight, then let us, in God's name, fight as peace-loving men.' – Neil Gillespie

In the final days of the election campaign there appeared a mischievous unsigned letter in the *Derry Journal*, under the title, 'Death of the Civil Rights Campaign.' It read, 'The following would be an appropriate notice to out in the obituary column of your newspaper: RIGHTS – In the Mid Derry and Foyle constituencies, after a short and fatal illness, lust for power, Derry Civil, aged approximately four months. Funeral arrangements will be kept strictly secret till after the result of the General Election.' I enjoyed the satire and the underlying point as to whether the Election heralded the end of the Civil Rights movement as a movement of street protest. John Hume and Ivan Cooper rode the Civil Rights tiger to victory, having, in the words of veteran Nationalist Councillor, James Doherty, 'used civil rights slogans, songs, emblems and colours.' In response, John Hume said that the achievement of civil rights would only a minimum and that there would remain serious social and economic problems to be tackled.

John Hume, my newly elected MP, went off to Stormont and made a maiden speech that began with a welcome of the Terence O'Neill's commitment to reform, which boded well for the future. However, it did not appear that we would be following a parliamentary trajectory as the radical left wing, in the persona of Eamonn McCann and Bernadette Devlin, called for more street demonstrations. At a St. Patrick's Day meeting in Guildhall Square, Bernadette reminded her audience that they had 'been off the streets too long.' Of course, street politics depended on an on-going state of perpetual protest, which became increasingly directed simply against the state and the police. It seemed to me that the newly elected civil rights MPs were being put under pressure to resume marches and they duly complied. The next policy matter with which to disagree with government was in relation to amendments to the Public Order Act, which the opposition viewed as draconian. Opposition MPs staged a sit down on the floor of the House of Commons after an eleven hour filibuster debate, in which none of their amendments was successful. Their next port of call was back to the streets. This seemed a negation of their parliamentary mandate and, not for the first time, the mob tail was wagging the parliamentary dog and we were back to law and order issues. Perchance, I was studying Gladstone and Ireland and learning how the PM had delivered on his promise to do 'justice to Ireland' by introducing radical reforms, I hoped that Captain O' Neill could do the same. In the title of a later movie hit, we appeared to be rapidly going, 'Back to the Future.' The Citizens Action Committee duly organised a march over the same route that William Craig had banned five months earlier. This time it was not banned and five hundred police were on duty to prevent a confrontation of the marchers and the Paisleyite counter demonstrators. All that had been gained from the November reform package and the 'Ulster at the Crossroads' address had been pissed down the sink. A new Northern Ireland had been rapidly submerged in the mists of its 'dreary steeples.'

Lest a reader should think that focus within Creggan was exclusively on issues of political reform, it is worthwhile pointing out that there were voices also calling for practical solutions to community problems. The Creggan Tenants' Association was lobbying for a police station on the estate to combat the recent rise of vandalism and a thousand residents took part in a sit-down protest on Creggan Heights against speeding traffic.

In the wake of the Stormont General Election, Northern Ireland was rocked by a series of bombings of electricity substations, water installations and reservoirs. Initially, these were thought to be the work of the Irish Republican Army, the IRA. It later transpired that they had been carried out by the outlawed loyalist Ulster Volunteer Force, the UVF. Its actions were designed to attempt to have republicans blamed, in the hope that this would help get rid of Terence O'Neill as Prime Minister and end any programme of reforms.

They say that momentum is an important factor in politics and, in early 1969, the momentum in the Catholic community was for continuing street marches and parades, rather than actively engaging in parliamentary opposition. Easter fell at the end of March, barely two months after the General Election. A sure sign of changing times was the decision of local republicans to organise a march through the city centre on Easter Sunday, commemorating the 1916 Rising, in Dublin. It was the first time, in living memory, that republicans had organised such a march in Derry. Previous commemorations had been low key and restricted to events in the Bogside and had not been attended by more than a few dozen people. In 1966, for the 50th anniversary commemoration events, republicans had gathered at a rally in Celtic Park, while the main event was held in Dungiven rather than in Derry City. In the intervening years, there had been virtually no commemorations. That was all to change as, on a sunny Sunday, the march attracted a crowd of about five thousand. Sundays in Derry were generally boring with everywhere closed for the Sabbath. A march promised some colour to an otherwise drab afternoon and it was no surprise that so many people turned out for the occasion. Eddie McAteer, the recently deposed MP, was in attendance but the newly elected MP for Foyle, John Hume, stayed away.

Leading republicans, in their best Sunday suits, marched in military formation with the Irish Tricolour at the head of the parade. The platform party consisted of Sean Keenan, a veteran republican, who had been interned for IRA membership, and Johnny White, one of the leading younger republicans in the city. You could tell who the committed republicans were by their serious demeanour. As the procession passed through Waterloo Place and on to Guildhall Square for the rally, the crowd was singing *The Soldiers Song*. This appeared to have replaced the Civil Rights anthem, *We Shall Overcome*, The Easter proclamation, which Patrick Pearse had read on the steps of the GPO, in Dublin, in 1916, was read by Leo Coyle, on the spot where Queen Elizabeth II had reviewed a Royal Navy guard of escort less than sixteen years earlier. Sean Keenan reminded everyone interested in listening, 'the enemy is still England.' Plus Ca Change. The unfinished business from the Civil Rights movement appeared to be the age-old dream of a united Ireland. This begs the question as to whether the Civil Rights movement should simply be viewed as another phase in the struggle between Nationalism and Unionism. That afternoon reminded me that there was clearly a re-emergence of a growing republican movement in the city.

In 1969, carrying the tricolour was a criminal offence under the Flags and Emblems Act but the police did not intervene on this occasion. A few days after Easter, however, five men were arrested and charged with public order offences. There was much talk that the carrying of the Tricolour was a symbolic gesture, reversing events in the early 1950s, when the RUC had batonned marchers trying to carry the Irish Tricolour through the city centre on St. Patrick's Day. There was much talk of another memorable day in Derry, when, in 1951, Eamon De Valera had visited the city to launch a Gaelic Week and large areas of the Bogside and Brandywell were festooned with Irish Tricolours and Papal flags. I was a bit perplexed to have learned that Papal flags would have been flown on such a political occasion, but religion and politics went hand in glove. It seemed somewhat appropriate that Jethro Tull, an English rock band, was soaring up the pop charts with lyrics 'we'll keep living in the past.'

The march that Easter Sunday was also an indicator of a power struggle that was taking place in Derry between the emergent republican movement and recently elected constitutional politicians. It was no surprise when a few months later a new organisation, the Derry Citizens' Defence Association (DCDA), was formed by republicans, with Keenan as its chairman and White as secretary. It was seen as a challenge to the authority of the John Hume led Derry Citizens' Action Committee. Moderate Civil Rights leaders had been calling for 'British rights for British citizens.' New voices or, to be more accurate, old voices of a generation that had unsuccessfully launched the IRA campaign in the 1950s, were now re-emerging to call for a united Ireland and seemed willing to advocate violent means to achieve their objective. I was reminded of the dialogue from one of my favourite films, *She Wore a Yellow Ribbon*, when US army Captain Nathan Brittles, played by John Wayne, tells Pony That Walks, his old Indian adversary, 'My heart is sad at what I see. Your young men painted for war...old men should stop wars.' In Derry, the old republican men, who had been involved in failed previous IRA campaigns, were to the fore in urging a renewed struggle to drive the British out of Ireland. Most Nationalists realised that a bloody civil war would have been required to achieve such an objective.

The veteran republican and writer, Peadar O'Donnell, saw the Civil Rights movement as the most progressive agitation in the North for a long time, as he believed it rekindled the republican flame. There was increasing rhetoric and words repeated from Wolfe Tone who in the later 18th century had talked of the aim 'to subvert the tyranny of our execrable government; to break the connection with England, the never failing source of all our political evils...' Republican sentiment had never had been very far from the surface and there had, consistently, been mutterings from politicians in the Republic that the Northern political crisis was the product of the evil of partition. From just over the Border in County Donegal, the leading Fianna Fail politician, Neil Blaney, was actually denouncing the Civil Rights leadership because it was not focusing on partition. It seemed to me quite ironic that while Ian Paisley and other unionists were saying that the Civil Rights movement had simply been a republican front, some republicans were branding it as having abandoned republican aspirations.

I did not buy into extremist sentiments and thought Tone's brand of republicanism very outdated. In the late eighteenth century, Tone had written that his means of ridding Ireland of English rule was, 'To unite the whole people of Ireland and to establish the common name of Irishmen in place of the denominations of Protestant, Catholic and Dissenter,' By contrast, in the second half of the twentieth century, I was more inclined to the political view that uniting 'the denominations of Protestant, Catholic and Dissenter,' should be an end rather than a means. As the bellicose noises of republicans intensified, it appeared to me that the only movement I could support was one that would employ only democratic and constitutional means to achieve its objectives.

While the extremes of Paisleyism and Republicanism were grabbing the headlines, it was also clear that there was some political thinking going on about the formation of new constitutional political parties. The problem was quite simple. Although Northern Ireland was a place of great diversity, there was no common loyalty that could bind it together. Nationalists and Unionists were reading from completely different scripts. Given such realities, it was refreshing that from within the liberal unionist tradition there emerged a new grouping, called the New Ulster Movement. Initially, it was a pressure group but by the middle of 1970 morphed into the Alliance Party of Northern Ireland. Meanwhile, on the nationalist side, there clearly was a need to have the old Nationalist Party removed from the scene and replaced by a new party espousing social democratic principles with constitutional nationalist credentials. It was therefore no surprise that the Civil Rights MPs, who were elected to Stormont in the General Election of February 1969, would, in the summer of the following year be the main figures in establishing the Social Democratic and Labour Party.

A few weeks after the Easter celebrations, there was a by-election in the Mid Ulster constituency for the Westminster parliament, as a result of the death, in the previous December, of the sitting Unionist MP, George Forrest. The constituency was in middle of Churchill's 'dreary steeples of Fermanagh and Tyrone' and had a small Catholic electoral majority. Its Catholic voters had often voted for republican candidates, who won the electoral contests but had refused to take their seats at Westminster. Tom Mitchell had won the seat in the 1955 General Election, refused to take his seat and was disqualified and a new writ issued. Forrest won the ensuing by-election. In the late 1960s, he was a staunch supporter of Terence O'Neill and incurred the wrath of O'Neill's Unionist opponents, Anna Forrest, his widow, was chosen to contest the seat as the Unionist Party candidate. What ostensibly could have been a by-election on O'Neill's reform programme reverted to a simple sectarian head-count and traditional Green versus Orange politics re-asserted itself. The loose coalition that made up the Civil Rights movement had, by now, become focused on 'anti-Unionist' unity, which seemed to emphasise sectarian division rather than civil rights. The turnout on Election Day was 91.5% and Bernadette Devlin, a student member of the People's Democracy won the seat as an anti-Unionist Unity candidate. When Ian Paisley ranted that Bernadette Devlin's veins 'were polluted with the venom of Popish tuition,' and Unionist politicians dubbed her 'a wild, irresponsible child, a danger to any civilized society,' the good Catholic, conservative voters took her to their hearts.

To a naive outside observer, it might have appeared that her election heralded a commitment to a course of parliamentary action as the way forward. Her maiden speech at Westminster was almost universally regarded as electrifying. Here was a twenty one year old student advocating, not moderate Civil Rights demands, but defiantly stating that she was not only a radical but a radical Marxist. Her politics appeared to be derived from Karl Marx and Frederick Engels and their urgings in in the Communist Manifesto of 1848; 'Workers of the world unite.' Mr. Sharkey urged us to study her maiden speech, which was easy to do as a number of newspapers printed it in full. It was a highly controversial speech in which she said; 'there are two ideals that are incompatible-the ideal of social justice and the ideal and existence of the Unionist Party.' The speech seemed a retrograde step, emphasising past divisions as well as consigning the Unionist majority in Northern Ireland to oblivion.

In her maiden speech, she started off agreeing with Robin Chichester-Clark, Unionist MP for Londonderry, who said, 'There was never born an Englishman who understands the Irish people.' However, that was the sole matter of agreement between them. The course of political action that she advocated was the abolition of Stormont, which suggested that the running of Northern Ireland would be handed back to Westminster. Her conclusion failed to match her analysis of the problems. Basically, she was stating a series of negatives-the Unionist Government could not solve the problems; the Government at Westminster could not solve the problems; economic sanctions against the Stormont government would not succeed. She branded Jack Lynch, the Irish Prime Minister as a Green Tory and said and the Republic of Ireland could not succeed in solving any of the North's problems.

A critical analysis of the speech revealed many flaws. Of course, it was better to keep our views very private as we would probably have been hanged from lampposts in the Bogside if we had ever published our critique. Bernadette Devlin was the local version of Joan of Arc and any criticism of her was regarded as heresy. While the speech made a good headline it was completely nihilistic. However, she had articulated an obvious change in policy from the demands first articulated by the Civil Rights leadership six months earlier. Top of her agenda was the abolition of Stormont. By such words, she reinforced Unionist perceptions that the Civil Rights movement was another republican front to smash Northern Ireland's constitutional position. On a personal level, I wondered how the convent educated Bernadette had morphed into a radical Marxist after she went to university. Was she the type of girlfriend to introduce to my mother? I thought not but thousands of women like my mother had voted for her in the Mid-Ulster by-election. With scruffy jeans and a cigarette forever drooping from her lips, when I did not dare to smoke, she was certainly different from a typical Westminster MP from the shires!

Within days of Devlin's election, the North Derry Civil Rights group announced that it was planning another march starting at Burntollet Bridge. It was immediately banned but a demonstration took place in the centre of Derry that resulted in yet another riot, as the police again forced rioters back into the Bogside. An incident then occurred that intensified Catholic hatred of the police. Rioters, fleeing from the police, pushed their way into a house in William Street. It was the home of Sammy Devenny, one of whose sons, Harry, had been in charge of our milk run at primary school. The police gave pursuit and burst into the house, giving Sammy a terrible beating. Within months he would be dead. The next day, the Bogside was saturated with policemen in riot gear and a major confrontation was only avoided by the smart thinking of John Hume. Like the Pied Piper, he led the Bogsiders to Creggan and gave the police an ultimatum to withdraw or face the consequences.

Fifteen minutes before the ultimatum ran out, the police withdrew. Some three thousand men, armed with sticks and iron bars, marched down from Creggan along the New Road to reclaim the Bogside. As they marched they sang '*We Shall Overcome*.' On the surface, Derry had settled down but the new normality saw a riot develop from the least provocation and the fighting between the police and the Catholic rioters would end up in the William Street/Rossville Street area. Another development was that large groups of Protestants would invariably come behind the police and throw stones and bottles at the fleeing Catholic rioters. At times, Derry was awash with rumours; one of which was that armed Protestants were going to attack St. Eugene's Cathedral. We all knew that a full blown confrontation had only been deferred.

As a postscript to the attack on Sammy Devenny, the family made a formal complaint that the incursion into their home and the beatings meted out by the police had not been fully investigated by the RUC. A year after the incident, an outside policeman, Kenneth Drury of the London Met, was then appointed to investigate their complaint. Drury confirmed that the Devenny family were 'God-fearing law-abiding citizens.' He was unable to identify the police officers who inflicted the brutal beating on Sammy Devenny. The Chief Constable said that Drury's investigation had been met with a 'conspiracy of silence…within the RUC.'

On the political front, scarcely a week after the latest Derry riots of April 1969, Terence O'Neill resigned as Prime Minister. Later that year, he went to the House of Lords as a life peer. Before resigning, he introduced a number of the reforms that were called for by the Civil Rights leaders and which had been outlined in the reform package of the previous November. These included legislation to establish an Ombudsman. The Unionist Parliamentary Party also voted to introduce universal adult suffrage in local government elections. One man, one vote, which had always applied to parliamentary election to the Stormont and Westminster parliaments, was now on the way for local government elections. Whilst unionist extremists were perpetually plotting against him, O'Neill resigned when there was no real pressure to so do. And he could easily have continued in office. I thought that he simply ran out of fight and chose an easy option.

I could never fully make up my mind as to whether O'Neill was a politician capable of delivering the necessary reforms or was simply all show and no substance. Just before he resigned he gave an interview to the *Belfast Telegraph* in which he was so condescending to Catholics saying, 'It is frightfully hard to explain to Protestants that if you give Roman Catholics a good job and a good house, they will live like Protestants because they will see neighbours with cars and television sets; they will refuse to have eighteen children. But if a Roman Catholic is jobless, and lives in the most ghastly hovel, he will rear eighteen children on National Assistance. If you treat Roman Catholics with due consideration and kindness, they will live like Protestants in spite of the authoritative nature of their Church.' There was me, living in a very modern house in Creggan, built by the Northern Ireland Housing Trust. It certainly was not a 'ghastly hovel.' Both my parents were working and I had no siblings!

O'Neill was succeeded by James Chichester-Clark, better known as Chi Chi, the name of a famous Chinese panda at London Zoo. Chi Chi was O'Neill's cousin and was also ex-Eton and Irish Guards and a member of the landed gentry. So, the cousins were to be the last of the Big House Unionist leaders to govern Northern Ireland. Chi Chi was regarded as a well-intentioned country squire but was also generally thought to be out of his political depth. Brian Faulkner was the brightest star within the Unionist Party, although he was regarded by Catholics as very cunning and devious and was described as having 'as many faces as the Guildhall clock.' However, in many ways, it was unfortunate that he did not become Prime Minister in 1963, instead of O'Neill. Politically, he came into his inheritance too late. Under Chichester-Clark, he became Minister for Development.

The political position in Northern Ireland appeared dangerous, but not desperate. The reality was that a reluctant British government stood on the wings, hoping that the Northern Irish would live happily ever after and that this problem would go away. The Labour government had continued to place its faith in Terence O'Neill to deliver the promised reforms. Now, it hoped that his successor could deliver. The recurrent problem in Northern Ireland, however, was the threat of violence on the streets that could upend the best laid of plans and that is precisely what happened in the ensuing months. There was a genuine fear that the 'marching season' could erupt in violence.

There was to be one other General Election before the academic year was over. South of the Border, polling day was set for June 18. I remember the election as it was possibly the first time that BBC Northern Ireland had reported on an Irish General Election. 'The Seventies will be Socialist' was the catchy slogan of the Labour Party and the BBC focused on the attempt of its high profile candidates to win seats. Conor Cruise O' Brien was a name that had gained fame as a diplomat seconded to work for the United Nations in the Katanga region of the Congo. The other star name candidates were Trinity College academic, David Thornley and former Health Minister, Dr. Noel Browne. All three were duly elected but there was no change of government and Labour actually lost a seat. Whatever was happening north of the Border did not seem to have any effect on the overall result.

As we neared the end of our first senior year in the College, my favourite football teams had come up short. Manchester United, the reigning European champions were beaten by A.C. Milan in the semi-final of the competition and only finished a poor 11th in the English first division. Derry City finished runners-up behind Linfield in the Irish League, in which Derry's striker, Danny Hale, was the top marksman. I had successfully negotiated another year of study in which I learned of Hannibal and his herd of elephants crossing the Alps, the Russians failing to seize Constantinople, and Gladstone failing to have the first Home Rule bill passed in the House of Commons. The Romantic poets wrote of an idyllic life, often under the obvious influence of wine and drugs, while the miserable Henry IV lamented about his profligate son and was haunted by doubts about the legitimacy of his reign, having deposed his predecessor, Richard II.

For the summer holidays, I was rather fortunate in securing a job, in the words from HMS Pinafore, 'as an office boy in an attorney's firm, ' working for Claude Wilton, whose offices were in Waterloo Place on the first floor of Ulster Bank Chambers. If I had been expecting to be immersed in cases like those of the redoubtable television attorney, Perry Mason, I would have been sadly disappointed. Most of my work consisted of filing, delivering documents to court and getting documents signed by Justices of the Peace. However, a few times I went to court in Bishop Street with Claude, carrying his files. The phrase, which was a part of the Derry vocabulary at the start of the Troubles became, 'Say nothing till you see Claude.'

Claude had been the Liberal Party's candidate in the Stormont election, earlier in the year and I had joined the Ulster Liberal Party, just as it was about to go out of business. I must have been something of a political anorak. While my contemporaries were chasing girls, I was immersed in reading of the great Liberal revival in Britain, where Eric Lubbock had sensationally won a by-election in Orpington. In Claude's office, I met Berkley Farr, a senior member of the Party but he was quite disconsolate about the emergence of a new liberal organisation, called the New Ulster Movement, which was drawing members of the Liberal Party to its ranks. Within a few years, the Liberal Party was finished as its former members became the nucleus for the Alliance Party. For a few months, at least, I was a member of the party once led by William Ewart Gladstone.

On the mantle place in Claude's office was a framed photograph of a Dublin University football team, a reminder of his university days when he was a very useful footballer. Beyond the frontiers of Derry, the excitement in July had little to do with my summer job or local politics but with the television pictures of American Astronaut Neil Armstrong becoming the first man to set foot on the Moon and uttering the immortal words *"That's one small step for man, one giant leap for mankind."* Man may have been conquering space but in Northern Ireland it appeared that we could not share our space. There was no major Orange parade in Derry on Saturday 12th July, as the main county march was twelve miles away in Limavady. However, that night there was fighting in the Diamond between Catholic and Protestant gangs and the end result was mayhem, as Catholic gangs roamed the area of Waterloo Street and William Street smashing shop windows and looting premises. It was described as the worst violence in the city in nine months and news reports confirmed that the police had drawn revolvers and fired shots when cornered in a cul-de-sac off Little James Street. The rioting lasted for three days but only seemed a prelude to the greater potential for violence a month later with the annual march by the Apprentice Boys, celebrating the Relief of the Siege of Derry in 1689.

As I walked down William Street on Monday morning, after the weekend riots, workmen were busy either boarding up shop fronts or the glaziers were having a field day fitting new glass. A week later, the political temperature in Derry went through the roof when news broke that Sammy Devenny had died. It was three month after he had being badly beaten by policemen in his William Street home. His police assailants were never brought to justice. His funeral was one of the biggest in known memory and was attended by almost twenty thousand people. Meanwhile, fourteen miles away in Dungiven, Francie Mc Closkey, a Catholic pensioner died after being hit on the head with a police baton during street disturbances. All eyes now turned to the Apprentice Boys of Derry parade, which was scheduled for 12th August.

Before all that, I had a break from Derry, as my parents took me for a week's holidays to Dublin, where we stayed at a B&B run by a Mrs Kennedy, in Fairview, on the north side of the city. Dublin was a challenge, as I planned to see as much of it as I could. What I first noticed about Ireland's capital was the large number of bicycles on its streets and the tall television aerials that dominated the skyline. I got an eye opener when I saw the array of tenements in the Summerhill/Gardiner Street area, which made Derry's public housing look palatial. The star attraction was visiting Claude Wilton's alma mater, Trinity College, or to give it its full name – The College of the Holy and Undivided Trinity of Queen Elizabeth near Dublin. In the middle of Dublin was this fifty acre university site, dating back to the 16th century, the oldest university in Ireland and one of the oldest in the world. I stood outside its entrance, looking across College Green at the Bank of Ireland building that had been the Irish Parliament in the 18th century.

As I walked through Front Gate, it felt like a modern equivalent of John Keats's 'Of first Looking Into Chapman's Homer.' The hustle and bustle of the city, with buses, cars and bicycles, suddenly gave way to the quiet cloisters of the College. It was the summer vacation and the grounds were teeming, not with students but with visitors, mainly Americans. One American woman bent over the railings and caressed the manicured lawn. 'Abner, it's real grass,' she hollered out and everyone on her tour group applauded. I walked along the cobbled squares and surveyed the architectural splendour of what was called Parliament Square, the College Chapel, Examination Hall, Dining Hall and the oldest buildings, which were called the Rubrics. After this visit I hurried to meet my parents who were having lunch in Davy Byrne's pub just off Grafton Street, immortalised in James Joyce's *Ulysses*. Excitedly I told them that I wanted to go to Trinity after St. Columb's. My father told me that this might be difficult as the Catholic Church had imposed a ban on Catholic students attending the College. A limerick seemed to sum up the attitude of the Catholic Church and, in particular, that of Dr. John Charles McQuaid, the Archbishop of Dublin:

Said Archbishop McQuaid in a Lenten tirade:
You may plunder and loot, you may murder and shoot.
You may even have carnal knowledge.
But if you want to be saved, and not be depraved,
You must stay out of Trinity College.

It wasn't that Trinity was refusing to admit Catholics. The College opened up admission to Catholics in 1793. However, the Catholic Church banned Catholics from studying at Trinity in 1871 on the basis that attendance constituted 'a moral danger to the faith of Irish Catholics.' It was a mortal sin for a Catholic student to attend unless he/she had obtained a 'letter of toleration' from the hierarchy. I was somewhat stunned to learn all of this. At St. Columb's College, we had heard a lot about Vatican Two and the reforms sweeping the Catholic Church worldwide. It therefore seemed that the Catholic Church in Ireland was living in the past. Civil Rights for Catholic students wanting to attend Trinity were what were urgently needed. So, the religious wars of the seventeenth century were not only being played out in the streets of Northern Ireland but also on a higher plane. I resolved to make further enquiries on this matter, without getting myself expelled *sine die* from St. Columb's. I returned to Derry and told Claude all about my visit to Trinity. He said that he remembered his student days there with great affection and encouraged me to follow my dream. When I asked him about the ban, he said that he was an optimist and expected that it would be gone within a few years as it had no part in modern Ireland.

A more pressing issue was the fast approach of the Apprentice Boys of Derry march in the city on 12th August, marking the 280th anniversary of the ending of the siege by Jacobite forces in 1689. In doing my deliveries to the courthouse on Bishop Street, I noticed that the city centre was awash with bunting and very large Union Jacks. Claude said that this year's Apprentice Boys' march was one of the biggest planned as there was great resentment in the Protestant community at what it perceived as the near treasonable activities of the Civil Rights/republican hordes who, in the last year, had breached the city's sacred walls and had paraded the Irish Tricolour through Guildhall Square. For good measure, the abolition of the Corporation was seen as an act of treachery.

The defence of Derry, the besieged city, had resonated with Ulster Protestants for generations. The Whig historian, Lord MacAulay, had written that the siege 'was a contest, not between engineers, but between nations; and the victory remained with the nation which, though inferior in number, was superior in civilization, in capacity for self-government, and in stubbornness of resolution.' The Rev. George Walker, civil governor of the city during the siege viewed the defeat of the Jacobites as a manifestation of divine providence. One of the city's defenders in 1688 had put it succinctly, 'To give up Londonderry is to give up Ireland.' More than a century later, Lord Castlereagh, architect of the passing of the Act of Union, regarded Derry as a loyal counterbalance to republican orientated Belfast. By the time I was born, most of Ireland had been given up and it was hardly surprising that there was thus a determination to retain control of the Maiden City. In 1848, Lord MacAulay had written, 'Five generations have since passed away; and still the wall of Londonderry is to the Protestants of Ulster what the trophy of Marathon was to the Athenians.' As we had been studying the third Home Rule bill, introduced by Prime Minister Asquith in 1912, we had been very familiar with the opposition of the Tory leader, Andrew Bonar Law, who had Ulster roots. He used language invoking the heroic deeds of the defenders of Derry in the siege. 'Once again you hold the pass,' he told a rally in Belfast; '...you are a besieged city. The timid have left you; your Lundys have betrayed you: but you have closed your gates.' Now, the ancient enemy, once dubbed by MacAulay 'the aboriginal peasantry' was back, occupying the marshland known as the Bogside and threatening the walled city again. Protestant Londonderry felt that it under a new siege.

On the Sunday afternoon of the 10th August, with nothing better to do, I took myself off to Celtic Park, not to watch a Gaelic football game nor reminisce on my school days of playing there and being chased by the strap-waving Brother Keane for dribbling 'Brandywell style.' A public meeting, ahead of the 12th march by, had been convened by the recently self-appointed grouping, the Derry Citizens' Defence Association (DCDA), whose leading lights were well-known republicans. The attendance was about a thousand. There were women with prams and the platform party consisted of men in the Sunday best suits. Even Eamonn McCann was wearing a suit! The event was like a pan-Catholic front with old style republicans like Sean Keenan, chairing the meeting. On the platform beside him sat John Hume, Eddie McAteer, Eamonn McCann and well known republicans like Eamon Melaugh and Finbarr O'Doherty. The speeches betrayed stoicism that violence was inevitable on the day of the Apprentice Boys' march. There was plenty of talk of putting up barricades and defence of the Bogside was to the fore in every speech. It was assumed that the Apprentice Boys' commemoration of the lifting of the siege in 1689 would be a catalyst for communal disorder. This was crossing bridges way before they had ever been reached.

A somewhat emotional McAteer made an emotional speech calling for tangible support from what he called 'our watching brethren,' on the other side of the Border. It was no surprise that the local Unionist party condemned the speech of Mc Ateer as inflammatory. Keenan said it was a very 'explosive time' and issued an ultimatum that if any group was 'remotely considering marching through the Bogside, he would warn them to think again,' All proposed action was predicated on the belief that the police and Paisleyite mobs would try to storm the Bogside. I was slightly perplexed as I believed that the route of the march by the Apprentice

Boys would not even touch the Bogside. I was quite impressed by John Hume's contribution. He readily admitted that the Apprentice Boys had a right to process through the city but questioned as to whether they should exercise that right.

Neil Gillespie, another veteran republican, who had no political mandate whatsoever, summed up the mood saying, 'If we are forced to fight, then let us, in God's name, fight as peace-loving men.' I left Celtic Park believing that the newly self-proclaimed and unelected leaders of the Bogside were gearing up for further confrontation with the state, rather than trying to calm a difficult situation.

It struck me that the speeches reflected a grim reality; that there would be no commitment to preventing violence and no attempt to steward the Catholic youths who were expected to gather at the bottom of William Street to stone the police and Apprentice Boys marchers. Rather than call for stewards to hold back stone throwers on the day of the march, the DCDA leadership called for 'volunteer guards' to protect the Bogside. Violence was either being accepted as inevitable or, indeed, was being deliberately fomented. I came away from Celtic Park convinced of the latter and thought that the leadership of the Derry Citizens' Defence Association was spoiling for a showdown with the police on 12th August. Given the trouble associated with events such as the marches of 5th October and more recently Burntollet, I was incredulous to see the newly elected parliamentarians, such as John Hume, who had an electoral mandate, now apparently ceding leadership to those whose aim was the destruction of the state and were openly prepared to advocate violence. The street politicians were literally calling the shots.

The march was to be held on the 12th itself, which was a Tuesday and everyone seemed to be expecting trouble. Ominously, Harry O'Hagan, our local milkman, remarked that few empty milk bottles had been returned in the run-up to the 12th, suggesting that they were being retained for an ulterior motive. A week later, the local dairies confirmed that forty three thousand milk bottles had not been returned in the run-up to the Twelfth.

Chapter Twelve
Battle of the Bogside

CS gas fills the air – 'Throw well, throw Shell,' urges Barricade Bill. Pitchfork wielding defenders arrive from Donegal on the back of cattle lorries. Belfast burns and finally the British Army rides to the rescue like the Seventh Cavalry.

The Twelfth of August 1969 was a Tuesday and was not a public holiday in Derry. Shops and offices were open for business as usual but there was a pervasive, nervous, tension. For the last few months, that day had been widely regarded as Armageddon. In early morning, the Apprentice Boys started their day of celebrations with a religious service in St. Columb's Cathedral, inside the city's walls. It was after lunch that the main parade got under way, marching down Shipquay Street into Guildhall Square and along Waterloo Place. Yet again, as an observer, I had a vantage point to view the parade, as Claude Wilton's office overlooked Waterloo Place. The police placed about half a dozen armoured vehicles around the public toilets and in front of Wellworths Store, as a screen between the Apprentice Boys and Catholic youths who had gathered at the bottom of the William Street. The police had also placed light metallic crush barriers there. There has been plenty of investigation and commentary on what happened next and a commission, under the chairmanship of Lord Scarman, carried out a detailed examination of the events.

The route of the Apprentice Boys' parade was a traditional one and it took them almost on the same route taken by Queen Elizabeth II a mere sixteen years earlier. From Guildhall Square, the Queen's Rolls Royce had gently purred across Waterloo Place, turned right along Strand Road and then made a sharp left turn up Great James's Street as it headed for a garden party in Brooke Park. Its route was guarded by soldiers of my father's old regiment, the Royal Inniskinning Fusiliers. You could say that in 1953 the Queen had come closer to Bogside, at Lower Gt James's Street, than the Apprentice Boys did in their procession in 1969. However, there was not any hint of any protest from the inhabitants of the Bogside to her visit. How times were to change.

I have been amused to read numerous accounts of the Battle of the Bogside by people who were never in Derry in those fateful days. Contrary to much that has been written, the march in Waterloo Place was not on the periphery of the Bogside. It was in the city centre. The route of the march was about forty yards from the bottom of William Street and the Bogside was a further five minutes' walk away.

Early afternoon, I noticed that there were very few stewards at the bottom of William Street, which was the most likely point for Catholic youths to attack the marchers. John Hume, Ivan Cooper and Eddie McAteer were there but, whereas they had mustered hundreds of stewards for Civil Rights marches, that day there was only a few dozen. From Claude's window, I could see that the Apprentice Boys had a large number of stewards on duty in Waterloo Place. I also noted that there was a large number of the media in attendance, almost in anticipation of trouble and ready for the inevitable photo opportunity.

Most of the Apprentice Boys had passed this likely point of confrontation in Waterloo Place and were heading down the Strand Road when the stones started flying from the youths gathered at the bottom of William Street. They seemed aimed more at the police than the Apprentice Boys marchers. Outside Claude's office, the police were very passive, standing firm in face of the stone throwing as they seemingly waited for the stewards to clear the stone throwers. The few stewards on duty were having little joy in this and Ivan Cooper was felled by a stone thrown from the growing ranks of rioters. There was no attempt to arrest the stone throwers or disperse the crowd. Behind the police lines, was a growing crowd of Protestant men, who appeared eager to get at the Bogside stone throwers. The police waited in vain for stewards to intervene and the stone throwing was to continue for a few hours.

Shortly after four o'clock, the first petrol bombs were thrown by the Catholic rioters at the ranks of police officers, before the order was given to the police to advance along William Street. By this stage the Apprentice Boys' march had long passed this point of possible confrontation. The police seemed poorly clad to deal with large scale rioting, even down to their uniforms. Many were wearing long trench coats and carrying small shields that would be useless against stones aimed at their legs, or worse, petrol bombs. There also did not appear to be enough officers on the ground to deal with a large scale uprising, without having to resort to firearms. Not surprisingly, on the first day of the riots there were over one hundred police casualties.

Claude Wilton thought that this was a good time to call it a day and closed the office, telling us that he would re-open when any trouble ended. Somehow, he conveyed the impression that he did not expect to be opening his office the following morning. All the stone throwing was being directed at the police at the bottom of William Street, which I decided to avoid. I made my way down Strand Road and then headed up Sackville Street, where all the shops were still open. There were policemen on Sackville Street as the junction with Little James Street led directly into the Bogside. Large crowds of supporters of the Apprentice Boys' parade had gathered at Great James Street. I doubled back towards the Bogside, where I found preparations were being made for battle. There was the expectation that there would be fierce fighting between the Bogsiders and the police. There have been many comments that there was spontaneity in the erection of the barricades within the Bogside. In my view, this is a distortion of reality. The Bogsiders were geared up for trouble. Barricades were being built in Rossville Street. From nowhere, hundreds of petrol bombs, which had obviously taken some time to make, appeared.

I was determined to avoid being caught up in the middle of any riot situation. By the time I reached Creggan I had formed the view that the rioting would be confined to the Bogside area but would be more intense than any previously seen in the city. I was at home by the time, around seven o'clock, when the police began their first assault turning from William Street into Rossville Street and the Bogside. Behind them swarmed a Protestant mob. If the strategy of the Bogside rioters had been to draw the police on to them, it had succeeded. For the next few days there was an almost ritual nature to the fighting as all attacks and counter-attacks seemed to be concentrated on the Rossville Street access to the Bogside. There were no serious casualties and no guns fired on either side.

The nearest that fighting came to Creggan was when there were petrol bomb attacks on the police station in Rosemount. The impression being given by the leaders of the Bogside insurrection was that Free Derry, an area of almost nine hundred acres and twenty five thousand citizens, was attempting to secede from the United Kingdom. However, away from the front line, life continued as before. Being at war with the Stormont regime was a far cry from wanting to be immediately incorporated into the Irish Republic. I had the distinct impression that the front-line defenders and their leaders did not want to be reconciled to any institutions of the northern state. On the other side, I doubted if the Stormont government had the ability to handle the situation. Very early into the disturbances, Eddie McAteer was calling for intervention by a United Nations peace-keeping force, while John Hume was calling for intervention by the British government and the suspension of the Stormont parliament. The IRA issued a statement that it was on 'full alert' and that some units had been on active service in the Bogside. This was certainly a red rag to Unionists and proof that an insurrection was a reality. Even at the early stage of the violence, it was clear that the police would either require outside support or would be forced to resort to firearms to subdue what Protestants saw as an insurrection. The tension within the Bogside and Creggan rose sharply when the Stormont government broadcast a call for all B Specials to mobilise. Armageddon looked to be on the horizon.

My father said to me that the breaking point would come when exhaustion overcame the limited numbers of policemen and that the situation would only end when British Army troops were committed. He was speaking from experience. He vividly remembered precisely what had happened in the 1930s when, as a young soldier in the Royal Inniskilling Fusiliers, he was despatched from barracks in Omagh to the streets of Belfast. His regiment was a buffer between rioting sectarian mobs. In spite of all the rhetoric and sabre rattling, he believed that the Irish Army was not going to cross the Border into Derry and there would be no United Nations' peace-keeping force. Interestingly, he was the first person I heard speak of the British Army being deployed on the streets of Derry as a short-term solution. By contrast, it was the prospect of the Irish Army or United Nations' peacekeepers on the streets that was exercising the minds of the local combatants.

In terms of military tactics, the charge of the RUC into Rossville Street on the first day of the rioting was akin to the charge of the Light Brigade. The advantage lay with the defenders, many of whom had taken up position on the roof of the of the nine storey Rossville flats from whence they poured a barrage of petrol bombs on the police, for whom it was a veritable 'valley of death.' The response of the police was to start firing CS gas into the Bogside to contain the Catholic mob. The Bogside was enveloped in palls of gas. A stalemate ensued as the standoff entered its second day. In the middle of the riots, I heard a humorous story of a well-known gay Bogside resident who was pegging stones at the police and was recognised by a local officer. 'Just wait till I get you next week and I'll stick this baton up your ass,' roared the policeman; to which the reply was; 'Promises, promises!'

It was obvious that Claude's office would remain closed that Wednesday and I did not venture into Waterloo Place for any confirmation of this. Mid-afternoon I went down to the Bogside and walked around Westland Street, there was a throng of about every leftie anarchist, who had escaped from Paris that summer and had made their way on the next leg of their own version of the Beatles' 'Magical, (revolutionary), Mystery Tour.' The lefties were busy spouting revolutionary fervour as they downed bottles of Guinness. However, I noticed that few of them wanted to engage in the rioting. Being in Derry would obviously look good on their CVs, when they returned to their ivory, academic, towers. The CS gas fumes hung heavy in the air and there were people walking around wearing old gas masks, the type you would see in World War I movies. Bernadette Devlin was telling people that they would get used to the CS gas and that it would not affect them, which was a bit silly. Like many locals I adopted a better deterrent, which was to wipe my eyes with a handkerchief that had been soaked in vinegar. There were bucket loads of vinegar at almost every street corner. Looking back, Bernadette was a convenient bête noire for the Prime Minister, Chichester-Clark, to rail against as the leading protagonist, inciting the Bogside to rebellion and to attempt to overthrow of the state. But, we all knew that she was a convenient scapegoat. However, in the shadows and on the streets were the real hard men, dreaming of another tilt at the northern state and eager to foment disorder.

More seriously, by early Wednesday, the place was awash with rumours and reports that fresh sectarian clashes were occurring at an interface on Bishop Street. Later that evening, there was consternation, when it was reported that the B specials had been mobilised and were patrolling Bishop Street. Some families began fleeing Derry and, in all, about five hundred people were evacuated across the border. The thought of leaving never even crossed the minds of my parents. The republican leadership of the Citizens' Defence Committee held a press conference, appealing for every able-bodied man in Ireland to come to Derry and help in the fighting. This was a call to arms and was backed up by a similar call from the Union of Students in Ireland for students and young people to go to Derry to join in 'the struggle for the final settlement of the Irish question.' If everyone, who had been summoned, had arrived there would have been a re-enactment of the Battle of the Boyne rather than the siege of Derry!

My most vivid memory of that second evening of the rioting was the television broadcast by Jack Lynch, the Republic's Prime Minister. It is known as the 'we will not stand idly by' speech. He did not utter the word 'idly,' as it was, apparently, dropped at the last minute. He called for a United Nations' peace keeping force to be sent to Northern Ireland He also announced that the Irish Army would be setting up field hospitals across the border in Donegal, which implied that Armageddon was at hand. The speech inflamed the position and people were on the streets of Creggan and Bogside actually believing that the Irish Army was going to be like the Seventh Cavalry riding to the rescue.

Similarly, the broadcast shocked Protestants, who believed that the republican insurrection was happening. Several hundred able-bodied Protestant men made their way to the centre of Derry from outlying areas to support the exhausted police. Many wore crash helmets and carried wooden staves and lined up behind the beleaguered police lines in Great James Street. There were rumours that they planned an attack on St. Eugene's Cathedral. There was little rational thinking but paranoia on both sides. The nearest I saw to a relief column was when a cattle lorry roared down Fanad Drive loaded with pitchfork and scythe wielding men from across the border in Donegal, who were en route to join the Bogside fray.

Not for the first time, in the space of less than a year, did Jack Lynch introduce the issue of partition into the debate, arguing that only reunification could provide a permanent solution. Was it any wonder that many young men of my generation took him at his word and joined the IRA? The continuing calls for an end to partition seemed irresponsible to me for two reasons. Firstly I greatly doubted if the Republic had any real interest in seeing a united Ireland as opposed to talking about it. Secondly, such language raised community tensions and put Catholics living in Protestant areas at great risk. At the time, however, in both Creggan and Bogside, Lynch's comments were greeted as confirmation that insurrection against the northern state was underway and that the Irish army would soon be on the streets of Derry. There was near hysterical jubilation that evening and the Bogside defenders raised the temperature by calling for nationalists in other parts of the North to organise demonstrations at police stations to stop reinforcements being sent to Derry. This was a spark that led to violence in other parts of Northern Ireland that claimed seven lives and witnessed widespread disorder, especially in Belfast. Within the Bogside, reports came in of the loss of life which resulted from the violence that followed the call for insurrection in other parts of the North. It seemed to me that the Bogside leadership had given little consideration to the reality that, by their words and actions, they had contributed greatly to the situation in which further loss of life occurred. They bore considerable responsibility for descent into anarchy and accompanying death.

Early the next morning, Thursday, the third day of the battle, my father walked into the house. I didn't dare ask him where he had been but he sat down, poured a cup of tea and told me that he had spent the night in the grounds of St. Eugene's Cathedral, which it was rumoured was going to be attacked. He told me that there were men armed and ready to repulse any attack. There was some shooting that night as a Protestant mob moved up Gt. James Street towards the Cathedral. No frontal attack materialised as the mob retreated down Great James Street. However, a neighbour of ours from Dunree Gardens, in Creggan, with whom I had played football, was shot in the stomach. Fortunately, he survived.

The strangest thing about that early morning conversation was that it was the only time that my father opened up to me about his wartime experiences. In 1939 he had been called up from the reserves as war was imminent and was attached to a newly formed battalion of the Royal Irish Fusiliers. Hitherto, the most I really knew of his wartime service was gleaned from a small cardboard box, tucked in a drawer in his bedroom in which he had a clutch of war medals, which included the 1939/45 Defence and War medals and Stars, the Africa Star and the Italy Star. I often wondered what he had done to win these medals.

That morning, in our kitchen, he talked with pride and a genuine affection for Malta and its people. With them and his Royal Irish Fusiliers, the Faughs, he had endured the siege by the German and Italian forces that lasted over two and a half years. His next theatre of war was in the Aegean and the island of Leros in the Dodecanese islands. It was rugged terrain, which was bitterly contested but captured by the Germans in November 1943. He told me that the Faughs' Commanding Officer was killed in the final days of the battle and that the Germans allowed his men to bury him before they were led away to be transported to POW camps in Germany. Listening to the story it seemed to me to be a modern version of the poem, *The Burial of Sir John Moore after Corunna*, by Charles Wolff. Life as a POW had been very unpleasant but he later discovered that the first telegram that arrived at the family home, in Bridge Street, reported that he was 'missing in action, presumed dead.' This triggered a lot of prayers and novenas for his safety and there was almost rejoicing when it was subsequently reported that he was alive but a POW. Having survived the war, he said he wasn't going to let a mob of armed thugs storm the Cathedral, where he had been married to my mother on his return to Derry. That morning as I sat in the kitchen talking to him, I knew that he would have had no reservation in using whatever force he would have deemed necessary to repel any attack. Maybe Divine Providence intervened and ensured that the would-be attackers didn't test his mettle, as I had little doubt that they would have come off second best.

Free Derry, as it was now dubbed by the Bogside defenders, was now in a state of insurrection. Both the Irish Tricolour and the Starry Plough, the flag of James Connolly's Citizen Army in the 1916 Rising, fluttered from the top of the Rossville Street high flats. Someone had also hoisted the Stars and Stripes but it was quickly removed on the orders of the left wing socialists. The area even had its own pirate radio station, Radio Free Derry, which broadcast at seven o' clock in the evening and after midnight. Police radio messages were also being listened to as they were picked up on local radio frequencies. On the former, we were treated to DJ Barricade Bill, exhorting young and old to 'throw well, throw Shell,' an obvious parody on a well known television ad for Shell petrol. Throughout his programmes, he played Irish rebel songs and gave updates on the situation on the ground.

Most of the music played on Radio Free Derry was woeful. There were plenty of maudlin tear-jerkers like the ballad of the IRA members who died at; '*the lonely woods of Upton*' in County Cork in 1921. The more modern ballads reminded us of the republican obsession that we lived '*in the cold chains of bandage*' and '*only our rivers run free.*' The most popular record played was the Rolling Stones' *Street Fighting Man*, whose lyrics chimed with local sentiment. Martha Reeves and the Vandellas had been singing *Dancing in the Street* but the Stones captured the Derry mood with lyrics such as 'summer's here and the time is right for fighting in the street,' and '*they, think the time is right for a palace revolution.*' Radio Free Derry also broadcast up to date statements from Bernadette Devlin and Eamonn McCann calling for the abolition of Stormont and the establishment of a constitutional conference on the very existence of the Northern Ireland state. Derry was literally going up in flames as Catholic mobs, armed with petrol bombs, set fire to a tyre depot and Ritchie's shirt factory in William Street that employed a large number of women. Next door, Stevenson's Bakery was also in flames. To me, it seemed crazy that the mob would now be destroying jobs.

A defiant and celebratory mood had soared on the third day as the police began to withdraw from the Bogside but dipped severely when it was rumoured that armed B Specials had been seen emerging from Victoria RUC barracks and were in Waterloo Place, making their way towards William Street. The Stormont government was about to make the last roll of the dice and unleash the Specials on the Bogsiders. It was reported that the Specials were armed. Behind the scenes, it was decision time in both London and Belfast and while the outbreak of the violence had been all too predictable, the end of the Battle of the Bogside took the Bogsiders by complete surprise. At around 5p.m. soldiers from the Prince of Wales Own Regiment took up positions at the bottom of William Street and at points around the Bogside. The police and B specials were withdrawn and the commanding officer of the troops agreed that no soldiers would enter the Bogside. So, it was the British Army and not the Irish Army, which was like the Seventh Cavalry, riding to the rescue in the final scene of many a good Western. The Battle was over and no one had died in Derry, although one hundred and fifty civilians and a similar number of policemen had been hospitalised and dozens of civilians treated at the first aid stations throughout the Bogside or across the Border. In the aftermath of the battle the big question was – what lay ahead? In Creggan, there was a mixture of relief and celebration when the police were withdrawn replaced by and the British Army.

The Prime Minister, James Chichester-Clark appeared on television to condemn the Bogsiders. 'This was not the agitation of a minority seeking by lawful means the assertion of political rights,' he said. 'It is the conspiracy of forces seeking to overthrow a Government democratically elected by a large majority.' The view in the Bogside was very different and was celebrating that they had repelled police force intent on attacking it with the support of Orange bigots. They were the same events with two completely different and conflicting interpretations. I wondered if there were elements of truth and falsehoods in both.

The Battle of the Bogside was over. However, we were very conscious that events elsewhere had ended in death and destruction. Bombay Street was burned to the ground by Loyalist mobs. It was alleged that they were led by none other than Johnny Mc Quade, local councillor for the area. The British Army did not move into the interfaces in Belfast between the Protestant Shankill Road and the Catholic Falls Road for another twenty four hours. In that period, there was civil war between the two communities and, on the morning radio news, I learned of further deaths on the Belfast streets. An eight year old youngster was killed in his bedroom in the Divis Flats as the RUC fired a Browning machine gun mounted on a Shorland armoured car. Undoubtedly, there would have been similar fatalities in Derry if the police had used such weapons and vehicles in their assault on the Rossville Street flats. We had the feeling that Catholics in Belfast were being left to their fate, while the Westminster government took its time to commit its troops. Meanwhile, behind the Bogside barricades in Derry, the hard core political activists were acting as though there was nothing happening in the rest of Northern Ireland. They issued a 'Barricade Bulletin,' which made no comment on the unfolding events in Belfast. Their bulletin was ambiguous in relation to the new situation, in which British Army soldiers were on the streets of Derry. 'This is a great defeat for the Unionist Government,' it began, before the more sobering judgment, 'we do not yet know whether it is a victory for us...the presence of the troops solves nothing...we do not go back to square one.' Mary Holland was reporting for The Guardian directly from the Bogside and her lead story began with the words, 'A gamble for peace in Derry.' I had the feeling that she was living in cloud cuckoo land as it had been a necessity to put British soldiers on the streets. The threat of civil war in Belfast had only been averted by the tardy intervention of the British Army.

The next day, the Derry Journal led with the headline, '*British Troops On the Streets of Derry,*' while spokesmen at the Ministry of Defence, in Whitehall, were briefing journalists that the soldiers would be back in barracks by the weekend! That day was my sixteenth birthday and I walked with my father through the city centre, viewing the novel sight of British Army soldiers at key vantage points. They were standing with their rifles and fixed bayonets at the makeshift wire barricade that they had erected at the bottom of William Street. I had the impression that they did not have a clue where they had landed and were, with some apprehension, awaiting a charge of Dervishes or Zulus on their position.

Thankfully, the bottom of William Street had not yet totally become Rorke's Drift. The sun was shining and, in the city centre, the shops were trying to get back to business as usual. I had been reading George Orwell that summer and well remember his salutary words in the essay, *The Lion and the Unicorn*, in which he wrote that, in any conflict, the British Army always saw each war as a repetition of the last one. This augured ill if the Army would now regard Northern Ireland as the latest colonial disturbance, like Aden, to be suppressed. As events transpired the Army fell into Orwell's trap very quickly and became agents of the Stormont government

Thoughts of Orwell were furthest from my mind that Friday afternoon. There was a new Relief of Derry and my father took me into his favourite pub, George Tracy's at the bottom of William Street. As I sipped a celebratory Coke, he reflected on the last few days. Northern Ireland had been portrayed as a police state, he told me, but for the past few days, the government had been content to attempt to contain the Bogside insurrection within the confines of the immediate area. The government's detractors had claimed that we were living in a police state but no police state, worth its salt would have tolerated the insurrection of the last few days. The government would have moved quickly to suppress any with armed force, which would have entailed shooting the petrol bombers on the top of the Rossville Flats. Maybe, it would have come to that in Derry, if it had not been for the intervention of the British Army on the streets.

To my father, the wheel of life had gone full circle. Inside the grounds of St Eugene's Cathedral he had been willing and able to defend it against possible attack by Protestant mobs. He spoke of his own father, a survivor the Great War, being in the grounds of St. Columb's College in the 1920s, armed and ready to repel attacks by the UVF. Turning to the matter of the troops outside, my father told me that while his deployment on the streets of Belfast in the 1930s had lasted only a few days, he was fearful that this time round the British Army was in for a long haul stay on the streets. In the annals of the British Army, the deployment of troops of the Prince of Wales' Own Regiment, on the streets of Derry that August 1969, was the beginning of Operation Banner. It became the longest British Army campaign and lasted thirty eight years!

That afternoon, in the snug of George Tracey's Electric Bar, he opened up to me about his last year in the British army after he returned to Derry in 1945, having been a POW for seventeen months. He was elated to be back in Derry for the first time since August 1939, when he had finished his days as an active soldier and was then a member of the Army Reserve. Within a month of being home, he had been recalled for active service as the war clouds gathered apace and, within a week of recall, he was posted to Malta. He smiled as he told me about a day, when back in Derry in 1945, he went to visit republican relatives who lived at the bottom of Bishop Street. He was in full army uniform, as he knocked on the door but there was no response. He heard voices inside and knocked again. An upstairs window opened and the head of one of his cousins stuck out, smiled and said, 'Johnny Murray, we are delighted that you have returned safe home. Come back here when you are dressed decent and we'll let you in.' With that rebuke, the window was slammed shut. He reminded me that there had always been a vocal anti-army sentiment in the city, which would not be comfortable with the presence of British soldiers on the streets of Derry.

To many, my father included, it appeared that the republican leadership of the Citizens' Defence Association had planned the whole thing as a conspiracy to overthrow the Stormont government. He wondered how they now felt with armed British army troops on the streets, being greeted by the majority of Bogsiders as saviours. Within a few years, quite a number of the leaders of the Citizens' Defence Association would emerge as the leading lights of the Provisional IRA. The Battle of the Bogside was the initiation for many of the young people into the cycle of violence as they progressed from throwing stones and petrol bombs to becoming members of the IRA and some of them became very prominent members. History has confirmed that immediately after the arrival of British troops on the streets of Derry and Belfast, in 1969, republicans had begun preparing for military action. It was just a question of when, rather than if, such a campaign would begin.

By coincidence, within a few days of the soldiers being on the streets of Derry, General Freeland, their commanding officer, suggested that the honeymoon period would be very short-lived. An example of the strange and almost farcical position that existed in the first weeks of the British army presence on the streets of Derry can be gauged from an incident that occurred just outside the Rosemount Factory, where my mother was working. During the Battle of Bogside, a brand new single decker Ulsterbus was hi-jacked and became part of a large barricade. The company was eager to retrieve it, whilst the locals wanted to retain the barricade. The newly-arrived soldiers, of 1st Battalion of the Queen's Own Regiment, worked out a compromise whereby Ulsterbus would provide an alternative bus for the barricade, an older bus, in exchange for the new bus. Two years later, a bus was hi-jacked on the same spot. However, there were no negotiations and it was quickly burned out!

At the start of the Troubles, I remember the bowling green at Brooke Park, just yards away from where the Ulsterbus was a barricade. Behind tall hedging, middle aged men in white trousers and women in flowing white skirts, all smartly dressed with accompanying club blazers, played lawn bowls, a game I associated with Sir Francis Drake. With the arrival of the British Army, an observation post was built in the grounds of the bowling club, which became a casualty of the Troubles and was forced to close. Two soldiers, members of the Royal Artillery, lost their lives when the IRA bombed the observation post at the beginning of my final year at the College.

By the end of August 1969, Northern Ireland was something of a political hybrid. British soldiers had been sent on to the streets of Derry at the request of both the Stormont government and the Bogside leaders, many of whom would have preferred an Irish army peacekeeping force. Politically, the situation within the Bogside had moved at a rapid pace and there were calls for the abolition of Stormont and the disbandment of the B Specials. Within days of the troops arriving, Harold Wilson installed his own senior civil servants at Stormont, suggesting that Northern Ireland was now definitely under London control. Logic suggested that Harold Wilson should have moved quickly and imposed Direct Rule but the thrust of government policy from London, for the last half century, was not to become enmeshed again in the politics of Ireland. Wilson's memoirs say that a simpler formula was proposed by Northern Ireland's Prime Minister that the British Army should take over total responsibility for security operations, including control of the RUC. The London government rejected this proposed solution. Resolving the conundrum of the army being in charge of security and the Stormont government continuing in operation would be one of the great problems in the ensuing period, until Ted Heath suspended Stormont in March 1972.

My father was glad to hear that I was looking forward to returning to the College for the year that would see me sit my O level exams. He said that it was good that I had something to look forward to and a target to achieve. He wondered what would become of what he described as the cannon fodder of the Battle of Bogside, the hundreds of young people, mainly men and youths who had borne the brunt of the fighting. The period had undoubtedly been, for them, one of excitement. But what awaited them as it appeared that the revolution was over, with reforms either on the statute book or in the pipeline. None of the reform packages would make the least difference to their lives in the immediate future. He speculated that it would only be a matter of time before the youth of Bogside and Creggan would be hurling stones and petrol bombs at the British army soldiers.

On television, we saw that over in America there was the Woodstock music festival of 'peace and music.' Joni Mitchell wrote a song summing up the mood of peace. Borrowing from the words of Isaiah, about turning swords to plough shares, she wrote:

> *"I dreamed I saw the bombers*
> *Riding shotgun in the sky,*
> *Turning into butterflies*
> *Above our nation."*

Meanwhile in Derry, August ended with a celebratory Liberation Fleadh Cheoil, a music festival in the Bogside. This was Derry's version of Woodstock and the organisers even printed leaflets talking about 'the manifestation of mass happiness.' The Dubliners played throughout the three days of the festival as did Tommy Makem, who wrote *Four Green Fields*, and sang it for the first time. Makem's song was not a song about Civil Rights but was filled with encouragement to retake the fourth Green Field from perfidious Albion and re-unite Ireland, by force, if necessary. It was about *Irlanda Irredenta*, the Irish version of Gabriele D'Annunzio writings about the Italy's lost lands of Fiume. In the Bogside Fleadh, while the craic was good and the mood upbeat, there was a definite message. Singer after singer called up the mythical Cathleen Ni Houlihan, who emerged from the shadows of the poetry of William Butler Yeats, to call for more blood sacrifice and the overthrow of British sovereignty over any part of the island of Ireland.

It is no exaggeration to say that in Derry, the modern IRA was born out of the Battle of Bogside. This opinion is shared by my old mathematics teacher, Sean McMahon, in his book, 'Battles Fought on Irish soil.' I tended to see it as much more. The Battle of the Bogside marked the definitive end of the Civil Rights movement. The stage had been set for the emergence of the Provisional IRA and a massive change from a campaign for Civil Rights to one seeking the overthrow of the state of Northern Ireland by violent means. In more ways than one, battle had been joined in a defining manner by the events of August 1969. It was naive to believe that the appearance of British Army soldiers on the streets of Derry and Belfast signified an end to conflict. It simply opened a new chapter.

Within a few years of the Battle of Bogside of 1969, the Wolfe Tones, a group that seemed to specialise in republican music, regularly appeared on stage in the Stardust Hall, in the Bogside, extolling armed resistance to anything British. Their lyrics went well beyond Jonathan Swift's dictum; 'Burn everything English but coal.' They were usually preceded by a local cheerleader, Barney Mc Fadden, who wound up the audience with the invective 'If you hate the British Army, clap your hands,' A one-armed caretaker would have been wise to take cover when Barney was in full flow, lest he be accused of not supporting the cause! Less than three years later, the same Barney Mc Fadden, stepped on to the altar in the Long Tower Church, grabbed the microphone and excoriated the priest who had just denounced the latest IRA atrocity. An inevitable by-product of this 'armed struggle' by republicans would be a continuing power-struggle within the Catholic community between the militants and the moderates. I had the clear impression that the militant republicans, apart from loathing the existence of the state of Northern Ireland, had little time for the democratically elected government of the Republic of Ireland.

At the College, there was some discussion about what was called 'the Green Book,' which was training manual for new IRA recruits. It was a far cry from Chairman Mao's Red Book. It was said that to own a copy of the Little Red Book, in Mao's China, was a way to survive. By contrast, to be caught by the police, in Creggan, with the Green Book, was a passport to jail. It proclaimed the Army council of the IRA was the legitimate government of a non-existent 32 county Irish Republic. It became quite clear to me that militant republicans were trying to hog the Irish Tricolour as their own as they proclaimed themselves the purist inheritors of the 1916 Easter Rising. Republican bands blasted out a new version of republican song written, in 1923, during the Irish Civil war, about the Republic's flag:

Take it down from the mast Irish traitors,
It's the flag we Republicans claim
It can never belong to Free Staters
You have brought it nothing but shame.

Before the Troubles I had heard the term Free State used as one of praise of the Republic, somehow reflecting that Northern Ireland was an unfree state.

The Monday following the arrival of British soldiers on the streets of Derry, I returned to Claude Wilton's office. As I entered the main gate of the Ulster Bank Chambers, I was greeted by a few British soldiers, who were billeted there and had been sleeping in the corridor. They looked only a few years older than me and one of them asked me where he was. When Claude arrived he told me to make them tea and get some buns from Sally's Bakery, in William Street, which had not been burnt out. They devoured the buns, suggesting that they had been half starved since arriving in Derry. It was a honeymoon period in Derry for the troops. Women were almost fighting with each other to invite soldiers to tea in their Bogside homes. When the soldiers told them that they were not allowed to enter the Bogside, the women brought trays of food, sandwiches and tea to the front line. The army quickly commandeered the old bus station at Victoria Market on Strand Road as their city side HQ.

The final piece of the Bogside jigsaw of the summer of 1969 was played out a few weeks later, when James Callaghan, the Home Secretary did a walkabout tour, accompanied by John Hume. In his memoir, *A House Divided*, Callaghan wrote that the main impression he had 'was one of being at the centre of a whirlpool of humanity bowling down the street' in which he was swept up and carried along. As I watched, it was like following the Pied Piper of Hamlin as hundreds pressed forward to see Callaghan, who took refuge in a house of Mrs. Diver, a few yards from Free Derry Corner. He sent the crowd into raptures of delight as he appeared to be talking to them directly, over the heads of the Stormont government. With megaphone in hand, he literally indulged in what has become known as megaphone diplomacy, and made a short speech from an upstairs window. He promised to ensure justice, equality and an absence of fear and discrimination. There was wild cheering when he said he was on the side of those who were deprived of freedom and justice.

With that, he departed and strode up Fahan Street and entered the walled city through Butcher Gate on his way to meet residents in the Protestant Fountain Street. His security detail must have been delighted when he left the Bogside. As he disappeared through the gate, I could not help but think that here was a real political leader, who wielded power and authority and had a good grasp of political reality and who compared very favourably with the political pygmies who bestrode our local stage. From the pages of *Derry Journal*, I learned that, in Mrs. Diver's terrace house, Callaghan had met leaders of the Citizens Defence Association, including leading republican, Sean Keenan. The delegation had demanded the abolition of Stormont. Callaghan had bluntly refused to countenance such a demand. I was sure that the members of the Citizens Defence Association delegation were far from pleased.

Just as a new political regime was being tentatively hinted at in Northern Ireland, the winds of political change were sweeping across my football life. Sir Matt Busby was no longer manager of Manchester United, having handed over the reins to his assistant, Wilf Mc Guinness. Some things did not change that quickly. The season started where the previous one had ended and United won only one of their seven games in the First Division, in August. The glory days were becoming a fading memory and I wondered when they would ever return. It was beginning to look as though winning the European Cup would be the pinnacle of achievement of that generation rather than the beginning of a new dawn. Sadly, my pessimism would prove to be true and would sum up my football experiences.

In the 1970s United would suffer the ignominy of being relegated from the First Division for the only time in my life.

Derry people have oft tended to draw a distinction between their city and Belfast, claiming that sectarian strife was very seldom to the fore in the Maiden City. However, it was never far from the surface and there was one incident during that summer that illustrated the point. It was only years later, that I found out this story from my wife, Nora, as the incident happened in her family home. I also talked about it with Paddy Doherty, better known as Paddy Bogside, who wrote about it in his autobiography. On Wednesday 27th August, 1969, a young man was driving through a barricade in the Bogside and was recognised. He was identified as Tommy Laird, a well-known loyalist, who had been allegedly involved in attacks on young Catholics and had allegedly taken part in the attack on Peoples Democracy students at Burntollet. He was also known to have joined the British Army.

On being recognised in the Bogside, he fled the car, pursued by a mob and sought refuge at the Gallagher household on Westland Terrace, battering at a window at the back of the house. On being let in, he hid in a cupboard under the stairs. Meanwhile, Nora's father, Hugh, was outside the front door remonstrating with the mob, which was in uproar, accusing him of harbouring a loyalist. Unaware that Laird had gained entry at the rear of the house, Hugh, better known as Sonny, was adamant in denying that Laird was inside. Nora came to his side. Tugging his sleeve, she quietly told him that there was a man hiding under the stairs. Fr. Tony Mulvey, a priest from the Cathedral and a good friend of the Gallagher family, had been summoned and confronted the mob, which was baying for blood.

Inside the house, Laird was brought from his hiding place under the stairs. Sonny, together with Hugh McLaughlin, a friend who been visiting with his wife, Monica, began asking him some questions. Hugh was a private detective and had acquired the nickname, Mannix, after a television detective of that name. Laird had identity papers, stating he was a British Army soldier, called Tommy McGarrigle. Paddy Doherty lived just around the corner and was the vice Chairman of the Citizens' Defence Association. He arrived on the scene and came into the house. Meanwhile outside, the mob was becoming very restless and threatened to burn down the Gallagher home if Laird was not handed over to their summary justice. A brick was hurled through the window. In return, Fr. Mulvey gave the mob the full venom of his clerical tongue and informed the mob that the man inside was British Army soldier called McGarrigle.

Some of the besiegers of the house shouted that he was Laird, as this was the name by which he was known, having been raised by a family of that name in the Waterside. Finally, the fugitive confessed that he was the Tommy Laird. One woman arrived and said that her son had been attacked by Laird, who had carved the initials UVF on him. She wanted to attack Laird with a Stiletto heel and when denied admittance, demanded an assurance, at the very least, that he would not be given a cup of tea by Mrs Gallagher. While Laird nervously drank a cup of tea, Paddy Bogside contacted the British Army, which confirmed that Mc Garrigle was a British soldier and requested his safe return. It was arranged that, at dawn, he be driven to the bottom of William Street at the junction with Waterloo Place and there handed over to the Army. A sergeant called Swaby signed a 'handing over receipt' and gave it to Paddy Doherty, as the Army whisked Laird away. Later that morning, a number of the besiegers, including the woman who had been wielding her stiletto-heeled shoe, came to visit Sonny Gallagher and apologised for their behaviour, when they had appeared demonically possessed. Laird should be forever thankful that he had sought refuge in the Gallagher home. The incident also demonstrated the raw, sectarian passions only a few weeks after the Battle of the Bogside.

Chapter Thirteen
Lull Before Another Storm

'All Kinds of Everything.' – Santa arrives in an army helicopter. O'Neill makes way for Chi Chi as young Stickies and Pinheads battle with the Army at Aggro Corner. Lord Hunt attempts to conquer policing as he had once done as a Mount Everest explorer. Rolls Royce goes bust and Rhodesia declares UDI.

As the Battle of Bogside receded into the mists of time, September arrived and it was back to the College. Derry had been transformed over the summer months and was emerging from its own version of the insurrection of the Paris Commune, a century earlier. It was clear that some of the voices that had been insurrectionary were now trying to cool the situation. Jack Lynch, the Irish Prime Minister, famous for his 'we will not stand by' speech of mid-August, had both rapidly and considerably moderated his tone. The Irish Army was no longer poised to cross the border and hasten a united Ireland. In a major speech to the Fianna Fail faithful in the republican stronghold of Tralee, in County Kerry, he said that Irish unity was not something to be forced but to be reached by agreement. I could hear the loud mutterings of discontent echoing around the militant circles in Derry.

There was, however, a new reality to be faced with a growing presence of British Army soldiers around the city centre and Military Police officers patrolling the Bogside and Creggan. The barricades were dismantled and the Derry Citizens' Defence Association was wound up. One morning, walking down Bligh's Lane on my way to school, I noticed that the Military Police had even taken over a wing of St. Cecilia's Secondary School for Girls. Outside flew a military flag of the Grenadier Guards, who were a support detachment. Similarly, at the library in Brooke Park, soldiers were now billeted. It was not uncommon to see a couple of car loads of Redcaps arrive at St. Mary's Church in Creggan for Mass and this was repeated in other city parishes. Meanwhile, in Belfast, the army started building 'peace lines' to keep the warring Catholic and Protestant factions apart as much as possible.

Policing had rightly been identified as one of the major issues to be dealt with and a committee of enquiry had been established under the chairmanship of the Everest explorer and mountaineer, Lord Hunt. His other claim to fame was that he could trace his ancestors to Samuel Hunt, who had been one of the young apprentices who had closed the gates of Derry against the advancing Jacobites in 1688. In October Lord Hunt reported and was certainly free free from any bias as the descendant of an Apprentice Boy who had been a leading light in the defying the Crown in 1688. He recommended that the Royal Ulster Constabulary (RUC) should become an unarmed force that the Ulster Special Constabulary (USC; the 'B Specials' should be disbanded and a new RUC Reserve should be set up. He also recommended that a new locally recruited part-time force should be established under the control of the British Army. This force was to become the Ulster Defence Regiment (UDR). There was quiet satisfaction in Catholic Derry at these recommendations, which had been some of the demands of the Citizens' Defence Association, when they had met James Callaghan. As Northern Ireland was a zero sum game, satisfaction in Catholic areas was mirrored by a storm of indignation and hostility from within the Unionist community.

James Callaghan, the Home Secretary returned to the Bogside, in October, with Sir Arthur Young, the newly appointed head of the RUC and former head of the Metropolitan Police in London, in tow. It was like motherhood and apple pie, as diehard republican Sean Keenan told the media that there would be no problem with the reformed RUC coming back in to the Bogside. This sentiment endorsed by John Hume's Independent organisation and Eddie McAteer of the Nationalist Party. The RUC was now, for the first time, an unarmed police service and within a month two RUC constables, were patrolling the Bogside, together with a military police unit. Life appeared to be returning to a lazy normality, except for the RUC issuing a growing number of summonses for the rioting during the Battle of Bogside. Bernadette Devlin received sixteen summonses for her part. Beneath the surface of a new normality, there was growing sullen resentment in militant circles.

It would have been naive to believe that a magic wand had been waved, dispelling the past hatreds and divisions. Before the month was out, there was yet another death of an innocent civilian, a Protestant called William King. There were sectarian clashes between gangs of Catholic and Protestant youths in the city centre of Derry and Mr. King, a middle aged father of four, died after being attacked by a Catholic mob and kicked to death. Officially, his death was recorded, like that of Sammy Devenny, as due to a heart attack. Barricades were erected in the Fountain Street area and his death marked the start of a mass exodus of Protestants from the west bank of the river Foyle to the Waterside. The British Army also clashed with Catholic youths for the first time and the army erected stronger barricades around the Bogside, indicating a policy of containment. Officially, the pretence was that the army was in Northern Ireland to 'support the civil power, the RUC.' My father told me that these infantry soldiers had probably served in places such as Aden in the last few years and that one thing for sure was that they were not trained as policemen. Interestingly, a number of years later, Michael Barthorp, a former soldier, wrote a history of the Royal Anglican Regiment, which was called *Crater to the Creggan 1964-74*. The attention of the international media had changed from the Golan Heights to Creggan Heights.

The day after Callaghan's latest tour of the Bogside, rioting erupted on the Shankill Road in Belfast, as a reaction to the recommendations of the Hunt Report, and the first policeman was shot dead in the Troubles, Constable Victor Arbuckle, aged twenty nine. The riot also showed that the British Army was fully prepared to shoot back, as soldiers from the Parachute Regiment shot dead two Protestant civilians during the rioting. The gun had returned to the streets of Northern Ireland and it was something of an irony that it was loyalists who fired the first shots. A week later, a member of the Ulster Volunteer Force (UVF), was severely injured when a bomb he was planting exploded prematurely at a power station near Ballyshannon, in County Donegal. He died the following day from his injuries.

An outsider, reviewing legislative developments in these months, would have concluded that it was full steam ahead for the reform programme, albeit at the insistence of the Westminster government. The demands of the Civil Rights movement were being addressed. Legislation was passed establishing a commissioner to deal with complaints against local councils and public bodies. There was a new electoral law, whose main provision was to make the franchise in local government elections in Northern Ireland the same as that in Britain. A new police authority was also established and an act, establishing a Ministry for Community Relations, was passed. In Derry, the Development Commission was busy building much needed houses, in Shantallow for Catholics, and in New Buildings and Kilfennan for Protestants.

At the start of 1969, the Stormont Government of Northern Ireland had set up a commission, under a Scottish judge, Lord Cameron, "to hold an enquiry into, and to report upon, the course of events leading to, and the immediate causes and nature of the violence and civil disturbance in Northern Ireland on and since 5 October 1968; and to assess the composition, conduct and aims of those bodies involved in the current agitation and in any incidents arising out of it." This became known as the Cameron Commission and it published its report in September. Its conclusions were seen by Catholics as a devastating indictment of Unionist government and John Hume said it was, 'a vindication of the Civil Rights movement.' Brian Faulkner, the Development Minister reflected that it was, 'a sober and reasonable report.' Rev Ian Paisley castigated it as being 'guilty of deliberate lying.'

Politics aside, it was back to the College and an important year lay ahead, with O Level exams at the end of it. In class, we were sorry to learn that Jimmy Sharkey would not be returning as our History teacher, which was the only change in the teaching personnel. The change meant that we would have Mr. O'Kane for both French and History. I was mindful of the excitement that had surged through my veins walking around the cobbled squares of Trinity College in Dublin and I determined to stay on track to do well in my O Levels. The biggest change in schooling was that we no longer had a half day of lessons on Wednesdays and Saturdays and the new school week consisted of a more conventional five day week. I think that the teachers had been pressing for this for some time, as school on Saturday morning hardly suited their weekend plans. The original school week had been established when the college was mainly a boarding school but there were probably no more than eighty boarders in the entire school population of over eleven hundred.

The main priority of the teachers was to ensure that, in each subject, the syllabus was comprehensively covered. Our Latin teacher, Fr. Farrelly, invoked the ancient muses, to advise us not to become involved in what was happening on the streets. He recommended that we should look down on it from the Olympian heights of the College, as the school dominated the Bogside skyline. It was sound advice, although we all found it difficult to remain detached. This difficulty would only increase in the coming months. Apart from class tests at Christmas, there was none of the mock exams to which we had been regularly subjected by Brother Keane in the run up to the Eleven Plus. Teaching examination technique was therefore restricted to being told to read the exam paper quickly from start to finish, make a mental note, where there was multiple choice, of the questions we would answer and the time to be spent on each question. We were then to read those questions in detail and begin putting pen to paper by answering the questions in order of how equipped we were for them, which meant the easy questions first. Of course, all of this was predicated on having worked throughout the year in each subject. We had good teachers for O Level and, provided we did your homework, a pass mark was easy to achieve.

In that period of my first term back at the College in the autumn of 1969, events in Derry were far from the anarchic days of the summer. The British Army was generally welcome and Santa even arrived in the city centre courtesy of an army helicopter. Bogsiders were even inviting troops for Christmas dinner. I remember a poster with the invitation 'Have a soldier for Christmas', to which one wag had added, 'they're delicious.' Young army officers were wandering around Brooke Park library, borrowing books. They seemed more interested in the poetry section than the history of Ireland, immersing themselves in which would have been very beneficial. There was a hearts and minds campaign as the army organised football tournaments for juveniles and discos to which they invited young women. The latter would prove a bone of contention with local youths, as it surely did in any garrison town in England.

It was the Christmas of 1969, when I finally tired of football boots and jerseys as presents and I was delighted when my parents bought me a reel to reel magnetic tape recorder. It looked like a small suitcase and such items are now only probably found in the Museum of Magnetic Sound Recordings in Austin, Texas. I had enjoyed Radio One's *Pick of the Pops*, presented each Sunday evening by Alan Freeman. In the confines of my bedroom, I was able to record the hits and play them over and over. It is no wonder I can easily remember the lyrics of the hits of my school days. My first gadget, however, was not my tape recorder but had been a Brownie 127 camera that I bought in Dixon's Chemist shop in Waterloo Place and from which I had endless hours of pleasure and still have the pictures to prove it. One of my first ventures was to take photographs of St. Mary's Church and I luckily got a very good pic of Fr. George McLaughlin, who was in charge of the altar boys. He was an avid Liverpool supporter, much to the disgust of my fellow altar boys, who were Man United mad.

By the time we had reached Easter and were fast approaching the exams, we were encouraged to think ahead to the A Level subjects that we would pursue. You could see a division opening between the boys who were better at Maths and Sciences and those who favoured the Arts subjects. For the former, the natural choice of A level subject was going to be Maths, Physics and Chemistry and there was little or no cross-fertilisation with arts subjects. As I enjoyed History and English, these appeared as easy choices for me. For a third A Level, I was drawn to French as I disliked Irish and was becoming bored with Latin. As the temperature in Derry seemed to cooling down, we were also encouraged to participate in the debating competitions against the three other grammar schools in the city, Thornhill College, Foyle College and Londonderry High School. Thornhill was the female equivalent of the College, a Catholic grammar school. Both Foyle and High School were state grammar schools, one for boys and the other for girls. Nominally state schools, they were, in reality, Protestant schools.

Foyle College traced its origins to the early years of the 17th century, when it was established, within the walled city as a Free Grammar School for boys. Its founder, Mathias Springham, was a member of the Merchant Taylors' company, one of the London companies involved in the plantation of Ulster. The school was built 'to the honour of God and the spreading of good literature.' Londonderry High School, set in the grounds of Duncreggan House, which had once been the home of the shirt manufacturer, William Tillie, had been established in the 19th century as an academy for young ladies. Debating in Foyle and High School was literally the first contact I had with Protestant pupils and guess what; they were not that different from us. The subjects for debate avoided any contentious issues relating to Northern Ireland and were dominated by topics such as 'This house Would Pull out of Vietnam,' and 'This House would prefer to be Dead than Red.' There were considerable efforts being made to promote contact across the great divide and debating was carried on throughout my remaining school years. The debates with Foyle and High School took place on their home turf. The College in Bishop Street may have seemed a bit too intimidating and was too near the Bogside to be regarded as a neutral venue.

While this cross-community activity was progressing in our school lives, on the streets, there was a new form of almost daily recreation emerging for other youths, not involved in inter-school debating. It became known as recreational rioting and began as schools emptied shortly after three o'clock. The rioting was not confined to secondary school pupils and it was not unusual to see children as young as eight participating. Soon, the corner of William Street and Rossville Street was christened Aggro Corner and army 'snatch squads' would attempt to arrest offenders; usually with little success. So frustrated did the soldiers become, that they would arrest anyone in sight and once accused of rioting there was an inevitable verdict handed down by the local magistrates, followed by a few months in jail. For such obvious reasons, I avoided that area as much as possible.

Saturday was the worst day for an afternoon riot, affectionately known as 'the matinee' and shops began closing at lunch time, a practice also followed by the local credit union, whose premises were on Rossville Street. There was some added concern in Creggan when the British Army uncovered an arms cache that mainly consisted of old rifles, which they said were still viable. It was pretty clear to me that the army was frustrated by the daily riots and its inability to get stuck into the rioters. It was, therefore, no surprise to me when years later a memo was uncovered from none other than General Ford, who authorised the Paras to invade the Bogside on Bloody Sunday. He wrote, 'The conclusion that the minimum force necessary to achieve a restoration of law and order is to shoot selected ringleaders among the DYH (Derry Young Hooligans) after clear warnings have been issued.' It all smacked of an army mindset that thought it was dealing with colonial outposts such as Aden. Before arriving in Northern

Ireland, the last active service that the Parachute Regiment had seen had been in the Sheikh Othman district of Aden in 1967, which was not exactly a good preparation for deployment in Northern Ireland, in support of the police.

Events on the streets again started to dictate their own agenda. Just before Christmas, the inquest in to the death of Sammy Devenny reached a conclusion of death by natural causes. On the same day, Bernadette Devlin appeared in the courthouse in Bishop Street and was sentenced to six months in jail for her part in the Battle of the Bogside. She was released on bail, pending an appeal. Throughout November and December, there were further prosecutions and an increasing number of local young men were jailed for their part in the summer riots. The smart move of any government would have been to have wiped the slate clean and declare a general amnesty. The New Year started badly when it was announced that no charges would be brought against sixteen RUC men, in connection with offences dating back to January 1969 and the incursion into the Bogside. It seemed a matter of double standards. On a political level, there was a growing belief that Harold Wilson was disengaging from Ulster and ceding too much power back to an unreconstructed Stormont regime.

Rev Ian Paisley was never far away from incidents of trouble and his presence in Derry's Guildhall, one Friday night in February 1970, was the catalyst for one of the first major confrontations with the army. There was a relatively small protest outside the Guildhall by about a hundred Catholic youths and an Irish Tricolour was waved and quickly seized by the soldiers, together with the young man waving it. A riot developed and this was the first time, in Derry, that there were accusations of brutality levelled against the army. The riot could almost have been scripted and followed the well-trodden path of previous confrontations with the RUC. There was a baton charge by the soldiers, and the Catholic rioters were pushed back towards William Street and the Bogside.

The honeymoon period was certainly over as we approached Easter, which marked the beginning of the long 'marching season' in Northern Ireland. In Derry, it was marked with the republican commemoration of the 1916 Rising. Harold Wilson had plenty of troubles in his own back yard, than to be concerned about riots in Derry. Rolls Royce, the manufacturer of the most British and expensive of cars and employer of thousands of workers, was bust and required a financial injection of £20 million. Four years after the declaration of independence, Ian Smith declared Rhodesia a republic, breaking all ties with the Crown. Wilson's reaction was simply to refuse to recognise the new state. Two months after his appearance in Derry, Ian Paisley became a Stormont MP, winning the by-election in the Bannside seat that had been held by Terence O'Neill, until the former

Prime Minister went off to the House of Lords, as Lord O'Neill of the Maine. We soon got used to the sight of Paisley leading his followers in singing '*Praise God From whom All Blessings Flow*,' when a Presiding Officer declared elections that resulted in victory for him and his candidates.

Within weeks of this rioting in the Bogside, there was celebration as Rosemary Brown, representing Ireland, under her stage name Dana, won the Eurovision Song Contest, in Amsterdam, with *All Kinds of Everything*. What made the victory even sweeter was that the UK entry, *Knock, Knock, Who's There?*' by the Welsh singer, Mary Hopkin was the favourite. None of us paid any attention to the Spanish entry sung by Julio Inglesias, who shot to international fame in the following years. The Browns had lived just round the corner from me in Creggan, before moving to the Rossville Street flats a few years earlier. I remember Rosemary as a Thornhill pupil. Out of school uniform, she was definitely 'a dedicated follower of fashion.' She would confidently step out, with a swagger and we nicknamed her Lady Penelope, after the marionette character from the television series, *Thunderbirds*. Rosemary returned to Derry and was feted as a heroine. From the balcony of the high flats, she serenaded the hundreds who had gathered with her winning song. She even shot to the top of the pop charts displacing Simon and Garfunkel, whose *Bridge Over Troubled Water* had occupied the top spot for three weeks.

There was singing of a different type in Derry a few weeks later. By Easter of 1970, we now had two IRAs rather than one. The playwright, Brendan Behan, had once written that the first item on the agenda of a republican convention was the split and it was no surprise that tensions between the traditionalists and young radicals would bring about a complete rupture. The traditionalists formed the breakaway Provisional IRA, while those who continued to give their allegiance to the Dublin leadership called themselves the Official IRA. In Creggan, the two wings of the IRA were initially simply known as the Pinheads and the Stickies. The Official IRA continued to use an Easter Lily that had a self-adhesive backing to attach it to the lapel. The Provisionals used the traditional Easter Lily, attached to the lapel by a pin. The term Pinhead soon faded and was replaced by the standard term Provos; whereas the term Sticky continued to be used, mostly as a pejorative one.

Easter Sunday, in Derry, thus saw two republican commemorations and serious rioting broke out after the Official IRA parade. The march passed the RUC station on the Strand Road and the marchers were incensed that the Union Jack was flying from its flagpole. The ensuing riot was described as the first serious confrontation between the British Army and Catholics in Derry, with the army being widely compared to the RUC for the force they used against the rioters. The sequel to the riot was that more young Derry men were charged, convicted and jailed, while General Freeland said that petrol bombers would be shot dead if they persisted after warnings given. In London, the government backed the general. Within a few days of the Derry riots, the television was broadcasting a similar, brutal confrontation in the Ballymurphy area of Belfast, involving Scottish soldiers and locals. It seemed to me that neither confrontation had happened accidentally but had been orchestrated as an opener for a summer of more mayhem. It also struck me that, given sectarian divisions in Scotland, it was a major error of judgment on the part of the British Army to put Scottish soldiers on the streets of Northern Ireland.

The newspapers were regularly stuffed with reports on daily rioting and the ritual condemnations of violence. I was quickly becoming immune to media reports. However, one story grabbed my attention. In March of 1970 Trinity College Dublin was celebrating the bi-centenary of the foundation of Edmund Burke's Club, the oldest student debating society in the world. There was a week of debates featuring prominent political figures such as American Senators Edward Kennedy and Eugene McCarthy, together with exiled Greek dissident, Andreas Papandreou and Michael Foot, a member of the Labour Shadow Cabinet n Britian. The Bicentenary Debate was on the motion 'That Emmet's Epitaph Be Now Written.' This was a reference to the United Irish leader, Robert Emmet, a Trinity graduate, whose speech from the dock, when convicted of treason in 1803, ended with the plea, '...when my country takes her place among the nations of the earth, then and not till then, let my epitaph be written.'

The debate was reported in in the pages of *The Derry Journal* for the simple reason that John Hume, my former history teacher from first year in the College, and now the M.P for Foyle in the Stormont Parliament, was one of the motion's proposers. I avidly read the transcript of the speech, which Edward Kennedy later read into the record of the American Congress. I came upon words that John Hume would use for the rest of his political life and which became his defining philosophy; 'The mental border of prejudice and distrust that exists between our people can only be removed by the promotion of better understanding and friendship,' he said and continued with the immortal words, 'it can only be removed by spilling sweat, common sweat, rather than by spilling common blood.' A clear line had been drawn between constitutional nationalism and physical force republicanism.

That distinction was more than evident a few months later with the dramatic news that Jack Lynch sacked two cabinet ministers, Charles Haughey and Neil Blaney, after revelations of a plot in smuggle arms into to the Republic for use in Northern Ireland. The government was rocked but Lynch survived. The incident was seen by Unionists in Northern Ireland as further evidence of the long-suspected conspiracy to bring down the state and official support for the emerging Provisional IRA, which was flexing its muscles in clashes with the British Army, particularly in Belfast.

Before the school year ended there was the more personal matter of the O level exams and an interesting Westminster General Election. A number of us decided that we would use the Reference Room at the Brooke Park Library, as a meeting place allegedly to work together on topics that might come up in History and English Literature. It was sunny exam weather and we were inevitably drawn into breaks, which simply became excuses to play football on the grass behind the library. One day, we were approached by one of the soldiers of the Royal Anglian regiment, stationed in Brooke Park, who asked if we would field a team to play them. We agreed and for a few weeks there were regular games, with coats for goal posts and no offside. The young soldiers would emerge from their billet in the bowels of Gwynn's Institution, dressed in army fatigue trousers, army tee shirts and wearing their black hob-nail boots. Their heads were almost fully shaven, which was very different to our Beatle cuts. A few junior officers would watch from the sidelines but never participated. It was both the first and last summer when such activities were to take place in Brooke Park. A few years later, the IRA placed bombs in the Gwynn's Institute building, in which the library was housed, and the library burned to the ground.

As we were playing football with the army, the real football deal was beginning in Mexico City with the World Cup. England were the defending champions and arrived, no doubt buoyed up with their official song, *Back Home*, which had gone to the top of the pop charts just before the tournament started. Playing at altitude, the European teams appeared at a disadvantage. Brazil were installed as the favourites and were hoping for redemption after the poor performance four years earlier. England were drawn in the same group as Brazil and lost the all-important game one nil to the favourites. The memorable moment of the game was not Jairzinho's winning goal but a fabulous save by England's goalkeeper, Gordon Banks to deny Pelé a certain goal.

As a result of the defeat, England had to play West Germany in quarter finals, a re-match of the 1966 final. While all eyes were on this much-awaited Italy emerged as dark horses, beating the hosts, Mexico, 4-1, in the quarter final. Gordon Banks suffered food poisoning and missed the game with West Germany. England led the Germans 2-0 after an hour but lost 3-2 after extra time and was eliminated from the competition. The squaddies that we played against in Brooke Park were speechless, as they anticipated meeting with Brazil in the final. Instead, it was the England song, *Back Home* that echoed in their ears as their team headed back home. Brazil went on to avenge the ignominy of the previous World Cup and beat Italy 4-1 in the final, with Pelé winning his third World Cup winners medal. It was carnival football, which chimed with the pop song, *In the Summertime,* sung by a band called Mungo Jerry, which was top of the pops for seven weeks. '*In the summertime when the weather is hot/You can stretch right out and touch the sky,*' ran the lyrics of the first verse.

On the political front, Harold Wilson called a General Election that he was expected to win comfortably. A few of my friends were Nationalists and the election in the Londonderry constituency was seen, by them, as the chance of some excitement. Eddie McAteer was the Unity candidate and, to my surprise, John Hume, who had defeated him in the Stormont General election just over a year earlier, was his election agent. I was a bit non-plussed but went along with them a few times to lick envelopes at the election headquarters in a disused tyre depot in William Street. The outcome of the voting in June was never in any doubt, as there was a solid Unionist majority in the constituency. My interest waned considerably and I reverted to concentrating on my revision for the exams. In the General Election, the Unionist Party won eight seats, while Ian Paisley became an MP, winning the North Antrim seat. Bernadette Devlin retained her seat as a Unity candidate, while Frank McManus was also elected as a Unity candidate in the neighbouring constituency of Fermanagh/South Tyrone. Gerry Fitt was re-elected in West Belfast. While the Northern Ireland Labour Party received almost 100,000 votes it failed to win any seats.

In the middle of the exams, there was a tragic and sad occurrence in Creggan in the house of one of my friends, John Mc Cool. On a Friday evening, there was an almighty explosion in his home at Dunree Gardens in which his father, Tommy and two sisters died along with two local men, Joe Coyle and Tommy Carlin. It transpired that the adults were making bombs in the kitchen, which were to be used in later attacks. Everyone locally, knew that Tommy McCool and his associates were involved in the Provisional IRA in Derry, some of whom had been involved in previous failed IRA campaigns and were members of known republican families. The Dunree Gardens incident was clear evidence that the Provisional IRA was upping the ante and preparing to go on the offensive against the security forces. The funeral of Tommy McCool and his children was a sad sight as it passed our front door in Fanad Drive. There were more than a thousand mourners, including Eddie McAteer and John Hume. The IRA provided a guard of honour, full military honours and a volley of shots over the grave.

The deaths in Dunree Gardens, coincided with the arrest of Bernadette Devlin, who lost her appeal against the six month sentence imposed on her for her part in the Battle of the Bogside. It was typical Derry theatre as Devlin had announced that she would travel to the city for a rally in the Bogside before handing herself over to the police at Strand Road station, which the IRA was planning to attack that same night. Fearing a riot, the police stopped her car a few miles from Derry and took her directly to jail. It was our local version of the board game, *Monopoly*, with Devlin going directly to jail, not passing Free Derry Corner and not collecting the adulation of her supporters. The end product was the inevitable riot, which went on for three days.

The British Army's response to the riot was to saturate the Bogside with CS gas, much the same response as had been adopted by the RUC, the previous summer. I was more than a disinterested observer as I was on the high ground of the College, sitting my O Level exams and the gas wafted over the school. A few times, exams had to be interrupted while boys went to wash out their eyes and get a drink of water. Below us in the Bogside, juveniles of our own age were pelting the army with stones, bottles and petrol bombs; Belfast was descending into further ugly sectarian clashes and gun battles. The college was an oasis. It was somewhat ironic that in our Latin paper we were translating the story of Aegialus, who received bad news from the battlefield and had to steady his men. I wondered whether Gladstone's domestic policies in his administration of 1868 to 1874, resonated with either the rioters or the young squaddies facing them. I was translating, from French, a passage from George Simenon's *Maigret*, – Rendez-Vous at the Pink Rabbit Club, which seemed light years removed from confrontation at the Bogside Inn, which would also have made a good title for a book.

In the excitement of the World Cup and the destruction on the streets throughout Northern Ireland, the change of government at Westminster was hardly noticed. Harold Wilson unexpectedly lost the General Election, and Ted Heath replaced him in Number 10 Downing Street. Reggie Maudling, the new Home Secretary, paid a visit to Northern Ireland and left us with a quote of the year. As he boarded the flight out of Northern Ireland, he was reported to have said: "For God's sake bring me a large Scotch. What a bloody awful country!"

The change in government also marked a change in the tone of government in relation to Northern Ireland and it appeared that the British Army was now being given free rein to deal with rioters. A military curfew was imposed on the Falls Road area of Belfast for a period of thirty six hours, at the start of July. The house searches lasted for two days and involved considerable destruction to many homes and their contents. I remember a television shot that really annoyed the Catholic population. It was of Captain John Brooke, son of a former Prime Minister, Lord Brookeborough, touring the Falls Road on the back of an army Land Rover. Even my mother, who was a moderate woman, was appalled at this sight of a Unionist aristocrat lording it over the vanquished Catholic area. As a retaliatory gesture, Patrick Hillery, the Republic's Foreign Minister, did a walk about on the Falls Road, a few days after the curfew had been lifted. During the period of the curfew, there were gun battles between both wings of the IRA and the Army, in which over fifteen hundred rounds were fired. Three civilians died as a result of shootings. There were now a growing number of fatalities, especially in Belfast and it was only a matter of time before a similar picture would emerge in Derry.

There were major ups and downs in the communal disorders in Derry that summer. July was relatively quiet and there was an expectation of a similar outcome in August, after a ban on all parades had been announced. This meant that there would be no annual Apprentice Boys' parade in the city, which had been the event from which the city had erupted in violence the previous year. However, as Harold Macmillan had once famously remarked, a political leader should fear 'events, dear boy, events.' In this instance, the events were happening in Belfast, and in Derry. A rally was called in the Bogside to protest about the shooting dead of a nineteen year old by the British Army, in Belfast. The protest degenerated into a week of rioting and the army used 'rubber bullets' for the first time. More ominously, the first shots were fired at the army, quite close to the College, in Bishop Street. Gelignite bombs were thrown and there was the first bombing of commercial premises when the offices of the Gaslight Company, on the Lecky Road, were destroyed in an explosion.

In record time, the government at Stormont had rushed through a draconian Criminal Justice Bill, which became law at the end of June, just before the much expected summer riots. It handed down a mandatory six month jail sentence to anyone found guilty of being 'in a riot situation.' What followed in the courts was tragic-comedy, except for the defendants, as soldiers swore they could positively identify the rioters, whom they often only fleetingly spotted under cover of darkness. Even before this legislation took effect, there was a notorious case, in Derry, of nine girls arrested by soldiers, who claimed that one of the girls had thrown a stone. In court, a policeman testified that all of the girls had clean hands when arrested and suggested that they had not been throwing stones. A soldier testified that he had not seen any of the girls throw stones. Three of the girls were released when soldiers made wrong identifications in court. However, the judge jailed three of the girls, two of whom were under seventeen!

In Belfast, a twenty year old docker, John Benson, painted 'No Tea Here' on a gable wall, a reference to the practice of giving tea to soldiers. He was hauled before the courts and the magistrate decided that the offence was an attempt to intimidate people and sentenced him to six months in jail. The new legislation was now regarded as the second most repressive piece of legislation on the statute book, surpassed only by the Special Powers Act. More importantly, the British Army was seen as delighting in implementing it. Derry wasn't Britain's only trouble spot. Police in London battled with rioters in Notting Hill. None of the rioters faced a mandatory six month prison sentence if convicted before magistrates. Before the year was out, the local Resident Magistrate in Derry, Paddy Maxwell, handed down a severe warning from the bench to innocent by-standers at riot situations. He told an unfortunate defendant that those who go along and call themselves innocent by-standers could be charged and convicted of disorderly behaviour or riot! Prior to his elevation to the bench, Maxwell had at one time been a Nationalist MP for the Foyle constituency, had welcomed De Valera to Derry in the 1950s and sat on a platform that included a former Chief of Staff of the IRA!

I was relieved to holiday in Galway that summer and again get away from Derry. The city was certainly different to Dublin but was also buzzing with vast numbers of tourists. Not surprisingly, we met a large number of Derry people who obviously had the same idea of escaping from the North. I stayed with my parents in Ward's, a small family-run hotel in Salthill. There was a long promenade along which to walk and forget about the troubles at home. Walking along the promenade, I could just about see the outline of Aran Islands in the distance and thought about John Millington Synge's essays of the same name that we had studied that year. I was always amused to read that Synge's play, *The Playboy of the Western World* had caused a riot outside the Abbey Theatre when it was first performed in 1907. While in Galway, I phoned the College and was pleased with my O Level results, which ensured that I would be able to continue my studies in any of the subjects to A level. I had little hesitation in deciding to embark on Modern History, French and English Literature for my remaining two years at the College and looked forward to a return to school. While I was in Galway, there was the news report of the first deaths of members of the RUC, caused by the IRA, as the Provisionals detonated a booby trap bomb in south Armagh killing two policemen. The IRA denied responsibly for this, which suggested that they were not yet fully ready for an all-out offensive campaign against the army.

It would be wrong, however, to portray this period as one in which the only actors were the British army and the Stormont government on the one side and the wings of the IRA on the other. There was a strong constitutional nationalist tradition in Northern Ireland, and particularly in Derry. In August, therefore, it was no surprise when six of the opposition MPs at Stormont announced the establishment of a new party, the Social Democratic and Labour Party, the SDLP. Gerry Fitt, the party's only Westminster MP, became leader and John Hume, my former History teacher from my days in Junior One, became deputy leader. Hume's Independent Organisation in Derry affiliated to the new party within a few months. Claude Wilton, for whom I had worked during the previous summer holidays, abandoned the almost defunct Liberal Party and threw in his lot with the SDLP, becoming a Senator in the Stormont parliament. The SDLP was going to have the time and opportunity to organise itself for any electoral contest as it was announced that local government elections would be postponed and the next Stormont and Westminster elections were a few years away.

A few days before we returned to the College, Robert Porter, then Minister of Home Affairs, resigned from the Stormont government. 'Beezer' Porter, as he was affectionately known in his native Derry, was widely regarded as a fair man of principle. The official reason given for his resignation was 'health' but he later said that he had not been consulted about the Falls Road curfew. Within a few years, Porter would resign from the Unionist Party and join the moderate Alliance Party.

An IRA member was killed in a premature explosion as he was planting a bomb at an electricity transformer in Belfast. A Republican from Derry, armed with a rifle and revolver, was arrested by the Irish police just inside the Republic's Border. He claimed that he was planning to attack British soldiers. It seemed as though we were going down another slippery slope and that the army's role had changed considerably from that adopted a year earlier. The summer in Derry ended with rioters hi-jacking cars, vans and buses.

On the international stage, the Popular Front for the Liberation of Palestine, the PLO, was hi-jacking five aeroplanes and forcing three of them to land in Jordan. Another terrorist organisation tracing its roots to the riots of the summer of 1969, the Red Army Faction, better known as the Bader-Meinhof Group, was established in West Germany and similar Anarchist groupings were formed in Italy and Spain. It looked as though the Seventies would be dominated by terrorism and that Northern Ireland would not be immune.

Chapter Fourteen
Life in the Sixth Form

The Trinity Ban lifted – The Wolves in the Brandywell as recreational rioting kicks off and the first British soldier dies in Ireland since the days of Lloyd George.

When I returned to the College in September of 1970 as a Sixth Former, it struck me that the first years seemed to be getting younger and smaller and they were still undergoing the ritual ducking. Our minds were on different matters and our first days were taken up with subject selection and finding out who our teachers would be for our final two years. Before finalising subject choice, we were given a talk by Fr. McElhinney, who was the teacher in charge of careers and university applications. Wee Willie, as he was affectionately known, was also our Religious Knowledge teacher for Lower sixth and he often used these classes to discuss careers and university choices. In the course of one discussion, I mentioned to him that I had been attracted to Trinity College Dublin and would like to know more about how to apply. I added that applying to Trinity might be of academic interest only as my understanding was that the Catholic Church had imposed a ban on Catholics attending Trinity. He smiled and enjoyed telling me that Rome had just given the Irish Hierarchy permission to lift the Ban. I almost whooped with delight and told him that, in that case, I would certainly be looking for information about the entrance requirements for Trinity.

For my chosen A Level subjects, I retained Mr. Frankie O'Kane for Modern History, which meant that he taught me either French or History throughout my four senior years at the College. For English Literature and French, I now had completely new teachers, Willie Donaghy and Jack McCauley, respectively. Our first week was spent familiarising ourselves with the syllabus in each subject and being told how each course would develop during the two years of study. All the courses were both exciting and challenging and it was soon clear that there was a big step up from O Level to A level. Extracurricular activities were going to be debating, in which we had advanced to the schools' senior competition, and membership of the Current Affairs Society that was restricted to sixth formers.

My mother marked the beginning of my sixth form years by buying me a bookcase at the Fraser and Mitchell auction rooms in Castle Street and they delivered it to Creggan. With pride, I started sorting the piles of books that littered my bedroom floor and created an orderly library. There were the Penguin novels I had gathered up and read in the previous two years. These ranged from an extensive collection by George Orwell, which included *Nineteen Eighty Four,* which had been on our O Level paper to other classics including *Animal Farm, The Road to Wigan Pier, Down and Out in Paris and London* and *Homage to Catalonia.* The last of these books reinforced my anti-communist sentiments, with lurid stories of the republican forces in the Spanish Civil War turning against each other. Our youth would not have been complete without J.D. Salinger's *The Catcher in the Rye* and F. Scott Fitzgerald's *The Great Gatsby.* Aldous Huxley's *Brave New World,* introduced us to version of the futuristic cinema called 'the Feelies', where the audience could hold a knob on their seats and feel the sensations of the movie. Irish literature selections included James Joyce's *Dubliners* and *Portrait of the Artist as a Young Man,* as well as drama of John Millington Synge and the poetry of William Butler Yeats. We also discovered that many of the books that we were reading were banned in the Republic of Ireland, under its austere censorship laws. They were deemed to be corrupting the morals of their would-be readers.

In my Lower sixth year, the French Revolution cast its shadow over all aspects of our studies in European, British and Irish history. The famous motto of Liberty, Equality, Fraternity was, somewhat incongruously, emblazoned on the flags of the French armies as they conquered and subjugated Europe. Roget De Lisle composed one of the most stirring anthems ever written, *La Marseilleise.* The happenings in France inspired either admiration or loathing in equal measures, as Tom Paine wrote forcefully in defence of the Revolution and its ideals, while Edmund Burke was scathing in his criticism. The French Revolution even intruded into poetry as we read the lines from Wordsworth:

> *Bliss was it in that dawn to be alive,*
> *But to be young was very heaven!*

I didn't share these sentiments. I was living in the war zone of Derry, where lessons were often disrupted by CS gas wafting through school and nights without sleep as gun battles raged in the street. On the streets of Derry, and elsewhere throughout Northern Ireland, the IRA was beginning its campaign of trying to stage a revolution and seek the establishment of a thirty two county socialist republic, by force of arms. I inclined to Edmund Burke's view of revolution as 'the very last resource of the thinking and the good.'

On my bookshelf, Beckett's slim *Short History of Ireland* was now joined by its larger successor, *The Making of Modern Ireland,* which formed the basis of our study of later 18th century Ireland. This was another turbulent period with the Volunteer Movement, threat of French invasion, the '98 Rebellion and the passing of the Act of Union. It was to prove an exciting time in our reading. We were introduced to the 19th century historians, Lecky and Froude as well as Thomas Pakenham's *The Year of Liberty*. For some of my classmates, it was the first time that they were faced with realities, rather than myths. I remember that a few of them, who had republican leanings, were astounded to learn that Wolfe Tone, the father and founder of Irish republicanism, had once proposed to the Prime Minister a scheme for the military conquest of the Sandwich Islands. He even outlined the military and commercial benefits that would accrue to the British Empire. I chuckled as I read this.

The second leg of the History A Level was British History. *England in The Age of Improvement,* by Asa Briggs, was the standard work on this period. The European History syllabus covered the period from the French Revolution to the Crimean War and another large book, *Foundations of Modern Europe,* by M.E. Barlen was our textbook. Together, this trilogy of history books made an impressive sight on my newly-acquired bookcase and my collection only grew in the ensuing two years. We were encouraged to read widely around the standard text books. Frankie O'Kane introduced us to the writings of Henry Kissinger and his work, *A World Restored*, was a fascinating insight into the diplomatic achievements of Lord Castlereagh at the Congress of Vienna in 1815. Castlereagh was a figure derided in Irish nationalist circles as having been the architect of the Act of Union that abolished the Irish parliament in College Green in Dublin.

Willie Donaghy, fondly nicknamed Cheyenne on account if his resemblance to the Clint Eastwood character, had a genuine love for English literature, which he wished to pass on to us. He also encouraged us to read widely beyond the set texts. Rather than simply study E.M. Forster's *Howard's End*, we read a fair amount of Forster's other works, including *A Passage to India* and *A Room with a View*. Similarly, with the works of Thomas Hardy, we went way beyond *The Mayor of Casterbridge,* which was the novel on our curriculum. Penguin paperbacks, at a modest price, opened a whole world of literature. Shakespeare had been an ever-present text since first year and in our A level studies we had *Henry IV Part II* and *Antony and Cleopatra*. The Puritan Milton and *Paradise Lost* complemented the romantic poets and T.S. Eliot's *Selected Poems* brought us into the modern world. I thought that Willie Donaghy was a great mind of knowledge on Eliot, as he took us through the Selected Poems, giving an erudite commentary. Years later, in a second-hand bookshop in London, I discovered *A Student's Guide to the Selected Poems of T. S. Eliot,* written by B.C. Southam and realised that Willie had used it extensively in class. However, this discovery did not change my appreciation of the enthusiasm for English literature that Willie had helped develop in me.

Part of the A level English Literature course was critical appreciation of pieces of prose and poetry. One stands out in my memory, lines taken from *The Leveller*, by Robert Graves. We read that one of the soldiers killed was 'a pale eighteen year old.' It struck me that at the time I was reading this poem, young British soldiers, some of whom were also only eighteen years old, were patrolling the streets of Derry. There were also young local lads, of similar age, on the streets. They had joined the IRA and would soon be looking to shoot and kill the soldiers.

French was a combination of language and literature, which ranged from Moliere to Camus with plenty of poetry in between, dominated by Victor Hugo and Charles Baudelaire. We were introduced to Albert Camus, the only goalkeeper to have won a Nobel Prize for literature. Any study of Camus inevitably brought with it the story of the Algerian resistance to French rule and the French Algerians, known as the Pieds Noirs, who were even prepared to attempt a coup in France rather than see an independent Algeria. We wondered about the similarities in Northern Ireland and the Unionist supporters of Bill Craig, who were advocating an independent Ulster rather than accept reform of the structures of government.

At the beginning of the academic year, we were subjected to the annual retreat in the College Chapel for senior pupils. This was conducted by missionaries, all of whom hailed from the wilds of southern Ireland and had hardly ever been in the North. Most of them had spent the greater part of their missionary lives in the Philippines. Attendance was compulsory, as was silence within the College grounds. It kicked off on a Friday evening with Mass in the College Chapel, followed by a homily. Saturday was a full day of prayer and reflection and the retreat ended with Mass on Sunday morning. At the outset of the retreat on the Friday evening, I remember the missionary urging us to 'enter into the same spirit as the Kerry team.' I was perplexed about this analogy until he told us that Kerry, the reigning All-Ireland football champions, were preparing to return for another final at Croke Park. Now, it was beyond me to understand just exactly what virtues we could take from this quest for football success and introduce them into our spiritual lives. One of the boarders in my year, who hailed from the Gaelic football heartlands of County Tyrone was equally unimpressed and turned to me in Chapel and whispered, 'Kerry are dirty bastards.'

The missionary would have made a deeper impression on me if he had talked about soccer, in a year that was to prove one of Derry City's last in the Irish League. The club had qualified for a new tournament, the Texaco cup, which was cynically dubbed 'the British Isles cup for also-rans.' The other Northern

Ireland team was Ards but the English participants included Wolverhampton Wanderers and Tottenham Hotspurs, the first teams I had seen, on television, win the FA Cup. Derry hit the jackpot in drawing the once-mighty Wolves, then captained by Northern Ireland's Derek Dougan, the Doog. The first game was scheduled for Brandywell, for the first Tuesday in December, at three o' clock. This presented us with a problem as we were due to be in school until an hour later. It was also the first time that I became aware that some of the Wolves players had grave reservations about playing in what was now called the 'No Go areas of Londonderry'. The football authorities, doubtless taking their cue from government, were determined that the game should go ahead.

So great was the excitement throughout the city that shops brought forward the half day from Thursday to Tuesday to accommodate their staff and the President of the College allowed us to leave the College, at 2.30 pm, to go to the match. There were ten thousand crammed into the Brandywell with many sitting on the roof of the stand. Sadly, the Doog did not play, due to a shoulder injury and Wolves were captained by the Scottish international, Jimmy McCalliog, who had scored for Sheffield Wednesday in their 1966 FA Cup Final defeat to Everton. Derry held out against Wolves for over eighty minutes until Bobby Gould broke our hearts with a goal that proved to be the winner. With the clock ticking by, Wolves made a goal line clearance to deny us a deserved and historic result.

My musical appreciation improved greatly, in Lower Sixth, as I had the good fortune to be introduced to some classical music in the form of *Mozart 40*. A version, by Waldo de los Rios, an Argentinean composer and conductor, shot to the top of the UK pop charts. Hitherto, I had regarded classical music as the preserve of the upper middle classes, like the Schlegels in *Howard's End*, who went to concerts to listen to Beethoven's *Fifth Symphony*. I was therefore greatly impressed by the Mozart piece and the fact that it became an overnight hit. A work of Mozart, who lived in the second half of the eighteenth century, was suddenly popular two centuries later. Some of our class had taken a subject called Musical appreciation and they regaled us with stories about Mozart and his works more than a decade before the film, *Amadeus*, hit the big screen.

The first six months of my Lower Sixth year saw a seemingly quiet Derry, while events in Belfast were fast moving to armed confrontation. The story of these years in Derry was one of peaks and troughs in street disorders. While discontent was steadily bubbling beneath the surface, its emergence remained restricted to the low level rioting, regularly condemned in the columns of the Derry Journal as 'worse than senseless'. However, not all voices were raised to condemn the rioters and it was quite a story when, in the aftermath of rioting in October, the generally sedate Nationalist Party condemned 'baton-swinging troops' and not the rioters. It described the soldiers as 'an occupation army, who use chemical warfare to preserve a corrupt state.' This was heady stuff and it caused a few resignations by very senior members of the party. However, such a statement reflected a growing alienation of Catholics from the institutions of the state. It was also manna from heaven for the growing Provisional IRA movement in the city.

The traditional republican mantra was that the state was unjust, sectarian and irreformable. It held that peaceful politics would thus be ineffective and that the state had to be destroyed by force. My old History teacher, John Hume, was ever to the fore in condemning riots. However, Derry was no republican fiefdom and the republican narrative was far from being the only story. What seemed to have been forgotten, by many, was that non-violent agitation by the Civil Rights movement had achieved more in six months than had been achieved by the Nationalist Party and Republicans in the previous forty five years of the existence of the state of Northern Ireland. There was an equally, if not stronger, body of Catholic opinion that earnestly yearned for normality and saw attacks on the army as symptomatic of mere hooliganism and destructive tendencies that threatened stability. My parents were strongly in this latter camp but my father acknowledged that the army's actions were a recruiting sergeant for both the Official and the Provisional IRA.

Early in my Lower Sixth year in October, I went along to a public meeting in Magee College, which was organised by the local branch of the United Nations Association. It featured an attractive panel of speakers, Professor Bob McKenzie, who was well known from his television appearances on Election Night on the BBC, Professor J.C. Beckett, whose Irish history book was our staple diet for our A level course and his fellow Queen University Belfast historian, A.T.Q. Stewart, whose work, *The Ulster Crisis,* was the authority on Ulster resistance to Home Rule. Mc Kenzie stunned the audience, when he said that the end of Stormont was nearer than most people believed and Stewart concurred with this assessment, saying that suspension of Stormont could be imminent. Beckett disagreed, saying that it was unlikely that we would reach the position of direct rule from Westminster. I wondered if McKenzie had some inside information on the thinking of the Heath government and whether he was floating a 'Hawarden kite,' to borrow a phrase from Gladstone's conversion to Home Rule almost a century earlier. Surprisingly, there was little take up of the story in the media and it did not even make the front page of the local papers.

While on the streets there was a steady deterioration in relations between Derry's Catholic community and the British Army, the all-out shooting war involving the IRA lay ahead. We were scarcely back at school, in our senior years, when I found myself, an innocent by-stander, in the middle of a riot situation in Francis Street. It was a sunny Saturday afternoon, ideal weather for recreational rioting, which by five o' clock had progressed from Aggro Corner to Francis Street, just below St. Eugene's Cathedral. One of my class mates, Eamon Gallagher, lived in Francis Street and we took refuge with him, rather than run the gauntlet of an army 'snatch squad,' get arrested for rioting and receive a mandatory six month prison sentence. As a bonus, we had a grandstand view of proceedings outside.

A company of Scottish soldiers started replacing their glengarries with riot helmets as they faced the rioters, many of whom were stripped to the waist and obviously enjoying the fun in the sun. Weighed down with heavy equipment, the soldiers could not possibly have been enjoying themselves and the sweat was dripping from them. In a lull in the stone throwing, a young boy dared to go as close as he could to the army lines, cupped his hands and shouted at the top of his voice, 'Hi Jocks, did you hear the score; Rangers 2 and Celtic 3, f… youse.' The reaction of the soldiers was a sight to behold. Some of them raised their arms in celebration while others started shouting, 'Fenian bastards,' and were clearly unhappy with the score. Within minutes some of the soldiers were fighting with each other. The rioters burst out laughing and started singing the Celtic anthem, 'It's a Grand Old Team to Play For.' In this near pantomime atmosphere, another contingent of British soldiers appeared from Great James Street and started shepherding their Scottish colleagues away from the riot. A tall, megaphone wielding soldier then emerged and addressed the rioters. In clipped, Sandhurst tones, he announced; 'Gentlemen, the British Army is going home for its tea and suggests you do likewise.' It was probably the first time that many of the rioters had been addressed as 'gentlemen.' With this, his platoon did an about turn and disappeared down Great James Street. The rioters thought it was an elaborate ploy to create an ambush and they held their ground. However, the army had been true to its word and retreated all the way to its base at Victoria Market on the Strand Road. When I got home, I found that the wee lad had been giving the correct score of the first Old Firm game of the season.

Of course, there was more to life than watching riots. In our lower sixth year, we had started going to dances, which consisted of ceilis, a form of traditional Irish music evening. They were unlike modern dances, where you took a girl out to dance and stayed with her until the music stopped or she told you to get lost. In a ceili, you asked a girl to dance but the chances were you would be dancing half the time with other girls as well as the dances were very regimented with a dance master ensuring that you adhered to all the right move and steps. The names of the dances still stand out in my mind, although I have long forgotten the steps. *The Walls of Limreick, the Siege of Ennis, the Haymaker's Jig* and *the Waves of Tory* were the main dance routines. The music was provided usually by an accordionist, although for a Ceili Mor, a big event around St. Patrick's Day, there was the Charlie Kelly Ceili Band. The first formal ceili had been held in Ireland in 1897, although the dances dated back much longer. Ceili dancing, which was promoted by An Cumann Gaelach, the Irish language society, was deemed part of Irish culture and just as important as the language, music and the national games promoted by the Gaelic Athletic Association. At the end of the evening's dancing, the musician always played the Irish National Anthem. The dances we attended were mainly in the Ancient Order of Hibernians' Hall in Foyle Street, although for St. Patrick's Day, either the Embassy Ballroom, in Strand Road, or the Guildhall was the venue. We weren't really interested in ceilis as expression of Irish culture. We simply saw them as social occasion and the opportunity to meet girls.

I think that the College authorities must have been well aware that we were now young males anxious to meet young females, as our Religious Knowledge classes were increasingly dominated by advice on courtship and chastity. Fr. McElhinney was a very spiritual man but no stranger to reality. However, when he started talking about matters such as impure thoughts, you could feel the tension and embarrassment in class. No one wanted to be asked a question. One day, Fr. McElhinney was talking generally about confessing sins of impure thoughts and what a confessor might ask a penitent. He nailed one of our class, saying directly to him; 'I would ask you, did you entertain these impure thoughts and what would be your response?' My unfortunate classmate, who shall remain anonymous, did not know where to turn or what to answer and blurted out the words, 'No, Father, they entertained me.' There was uproar and even Wee Willie could not suppress a smile.

The dance scene in Derry soon brought us to the Embassy Ballroom, on the Strand Road, not just for ceilis, but for run-of-mill Saturday night dances and discos. It was still the age of the show bands, which had a large following. I recall that the Embassy held a number of competitions, one of which was called the Dandy Diddler Award for the best dressed man at the dance. As fate would have it, one of the weekly winners was a classmate called Jim Norris. He enjoyed his few days in the spotlight until, one morning, Monsignor Coulter, the President of the College, made an unannounced visit to our English Literature class as Willie Donaghy was in full flow on Shakespeare.

After a few pleasantries, Bunkum, as the President was nicknamed, cut to the chase. 'And how is Norris doing, Mr. Donaghy?' he asked. Willie was somewhat non-committal, which led to Bunkum beginning a eulogy on my classmate, whom he described as 'public spirited' and a member of the Knights of Malta. Then came the punch line; 'Did you know, Mr Donaghy, that Norris was the winner of the Dandy Diddler event in the Embassy Ballroom last weekend?' We could hardly suppress our giggles and Willie Donaghy had similar difficulties. Jim blushed. Bunkum was in full flow by this stage. 'Norris, would you tell the class, Mr. Donaghy and me, what you had to do to win this illustrious prize?' He said the words 'Dandy Diddler' through gritted teeth. Jim, who was sitting in the row beside me, quietly explained that he won because he was the best dressed man at the dance. Before he departed, Bunkum said, 'Norris, at least you weren't wearing your College blazer,' to which Jim responded, almost under his breath, 'I know Father, because I would not have won if I had been wearing it.' Bunkum pretended not to hear and left, having made his point.

There was a game of cat and mouse and some boys deliberately grew their hair longer than Bunkum permitted and a few attempted to grow beards, or at least stubbles. When confronted by our President, they often heard the sarcastic question, 'Are you doing it for a bet, son?' The usual punishment was to be sent to Seamus McColgan's barber shop in Waterloo Street, where hair was cut to an acceptable length before the return to the College.

Bunkum had more to worry him than Jim Norris being awarded the Dandy Diddler award. There were growing signs of antagonism between the British Army and the civilian population. The Army had a sand-bagged look-out fortification on the Walls, just above Bishop Gate, through which College boys made their way to the city centre. There were problems, especially when it was manned by Scottish soldiers. One day, the soldiers started hurl bottles, as well as abuse at College boys as they made their way through the Gate. A few of us went to Bunkum, who was horrified by such behaviour and said he would immediately contact a senior military commander. The behaviour ceased but you could discern a change in the relationship between Derry Catholics and the British Army. Inside the College, there was the growing problem for him that some of my contemporaries were attracted to, if not actively involved in, the IRA.

By the beginning of 1970, the patrons in the Embassy now also included soldiers stationed in the city and from the outset, there was a tension between the local young men and the soldiers for the affection of the young ladies. Our History teacher, Frank O'Kane, told us that Von Clausewitz, the famed Prussian General and military theorist, had once remarked that war was the continuation of politics by other means. It seemed to me that the Embassy Ballroom was becoming the alternative location for direct confrontation between local youths and British soldiers. It was rioting by other means and most of our sport was confined to watching from the balcony, as the stand-offs developed on the dance floor. We even had a spot light on the balcony and there was one occasion when we used it to great effect. One of the College's teachers was on the dance floor, doing his best to chat up a very good looking young woman. He was somewhat better dressed than the other locals of similar age, wearing suit, shirt and tie. One of our gang suddenly trained the spotlight on him and, leaning over the balcony, shouted to the a group of young men on the sidelines, 'Hey, your man's a Brit.' We made a hasty retreat before we were identified by the teacher in question but later discovered that he was more concerned in making a hasty retreat himself, rather than be confronted by the locals. The art of walking home to Creggan from ceilis and dances was to ensure that you avoided William Street, the epicentre of any disturbance and where you were most likely to be in danger of being arrested if any riot took place, which it normally did at the weekend.

The alternative to going to the Embassy or the Stardust dance halls was to go to the cinema and my final years saw a plethora of good films on show. *Butch Cassidy and the Sundance Kid, The French Connection, Dirty Harry, Ryan's Daughter* were but a few of the big movies to be screened in the ABC Cinema. However, it is the Dracula films, starring Christopher Lee, that stand out in my memory. *Taste the Blood of Dracula* and *Dracula Prince of Darkness* are two of the titles. The reason I remember them so fondly was because we would usually go in a gang and try to get seats behind a row of young women. Just as Count Dracula was about to sink his fangs into the neck of the unsuspecting maiden, we would lick the nails of our thumb and index finger and lean forward and gently bring them to bear on the neck of the girl directly in front of us. There would be a howl of anguish and indignation. Most of the time, such antics were quickly laughed off by the victims but on one occasion we were nearly ejected from the ABC.

A more serious and sinister development occurred, at that time, although we only became aware of it sometime later. Early in the New Year of 1971, the Provisional IRA Army Council sanctioned offensive operations against the British Army. The inevitable soon happened in Belfast. In February, Gunner Robert Curtis of the Royal Artillery Regiment, became the first British soldier shot dead in Ireland since the days when Lloyd George was Prime Minister, half a century earlier. It had been almost eighteen months since the British Army had been deployed on the streets of Northern Ireland. Gunner Curtis died in a situation that was fast becoming the norm. Increasingly, there was organised rioting to lure soldiers into situations where they were vulnerable to IRA snipers and blast bombs. There was widespread shock and revulsion when, a month later, the IRA in Belfast shot dead three young Scottish soldiers, lured to their deaths while off-duty, drinking in a Belfast pub. There were immediate calls for tougher security measures and over 4,000 shipyard workers marched on Unionist Party headquarters in Belfast, demanding the immediate introduction of internment.

In the same month, the army suffered its first fatality in Derry when a young soldier died as a result of a petrol bomb attack on his Land Rover, in Westland Street, in the Bogside. In an Easter address, the Provisional IRA confirmed that it would be going on the offensive against the security forces, an announcement post fact. However, in Derry, the shooting war with the army had not commenced and it was rumoured that the IRA leadership in Belfast sent two of its leading gunmen to Derry to kick start it as they felt that the local IRA units were not pulling their weight. James Chichester-Clark, who succeeded Terence O'Neill as Prime Minister, signalled the severity of the situation declaring 'Northern Ireland was at war with the IRA Provisionals.' Within a month, he resigned but the war continued.

Politically, in March, the picture had changed, as Brian Faulkner had finally realised his ambition by becoming Prime Minister. In his first broadcast, he announced that the kernel of the immediate problems was the law and order situation and that his priority was the elimination of terrorism, sabotage and the ending of riots and disorder. The IRA's bombing campaign had begun in late 1970 and the army introduced a new term into our vocabulary, 'organised terrorism.' Faulkner appointed Albert Anderson, the MP for the Londonderry constituency, as a Parliamentary Secretary with responsibility for the 'security situation on the ground.'

Within a few months of Faulkner taking office, the loyalist leader, John McKeague, became the first, and, as it transpired, the only person to be prosecuted under the Prevention of Incitement to Hatred Act that had been put on the statute book the previous year. A jury acquitted him of all charges. McKeague had published a loyalist version of the lyrics of the song '*I was born Under a Wandering Star*,' taken from the film, *Paint Your Wagon*. The lyrics of McKeague's publication, for which he was prosecuted, included the lines:

*"If guns were made for shooting, then skulls were made to crack
You've never seen a better Taig (slang for Catholic) than with a bullet in his back."*

Politically, the new Prime Minister, Brian Faulkner, balanced a tough law and order agenda with an offer to the SDLP of participation in government through the chairmanship of important parliamentary committees. To the suggestion that the SDLP could share in government, he was dismissive, describing such a scenario as 'A Bedlam cabinet-a kind of fragmentation bomb virtually certain to fly apart at the first meeting.' At least, there was the beginning of a thinking process as to how the Catholic/Nationalist minority could be accommodated in the state, without tearing it down. As the Provisional IRA was commencing its bombing campaign in Belfast, the initial SDLP reaction to Faulkner's offer of committee chairmanships was very positive, indicating a willingness to find a peaceful and parliamentary resolution to division. Paddy Devlin described it as Faulkner's 'finest hour.' However, even as we had been finishing our Lower Sixth year at the College, the centre of political gravity had been moving from the marble halls of Stormont to the streets. In Derry, the IRA's response to political developments was an escalation of terrorist violence.

Chapter Fifteen
All Hell is Let Loose

Internment and 'Chirpy Chirpy Cheep Cheep' – Young women are 'tarred and feathered' in the No Go Areas – The end of senior football as Ballymena FC team bus is burned out at Brandywell

The summer of 1971 saw an increase of violence in Derry and beyond. After a year in which the British Army had been attacked with hand-thrown missiles, hundreds of rounds were now being fired by the IRA in the space of a few days in July. It seemed that the situation had moved from isolated incidents to a full-out attack on the Security Forces. In July, there were four continuous days of rioting. Amid both daily and nightly rioting, during which the army had been fired on more than sixty times, soldiers returned fire in the Bogside and shot dead two local civilians, Seamus Cusack and Dessie Beattie.

The army alleged that Cusack was carrying a rifle and that Beattie was about to throw a bomb. These allegations were strongly denied by the local populace. Seamus Cusack came from a large, well-known family in Melmore Gardens Creggan, a stone's through from my home. He was believed not to be involved in the IRA. There was widespread anger and shock at his death and barricades were erected in Creggan. When he was shot, Seamus Cusack had been removed to a hospital in Letterkenny, across the Border and a half hour's drive from Derry. It was becoming common practice to take Catholics injured in clashes with the army to Letterkenny as it was believed that if they had gone to the hospital in Derry, Altnagelvin, the details of their injuries would have been passed on the police. On this occasion, if Seamus Cusack had been taken to Altnagelvin Hospital, in Derry, he might have survived. In the wake of these deaths, for the first time there were gun attacks on the British Army post at Bligh's Lane. It is no exaggeration to say that with this first instance of a return of fire by the Army, the Catholic community in Derry went, in the words of one Army commander, 'from benevolent support to complete alienation.' There was a distinct possibility that any political vacuum would be quickly filled by both wings of the IRA.

A few days after the funerals, the Provisional IRA held an open-air rally in the Bogside. Mrs Maire Drumm, a leading republican from Belfast addressed the meeting and made a public appeal for volunteers. She told the assembled youth that it was past time to be shouting, 'Up the IRA.' It was time, she said, for them to join the IRA. There was a surge of young men of my age who queued up to join up. In a statement, the IRA vowed to avenge the killings. The majority of those who joined the IRA did not come from families steeped in republicanism but simply joined as a way of hitting back at the army, the police and the whole apparatus of government. As the Troubles intensified in Derry, more young men of my generation rushed to join the IRA, I was impressed by the words from J.D. Salinger's *The Catcher in the Rye*, 'The mark of the immature man is that he wants to die nobly for a cause, while the mark of the mature man is that he wants to live humbly for one.' There were unfortunately, too many young men who not only wanted to die for Ireland but were prepared to kill for Ireland as well.

A few hundred yards away from the IRA rally being addressed by Maire Drumm, there was a crisis meeting in John Hume's home, as the most of the SDLP leadership toyed with finding a response to the killings and attempted to ensure that a brake was put on the efforts of the IRA to become the sole spokesmen for the Catholic community. The SDLP issued an ultimatum to the British government that either there would be an impartial public inquiry into the deaths of Beattie and Cusack, or else the party would withdraw from the Stormont parliament. In politics, once you make a threat you have to be prepared to carry it out. A few months earlier, Brian Faulkner had won plaudits from the SDLP for his initial statements about involving the Opposition MPs in the process of government as committee chairmen, He now expressed disappointment at what he termed the irresponsibility of the SDLP for indulging in 'the instant politics of every issue as it arises without consideration of the long-term effects.' The threat to withdraw from Stormont looked like an empty gesture as parliament was in its summer recess. I greatly doubted if the British government would give way and there were very few people, in Derry, who believed that any inquiry would be established. The British Army was the last line of defence in Northern Ireland and neither the British Government nor any member of Brian Faulkner's Cabinet at Stormont openly questioned the army's version of an increasing number of shooting incidents in Derry and elsewhere. No official inquiry was established. An unofficial inquiry, headed by Lord Gifford, QC, concluded that neither Cusack nor Beattie had been armed, when shot.

I wondered if the withdrawal from Stormont signalled an end to politics and a return to street protests as a norm. Any prospects for political progress came to an end and the reality was that the SDLP was becoming irrelevant as we were facing direct confrontation between the IRA and the British Army. Reginald Maudling, the Home Secretary, repeated the phrase, initially used by James Chichester-Clark, that a state of war existed between the IRA and the British

Army. The remaining July days were dominated by gun battles between the IRA and the Army. There was alarm when John Taylor, the Minister of State in the Ministry of Home Affairs at Stormont, spoke about the shootings in Derry of Seamus Cusack and Dessie Beattie. He said that prompt action was needed to bring the IRA's growing campaign to and end and that it might be necessary for the Security Forces to take an even firmer line with rioters. With the prospect of more shootings of civilians, I was glad to be going to the Donegal seaside resort of Bundoran, sixty miles away from Derry, with a few of my classmates.

In the mid 1970s, Bundoran, like many seaside resorts in county Donegal, acquired a reputation as a haven for IRA gunmen on the run from the authorities in Northern Ireland. In 1971, however, it was still a major holiday resort with plenty of hotels, bars with nightly music, sandy beaches and the Astoria dance hall where the show bands played nightly. There were big names, such as Brian Coll and the Buckaroos, Big Tom and the Mainliners and Joe Dolan, playing there during the summer months. Together with two of my classmates, Gerry Conway and Aidan Mc Grath, I stayed in a B&B in the Main Street, the *Stella Maris*, Star of the Sea, and had a leisurely break away from the troubles in the North. On the Monday morning of 9th August, we were surprised to hear on the radio that interment without trial had been introduced in Northern Ireland. The British Army called it *Operation Demetrius*. It was not named after the young Athenian lover in Shakespeare's 'A Midsummer Night's Dream' but more likely after the Macedonian military leader from ancient history.

Internment was accompanied by a ban on all marches for six months, which, at least, meant that there would be no Apprentice Boys' parade in Derry a few days later. From television and radio reports as well as from the pages of *The Irish News*, we learned that Northern Ireland literally went up in flames when internment was introduced. Barricades again went up in Derry and the RUC police station at Rosemount became the focal point of day long attacks by stones and petrol bombs. Several bursts of machine gun fire were directed at troops. In the two days following internment, twenty four people were killed in Northern Ireland. The number was made up of twenty civilians, two British Army soldiers and two members of the IRA. In the housing estate in Ballymurphy in West Belfast, eleven Catholic civilians were killed by the British paratroopers, the same troops who, within six months, would be involved in Bloody Sunday in Derry.

The day after the introduction of internment, Bombardier Paul Challoner of the Royal Horse Artillery became the first British Army soldier shot dead in Derry, killed by a sniper's bullet as he manned an observation post in Bligh's Lane. The shots were fired from Eastway Gardens in the Creggan, just a few hundred yards from my home. He was the 100th person to die since the first UVF killings of Catholics in 1966. Within three months, a further half dozen British soldiers had been killed by the IRA, in Derry, in a campaign that increasingly seemed to have been planned well in advance. In our first month back at the College, two soldiers were killed at the Bligh's Lane army post, which was on our route to school.

No loyalist paramilitaries had been lifted in the swoops. This did not go down well with the wider Catholic community as Loyalist paramilitary violence had been ever-present from the Malvern street killings of 1966, through explosions designed to topple Terence O'Neill and the shooting dead of the first policeman on the Shankill Road in a weekend of violent protest against the Hunt Report on policing.

More than three hundred men were lifted in the first swoops, which included only sixteen from the Derry area, including leading republicans Sean Keenan and Johnny White. Another of the internees was Mickey Montgomery, a leading member of the Official IRA. Within a few weeks of being interned, a statement by him was smuggled from prison. In it, he alleged being subjected to what amounted to torture by the police and army. It wasn't just about roughing up men, who had been lifted, but involved what became known as 'the five techniques' of interrogation. This involved placing a hood over the head, forcing the internee to stand spread eagled against a wall for long periods, denying regular sleep patterns, providing irregular and limited food and water and subjecting internees to white noise in the form of a constant humming sound. He was not alone in making such allegations.

With internment, Northern Ireland erupted in violence and gun battles. I phoned home and my mother advised me to stay in Bundoran as long as possible, as life in Derry was both grim and dangerous. I returned to Derry on the Saturday afternoon of 14th August, just as an anti-internment was taking place in Guildhall Square. Surprisingly, there was a very small turnout of less than one thousand people, which may have spoken volumes in itself. The wider Catholic community was fed up to the teeth with IRA violence and wanted to see gunmen removed from the streets. The only point of dissent was whether it should be by way of internment or bringing them before the courts. A year earlier, Jack Lynch had said that he was prepared to introduce internment in the Republic, if circumstances of a threat to the Republic demanded it. At the Guildhall Square rally, I remember Bernadette Devlin making an impassioned speech. She said the time for talking was over and that it was time for action. I wondered what action she had in mind and whether she was, in reality, giving Jack Lynch the green light to introduce internment in the Republic.

Back in Creggan, I found a significant difference. The following week, over one thousand soldiers descended on Bogside and Creggan and there was intense rioting as the army made further arrests and attempted to dismantle barricades. As soon as the soldiers dismantled barricades they were rebuilt. The barricades were destined to stay in place for the next eleven months. The fighting was taking place literally outside our front door, rather than being contained within the Bogside. Creggan was saturated with tear gas. The soldiers fired a canister through the front room window of the home of one of my friends, Kathleen Grant, in Malin Gardens. Attacks on the army post at Bligh's Lane were met with volleys of CS gas and rubber bullets. Fr Martin Rooney, the administrator of St. Mary's, normally the mildest of men, called for the removal of the army post to allow normality to be restored. The IRA carried out a propaganda coup by holding a press conference in the Bogside, while soldiers were literally outside the front door. Taking part were Sean MacStiofain, Seamus Twomey, Daiti O'Conaill and Martin McGuinness, all of whom were presumably on the wanted list. On a gable wall on Cable Street was painted the words, BA-HA HA. They were not meant as a sneer at a Bachelor of Arts degree but at the British Army!

Within a month of the introduction of internment, the government had created POW style camps to house the internees. Only perimeter security was maintained by the state and the internees were free to run their own compounds. In reality, the British were creating terrorist universities in which the IRA were to plot and plan the future of their armed struggle. There were also signs of a questioning of policy at the highest levels of government in London. In September, in the House of Commons, the Home Secretary, Reginald Maudling recognised that Catholic grievances had moved on and that the government was trying to devise a formula for the 'permanent and guaranteed role of the minority community as well as the majority in the life and public affairs of the Province.' Few paid any attention to his words, which signalled a major change in government policy. It was the right political aim but, amidst the mounting violence, it looked like a utopian dream to me. There were two separate issues to be addressed, the security situation and the political situation. Although separate, they were interlinked and one reacted on the other. Internment applied exclusively to Nationalist and Republican areas, and accompanied by the interrogation techniques, simply increased alienation among the minority.

Internment also brought to a head the growing divisions between constitutional nationalists and physical force republicans. Just before internment, Fr. James Coulter, the President of the College delivered an insightful address to a conference in the seminary in Kiltegan, County Wicklow. The title of his paper was 'Catholicism – Its impact on the Northern Situation.' In the course of his address, he said, 'In practice, Catholic support for the IRA was very little but emotionally it was considerable.' He bluntly asserted, 'Too many soldiers had sworn perjured evidence against alleged rioters; too many people had been beaten up after arrest...'

In such an environment, constitutional nationalist politicians were trying to channel popular opposition through peaceful means and advocated a campaign of civil disobedience and passive resistance, which included a rent and rates strike. The political leaders took the line that there would be no engagement with, or participation in, the state bodies such as district councils until internment was ended. They argued that 'political' detainees should be released and those not released should be charged before the courts. I was doubtful if this situation would came to pass as it seemed to me that there was a real problem is applying the criminal law in situations where it was difficult, if not impossible to get the necessary evidence against alleged paramilitaries, given the potential threats to witnesses. A one day strike was called for in Derry. In sharp contrast the paltry numbers who had attended the Guildhall Square demo, it was reported in *The Derry Journal* that eight thousand people had taken part in the strike. In contrast with the policy of peaceful protests urged by constitutional nationalist leaders, republicans had launched an all-out shooting war against the state and its Security Forces. As violence escalated, there did not appear to be any possibility of internment being dispensed with as a weapon in the fight against republican paramilitaries. The internees were soon housed in a specially built camp at Long Kesh, which was near to Lisburn. Long Kesh was a series of compounds of Nissan huts, reminiscent of the old Springtown Camp on the outskirts of Derry.

It was a classic chicken and egg situation. Which came first, the violence of the paramilitaries or the coercive measures of the state? From my O level study of Irish history, I was reminded that even Gladstone had introduced a very draconian Coercion Act in 1881. The constitutional lawyer, Dicey, had opined that the Act, which suspended Habeas Corpus, enabled the Viceroy in Dublin Castle to lock up anybody he pleased and detain them as long as he pleased while the Act was in force. It seemed that little had changed in the intervening seventy years.

Just over a week after the introduction of internment, there was an anti-interment protest on Laburnum Terrace, which is the main road marking the divide between Bogside and Creggan. Constitutional nationalist leaders such as John Hume, were now to the fore of opposition to internment, which may well have appeared to Unionists as being supportive of the IRA. The British military moved along the Lone Moor Road, towards the crowd, and tried to break up the protest with riot squad and water cannon, which sprayed coloured dye. The idea behind the dye was to enable soldiers to arrest people covered in it, maybe hours after the protest itself. John Hume instructed the demonstrators to sit down on the road, which they duly did and many were arrested, including Hume and his fellow MP, Ivan Cooper. It has transpired that the Royal Marines officer who arrested Hume was none other than Paddy Ashdown, later leader of the Liberal Democrats at Westminster. Getting arrested did Hume's street credibility no harm whatsoever as he followed in a long lineage of nationalist leaders, including Charles Stewart Parnell, who were arrested under previous Coercion Acts.

I watched from the iron steps that led from the Beechwood Avenue to the New Road as baton-wielding soldiers weighed into the protestors and showed no mercy. As I started making my way back towards Creggan, there were a few young men, who were watching the demonstration impassively. I recognised one of them as one of my former classmates from the Christian Brothers, who came from a well-known republican family. We started talking about Hume being arrested and he was contemptuous of the protest taking place. He coldly said that there was only one form of action that would get the British out of Ireland and that it would be the IRA that would carry out such a campaign. It was clear that the shooting war was about to begin in earnest in Derry. Within hours there were fierce gun battles, mainly in the Creggan and Brandywell areas. In all, there were twenty three shooting incidents in Derry, within a period of two hours. Barely a week after the death of Paul Challoner of the British Army, Eamonn Lafferty, aged nineteen became the first IRA member shot dead in Derry, by the army in a gun battle. He was related to me on my father's side. His family had been my father's cousins who had famously told him not to return to visit them in Bishop Street until he had changed out out his British army uniform in1945. Eamonn Lafferty's funeral was attended by more than two thousand mourners and hundred lined the funeral route. Three men wearing black berets walked on each side of the hearse as a guard of honour and the coffin was draped with the Tricolour.

There was now almost daily rioting at the Army post in Bligh's Lane. People used to park their cars on Eastway Road and watch this new form of recreation until the Army hit a few of them with rubber bullets. Three weeks later, as we returned to the College to begin our Upper Sixth year, it was fair to say, in the words of William Butler Yeats, that 'all changed, changed utterly.' One of my classmates, Tucker Doherty was stunned as he told us that his father's apprentice butcher, a young Martin Mc Guinness, was now head of the IRA in Derry.

As we returned to the College for our final year, Cardinal Conway and the five, northern Catholic bishops issued a statement, denouncing the IRA and criticising internment. Their statement attacked the 'Small group of people, who are trying to secure a united Ireland by the use of force,' and posed the question, 'who in their sane senses wants to bomb a million Protestants in to a united Ireland?' The statement fell on deaf ears. The Provisional IRA's response was quick and pointed and, within a few weeks, it exploded a bomb in a bar in the Shankill Road, killing two men and injuring thirty others. The Provos seemed intent on provoking a loyalist backlash. It was therefore no surprise that the same month saw the establishment of the Ulster Defence Association, merging a wide range of loyalist vigilante and paramilitary groups. Within a few months there was a spate of tit for tat sectarian killings carried out by the IRA and loyalist paramilitaries. We appeared to be heading for Armageddon.

Killings were not confined to republican and loyalist paramilitaries. Within weeks of our return to the College, the British Army shot dead Billy McGreanery, He had worked in McLaughlin's Shoe Shop in Waterloo Street, and, for years, I had bought my football boots from him. He was shot from a look out post in the army base at Bligh's Lane, where earlier that day a soldier died, shot by an IRA sniper. Billy was the most civil, inoffensive, person you could ever meet and his death was regarded simply as retaliation for the killing of the soldier. A few weeks later, Annette McGavigan, the sister of one of my school friends, was shot dead by the army, whose press release said she was shot in crossfire in a gun battle with the IRA. Locals disputed this saying there was no gun battle at the time of her death although gunmen were seen in the vicinity. Gary Gormley, a three year old child was killed along the Foyle Road, when he was struck by an army armoured vehicle. An army major in the Royal Green Jackets was seriously wounded in a shooting incident in William Street, as his platoon was protecting firemen tackling a blaze. Five months later, he died of his wounds, on Bloody Sunday, 31st January, 1972.

Cryptic humour was provided by the television coverage of a confrontation between rival Protestant and Catholic mobs in Belfast. The Protestants were gleefully singing their own lyrics to a pop tune that was at the top of the charts, *Chirpy Chirpy Cheep Cheep* by a group with the singularly inappropriate name, *Middle of the Road*. Taunting the Catholics over internment, the Protestant mob was singing:

Where's your Daddy gone?
Where' your Daddy gone?
Far Far Away
Woke up this morning and your Daddy was gone
Chirpy Chirpy Cheep Cheep

Internment marked the beginning of a sad and sorry sight. It continued for years for the families of those in prison as they were taken in minibuses to visit their relatives and bring them food parcels as well as company. I would see the visitors, who were mainly women, waiting to be collected at the Creggan shops. They looked both miserable and despairing. I am sure they often wondered why and how their sons and daughters had become involved in the paramilitaries A new organisation was formed, the Prisoners' Dependants' Fund and its members stood outside Mass every Sunday, with large sweet jars, collecting money. Inside the churches, prayers were regularly said from the altar for an end to violence and for the 'prisoners.'

Against this backdrop of intensified violence, I returned to the College. Many of my school friends in Creggan had been a year ahead of me and they went off to university, in the autumn of 1971. Hugh Morrison went off to Queen's, in Belfast, to read Mathematics, while Tony Peppard headed to London to read English. A number of the girls, Gay Callan and Kathleen Grant, also went to Queen's. Arthur Duffy went off to Maynooth to study for the priesthood. Each morning, in the past, we used to meet at the roundabout at the top of the New Road. It was now a lonely place each morning. Christmas was the first time I met up with them when they returned to Derry for the end of term holidays. They seemed changed by their university experience and their fashion senses and musical tastes had certainly changed. Hugh Morrison and Tony Peppard had grown their hair quite longer than the College would have considered acceptable. Flared trousers were all the go, together with a return of Oxford Bags and Gay took to them with relish. Sandy Denny and *Fairport Convention* had replaced the Beatles in their musical tastes. By contrast, I had started going to Borderland, a dance hall just a few miles over the border in Muff, on a Friday night and was revelling in jiving with Margaret Hannaway, the best jiver with who I have ever had the pleasure of jiving. My friends, who were now at university, probably thought I was a Neanderthal.

On a serious not, my university friends also told me that life in Belfast had its increasing pattern of gun battles. The girls, who were staying at the Aquinas Hall of Residence, on the Falls Road, said they had to lie on the floor as the nightly gun battles took place between the IRA and the British Army. All of which convinced me that Belfast would not be my chosen university location.

As a result of the continuing violence, the Current Affairs Society at the College, of which I was then chairman, had to plan a more restricted series of meetings. Early in first term, we held an evening meeting, which was addressed by Robert Cooper, who was a leading member of one of the new political parties, the Alliance Party of Northern Ireland. Although educated at Foyle College in

Derry, Cooper admitted that this was the first time he had set foot inside St. Columb's. His talk was very instructive. For the first time in our lives, we heard someone espouse a unionist philosophy, based on a party drawn from Protestants, Catholics and Dissenters, united in wanting Northern Ireland to succeed. Alliance sounded a very attractive proposition.

Our committee planned a series of meetings with other political leaders. In particular, we were eager to hear our former history teacher, John Hume, on the apparently revised SDLP policy of pressing for the suspension of the Stormont Parliament. In addition, the party seemed to be advocating Irish unity, rather than reform. However, Monsignor Coulter, the College President, advised us that in the current atmosphere, it would be inappropriate to bring students back to the College for evening meetings and advised that we defer any meetings until the Spring. The Current Affairs Society became one of the first victims of the renewed upsurge of street violence and never met again. The senior debating committee, consisting of student representatives of Thornhill, Foyle, High School and the College continued to meet and planned a series of debates that were held in the afternoons, straight after school. All schools, apart from the College, hosted these debates as our location, on Bishop's Street, was not regarded as neutral territory. The *Derry Journal* continued to sponsor senior debating competitions, which was one of the few forums in Derry where Catholic and Protestant students met socially. After school debates became one of the few pastimes now available. The new norm was that we went home after and stayed there most evenings of the week. We felt we were victims of the Troubles but, at least, we were still alive with the prospect of getting out of Derry and Northern Ireland by going to university. A Level examination success would be our passport to escape!

Both the committee and members of the Current Affairs Society in the College had been eager to hear the SDLP explain its withdrawal from Stormont Their withdrawal had been followed at the end of August by the withdrawal of thirty prominent Catholics from public bodies such as the Development Commission, the Police Liaison Committee and the Board of Governors of the Technical College. My father remarked, acidly, that at some stage the boycotters would have to swallow their pride and return to these bodies. In an attempt to show total alienation from the structures of government that had pertained at Stormont for half a century, the SDLP and other Nationalist politicians met in an alternative assembly in the Castle in Dungiven, a town twenty miles from Derry, on the main road to Belfast. My father was equally dismissive of the establishment of what became derisively dubbed 'the Dungiven parliament,' as an alternative to Stormont. It met only once.

In its only session, John Hume quoted words of Edward Carson's defiance of the Home Rule Bill of 1912. He gave a modern twist with his statement; 'We do not recognise the authority of the Stormont Parliament, we do not care tuppence if this is treason or not.' We analysed these words in our history class and noted that Hume had not refused to recognise the authority of the Westminster parliament but no journalist had quizzed him on this issue. In chats at the schools' debating committee, my friends from Foyle said they were aghast at the course of action being taken by so-called moderates in the Catholic community, who a few months earlier were welcoming Brian Faulkner's initiatives. One of them went as far as to say that Hume was really giving cover to the IRA attacks on the existence of the state. The gulf between Catholic and Protestant perceptions was becoming a chasm that extended to our generation.

While prominent Catholics were withdrawing from public life to register their opposition to internment, I was witnessing what I regarded as a far more important sequence of events unfolding, with the beginning of the end of senior soccer in the Brandywell stadium. Ballymena United arrived for an Irish League game in September and the team bus was burned out, just outside the Brandywell. As a result, most of the teams in the Irish League joined Linfield in refusing to play in Derry. The Irish Football Association, with whom Derry City had enjoyed a fractious relationship, directed that home matches were to be transferred to Coleraine, thirty miles away. In the long term, this was financially unsustainable for Derry City and a year later the board of directors formally requested permission to return to Brandywell. The matter was put to a vote of the clubs and despite support from Ballymena United, the motion to return was defeated by six votes to five with Coleraine abstaining. The formal response from Derry City was to withdraw from the Irish League, thus bringing down the curtain on senior football in the city that went back to 1929. Senior football did not return to Brandywell until 1985, when Derry City was admitted to the League of Ireland in the Republic, rather than the Irish League in Northern Ireland.

As a result of interment, the barricades had gone back up in Creggan and Bogside and both wings of the IRA soon started to hold themselves out as the legitimate authority within what became known as the 'No Go' areas. The Provisionals' way of enforcing their authority began with the tarring and feathering of three men who they claimed were involved in petty crime. They also warned local girls not to 'fraternise' with British soldiers. In three separate incidents at the beginning of October, three young women were taken from their homes in the Bogside, tied to lamp posts, their heads were shaved and tar and feathers were poured over them. A placard was then hung over their shoulders, which read 'soldier doll.' One of these unfortunate girls was Marta Doherty, who was due to marry a British soldier a few days later. Larry Doherty, the Derry Journal photographer, captured the moment and overnight, the photograph of Marta Doherty, tied to a lamppost, head shaved, covered in feathers and dripping with tar, went worldwide or viral, to quote the modern term. There was widespread outrage in Derry.

A few weeks later, in Creggan, just behind the community centre a few hundred yards from my home, the IRA attempted to emulate the feats of their Bogside comrades and dragged a young woman from her home, accusing her of fraternising with soldiers. The scene was set for a repetition of the earlier incident, as the scissors, tar and feathers were produced. However, a local priest had been summoned and he attempted to dissuade the IRA from carrying out their punishment. The woman allegedly had a reputation for loose morals but not for fraternising with British soldiers. The IRA was insistent that she had been in the army post at Brooke Park the previous night. The priest asked her to tell her would-be attackers where she had been. 'Father, I couldn't tell them that,' she replied. Drawing on some kind of divine inspiration, he said, 'Tell me aloud as if you were in the confession box.' After an embarrassed delay and as the would-be attackers were about to lose any patience, she blurted out the words, 'Last night I was on my back on a spud boat.' The growing circle of onlookers burst out laughing and the IRA unit quickly withdrew, leaving their tar and feathers behind them. There weren't any further incidents of tarring and feathering in Creggan but a few girls, who were engaged to British soldiers, left Derry quickly. Their number included Margaret Thompson, who was a close friend of my cousin Mary Mc Daid.

While Marta Doherty became known worldwide as a result of the attack on her, there was no similar publicity for a woman called Kathleen Thompson who was shot dead by a British Army soldier, as she stood in her garden, in Creggan, a few weeks later. It was another funeral I attended as I knew her sons from primary school days. There was widespread anger in Creggan at the death of Mrs Thompson and the local Tenants' Association compared the action of the British Army to those of the notorious Black and Tans, half a century earlier.

In the months leading up to Christmas, the British Army carried out a few major raids, in the middle of the night, into Creggan as part of follow-up internment swoops. I think they were also testing out the IRA defence of the area. When the soldiers appeared, the bin lids would be rattled on the estate as signal of the army's approach. It reminded me of what we were then studying about the tocsin being sounded in Revolutionary Paris in the 1790s to summon defenders. One night, a platoon was pinned down at the side our home. The soldiers had the protection of a sturdy wall but their assailants began trying to bounce nail bombs off the gable of our house onto the soldiers. I was lying in bed when there was the crash of a bomb exploding outside and the window shattered. The venetian blind came to my rescue but I got out of bed and crouched against the wall, calling to my father and mother that I was safe and advising them not to come into the room. I gathered that the soldiers were becoming a bit desperate to stop this assault. I heard an English voice give the order, 'Shoot any bomber.' A few shots were fired by the army. However, the next morning there were no reports on the radio of any casualties and there were no signs of any blood having been spilt or any empty cartridge casings. The immediate task at hand was to arrange for wire mesh protection for the windows and for years, until the IRA ceasefire in 1994, these became permanent features in Creggan.

On one of these army sorties into Creggan, a young soldier was left behind in the confusion. A similar incident had occurred in Belfast when the IRA had shot dead a soldier and stolen his weapon. In the Creggan incident, the errant soldier was much luckier. He took refuge in the outbuildings of the parochial house at the bottom of Broadway, which used to be a farm. This particular outhouse was used as a garage by the priests, one of whom discovered the soldier when he was getting his car as he was going to say early morning Mass. He made the young soldier change clothes from his combat gear to a black clerical suit and drove him to Ebrington Barracks in the Waterside. The story only emerged years later.

By the end of the year, there had been a litany of deaths in Derry and throughout Northern Ireland and it was virtually impossible to keep up to date with the death count. Nineteen people were killed in Derry that year, including nine British soldiers. The Official IRA took to using dumdum bullets in its attacks on soldiers. The Provisional IRA introduced its latest weapon, the car bomb, that destroyed many city centres. In Derry, as elsewhere, women were increasingly involved in IRA attacks and were widely regarded as more uncompromising than their male counterparts.

One night, just outside the grounds of St. Mary's Church, and less than a hundred yards from my home, a British soldier, leaving a local girl home from a dance, was apprehended by women members of the Official IRA. There was general commotion, which I heard and went to investigate. The women wanted to hang him from a lamppost, there and then. Someone even went to get them a rope. A crowd gathered and there was considerable debate about the young soldier's fate. Again a priest was sent for. He arrived at the same time as a car load of IRA men pulled up. They clearly didn't want to see such an execution carried out that evening. It was not that they cared for the fate of a British soldier, whom they would have had little compunction killing with a sniper's bullet. However, coming shortly after the Marta Doherty fiasco, it would simply have been unwelcome publicity for the IRA. They gave the priest their assurance that the soldier would not be harmed if he could secure his release. This was going to prove a hard task as the Amazons were in full cry and demanding a lynching. Staring the ringleader straight in the eye and addressing her directly, the priest asked, 'Was your husband not wearing a British Army uniform the morning I married you here in St. Mary's?' There was a hushed silence, broken only by the comment of a fellow Amazon, 'We didn't know your man was a Brit.' In the ensuing disorder, the IRA men grabbed the soldier, threw him into the back seat of their car and sped off. They kept their word to the priest and released the soldier, unharmed, near Derry Walls, and told him never to return to Creggan.

Far from the madding crowd, our first term in Upper Sixth was ending. We had the a pleasant surprise to learn that Fr. Devine, the college Dean and our Religious Knowledge teacher, had been replaced by the recently ordained Fr. Colm Clerkin. It was like a new broom sweeping away the cobwebs. There was much rejoicing throughout the College when the Monk packed his bags and headed to Maghera, where he became Principal of St. Patrick's High School. Fr. Clerkin was a breath of fresh air and our studies took on an interesting dimension.

Within a few months, we were studying the documents of Vatican Council II and grappling with the debate on the theory of a Just War. Our focus was on the Church teaching contained in 'Gaudiam et Spes,' which proclaimed 'any act of war aimed indiscriminately at the destruction of entire cities of extensive areas along with their population is a crime against God and man himself. It merits unequivocal condemnation.' Fr. Clerkin turned this in the direction of the IRA's campaign of 'armed struggle' and there was lively debate as atrocities such as the Abercorn Restaurant bombing of March 1972 and the whole question of the alleged legitimacy of the IRA's 'war.' While the majority of the class was strongly opposed to the campaign of violence on the streets, there was a significant and vociferous minority that felt that the IRA was justified in its actions. The debate in the classroom could never be duplicated on the streets of Creggan, as openly voicing opposition to the IRA would have left one vulnerable to being dubbed a 'Brit lover,' attacked and intimidated out of the estate.

Reading the tabloid press, one could have been forgiven for believing that the No Go areas of Creggan and Bogside were havens sheltering hundreds of IRA gunmen, backed and protected by the vast majority of the local population. Nothing could have been further from the truth. The vast majority of people did not support the IRA but were very critical of army tactics. Common sense dictated that if you disagreed with the IRA, the safest thing to do was to keep your head down, keep your opinions to yourself and try get on with everyday life. Contrary to popular myth, the overwhelming majority of young men of my generation did not join the IRA but instead tried to live normal lives under exceptionally abnormal and stressful conditions. Walking to the college each day, we watched, as the Provisional IRA set up headquarters inside the Gasworks complex in Stanley's Walk and openly paraded through the streets of the Bogside with rifles. They also set up a headquarters in an unoccupied shop in Central Drive.

In Germany, Baader Meinhof, the left-wing terrorist grouping, had a penchant for stealing top of the range BMWs to such an extent that the car was soon dubbed the *Baader Meinhof Wagen*. In the No Go area of Derry, however, our Provo 'liberators' were content to drive round in Ford Cortinas, that they had hi-jacked from Desmond's Garage on the Strand Road. Meanwhile the Official IRA had to make do with cars hijacked from members of the public. One morning, it was somewhat ironic to encounter a carload of hooded IRA men outside Mc Cool's newsagents, after their night shift. They parked their hi-jacked Ford Cortina, took off their balaclavas and queued up to buy the *Daily Mirror* and the *Sun*, two of the most anti-IRA tabloid newspapers. In Belfast, the IRA had blown up the *Mirror*'s print works! Obviously the leadership had not conveyed to the foot soldiers that the *Daily Mirror* was off their reading lists. While both wings of the IRA were violently opposed to the British Army, you could detect the tensions between them that sometimes spilled over into brawls in the few pubs within the No Go area. In Belfast, such feuds were resolved with guns not fists.

One Saturday, just outside our home in Fanad Drive, hooded Official IRA men tried to hijack a fruit and vegetable van, belonging to a very popular man called John Morrow. To say there was an altercation was to put it mildly and Fr. Joe Carolan appeared on the scene and told the hijackers to get lost. One of them said he would gleefully have given Fr. Joe the edge of his rifle butt if he had not been a priest. Fr. Joe said he had never regarded the clerical collar as an obstruction from doing what he felt he needed to do. In a flash, he chinned the would-be hijacker with a right hook that Muhammad Ali would have been proud of.

I remember one evening when I was returning from Ramsey's fish and chip shop on Central drive, when an ambulance pulled up and the driver rolled down the window and said they had received a phone call that a man had been shot in the knees behind the shops. A hooded IRA member appeared and told the driver to return in ten minutes as they had not yet carried out the shooting. The hand gun to be used to administer the shooting had not arrived! In another incident, a young IRA member was kneecapped behind the shops because he had used his OC's Cortina to transport a bomb, rather than hijack a car from a member of the public! Outside our front door, the two wings of the IRA stage-managed checkpoints for a visiting foreign television crew. From behind the barricades, the IRA held a press conference promising to fight on until a 32 county socialist republic was achieved. It is something of an irony that some of their leading spokesmen subsequently finished their republican careers helping administer a London funded, power-sharing Executive at Stormont, in tandem with their erstwhile enemies, the DUP.

For a short period of less than a year, life within the No Go areas resembled something from the Wild West. In the Stardust dance hall on a Saturday night, there was one young man, brandishing a pistol, challenged another outside for a gunfight at twelve paces over a girl. It was like *Gunfight at the OK Corral*. One afternoon after school, I was walking through the Bogside when a young man, who was about my own age, appeared from a doorway and started firing a sub-machine gun at a helicopter overhead. I recognised him. His nickname was Scatter. His reputation was that he could not hit a barn door from ten paces and that whenever he appeared with a gun, the safest thing to do was to scatter, which was the reason for his nickname. He was in the words of the historian, Thomas Pakenham, describing the Irish Militia in 1978, 'formidable to all but the enemy' and there was a sigh of relief when he was eventually lifted by the army in a pre-dawn swoop.

In the Telstar Bar in Creggan, there were rifles stacked neatly in the corner while their IRA owners had a break, before returning to 'active service.' One of my College friends, who lived on Bishop Street, was lifted by the Provisional IRA whilst walking through Creggan. He was deemed suspicious because he was carrying an umbrella! He was on his way to Creggan Heights to meet a girl and the explanation was eventually accepted. Carrying an umbrella was obviously not regarded as acceptable civic, republican behaviour. The Official IRA hi-jacked a lorry load of butter, which they distributed as having been 'liberated.' Ulsterbus suspended all bus services to Creggan, which played into the hands of the republican paramilitaries, who set up what they called 'the Peoples' Taxis,' as a means of funding their organisation. They even purchased the limousine once used by Bishop Neil Farren as part of their fleet. However, the Lough Swilly Bus Company continued its school run bus service, which took girls from Creggan and Bogside to Thornhill College, which was situated about five miles away on the Culmore Road.

The Catholic Church tried to fill the vacuum created by the removal of policing from Creggan by establishing an unarmed peace corps to patrol the estate. I joined up and, one Sunday afternoon, wearing my best and only suit, I found myself on patrol along Creggan Broadway heading towards the shops at the top of Beechwood Avenue. The only identification of my new-found status was an arm band. All of a sudden there was a burst of rifle fire, which appeared to be coming from behind the shops and being directed towards the RUC station in Rosemount. We took cover behind the high walls that surrounded the parochial house and when the shooting had subsided, walked towards the shop. A few minutes later, two young men, one of whom I knew as a leading local Provo, emerged in front of the shops. They were heavily armed and appeared high on the adrenalin of having been involved in a shoot-out, although I greatly doubted if any fire had been returned from the police station. They threw their weapons into the boot of a waiting car and soon sped off.

So, what was I supposed to have done at that moment? I thought it prudent not to attempt to arrest them, although they had just committed firearms offences. I quickly concluded the Peace Corps was a sham and promptly decided to walk away from both it and the incident. The simple truth was that authority, in the days of the No Go areas, was vested in the IRA, not the government, not the security forces, not the Catholic Church and not the SDLP. The IRA appeared to have learned one thing from Chairman Mao's Little Red Book, 'political power grows out of the barrel of a gun.' I derived some comfort from a tale of the Abbé Sieyes, a leading figure in the French Revolution. The historian, Francois Mignet was writing a history of the Revolution in the 1820s and went to visit the Abbé, then an old man. Mignet began their conversation with the question, 'What did you do during the Revolution?' and received the curt by clear response, 'I survived.' Survival was the name of the game inside the No Go areas.

By the end of 1971, Belfast had descended into tit for tat sectarian killings. The UVF blew up Mc Gurk' Bar, killing fifteen people and a week later the IRA carried out a similar no-warning bombing of a furniture store on the Protestant Shankill Road, killing four people, including two infants. As I approached the end of my first term in Upper Sixth, it was down to the nitty gritty of completing university application forms. My main goal was to secure a place at Trinity College in Dublin, for which there was a separate application form from that used for universities in the UK. I had given a lot of thought to choice of subject and plumped for the degree in History and Political Science. My parents had hoped that I would study law. As a matter of routine, I went through motions of completing the UCCA forms to apply for a place in a UK university and received provisional acceptance from all six institutions, from which I finally selected Queen's University Belfast as my number one choice, with Leeds University as a back-up.

In reality, I had no intention of going to Queen's, which I considered to be in the middle of a war zone that was much worse than Derry. Its halls of residence were too close to loyalist Sandy Row for my liking. A number of my contemporaries opted for the Mecca of De La Salle Teacher Training College, in Manchester, which gave them an escape from the Troubles of Northern Ireland, with the bonus of being able to see Manchester United on a regular basis. With forms in hand, I went along for my meeting with Monsignor Coulter, the College President. He placed the forms on his desk and the first question that he asked me was, 'Have you considered the priesthood?' I gave him an honest answer, which was that I had considered this but that I did not have a vocation for the priesthood, which he accepted, without demur. He then went through my applications and was pleased with my Trinity application. He asked me why I had chosen History, a subject he had taught. Somewhat sheepishly, I told him the choice seemed a safe bet. I had consistently been getting top marks in essays and examinations. I had also been greatly impressed by the recommendation of the historian, David Thompson, in his book *Europe Since Napoleon*, that he believed 'The study of history to be the best liberal education a student can have in the modern world.'

As my first term in Upper sixth drew to a close at the end of 1971, that year was one in which a record number of people, one hundred and seventy three, died as a result of the Troubles in Northern Ireland. The previous year the figure had been twenty five. While Ted Heath may well have believed that Northern Ireland was on the verge of complete anarchy, he also had plenty to occupy him in domestic politics. The National Union of Mineworkers went on a strike that was to last for seven weeks, while unemployment exceeded the one million mark, almost double what it had been when he took office in July 1970. However, Northern Ireland was soon to return to the top of British political priorities, in the aftermath of Bloody Sunday.

Chapter Sixteen
Annus Horribilis

From Magilligan Strand to Bloody Sunday-funerals as 'the skies wept too' and 'a United Ireland or nothing' becomes the new mantra – More killings in final months at the College.

The year 1972 was my last at the College and it followed a long period of mounting violence in Northern Ireland. We had our first glimpse of the methods of the Parachute Regiment when, in January, they were deployed to police an anti-internment march along the beach near Magilligan Prison, in County Derry, where a number of the internees were held. Many of the protestors had crossed the River Foyle by boat from Greencastle in County Donegal. On the evening news I watched as the soldiers, identifiable by their maroon berets, severely beat protestors. An angry John Hume accused the army of 'beating, brutalising and terrorising the demonstrators.' The same paratroopers were to be deployed on the streets of Derry, a week later. My father told me that the Paras were formed for landing behind enemy lines, in war, and were totally unsuited, by their training, for deployment in a situation such as policing a Civil Rights march.

The steady turmoil that the country endured saw roughly 100 bombs explode per month and the death toll within the first two months amounted to 49, with 257 people injured. In Creggan, there were daily gun battles between the IRA and the British Army. There was an escalation of violence and the army's forward operating base at Bligh's lane was targeted by sustained gunfire on a nightly basis. Hundreds of shots were fired but there were no casualties on either side, which said a lot about the standard of marksmanship. I would lie in bed, unable to get to sleep, against a background that made the final movement of the 1812 Overture sound like a lullaby. In one incident, the IRA was firing from the City Cemetery and aimed shots at an army helicopter flying overhead.

On the Wednesday of the week leading up to Bloody Sunday, William Craig was in Derry addressing a meeting of the Loyalist Association of Workers in the Apprentice Boys' Memorial Hall. This was the first of his planned series of rallies that would culminate in a massive rally in Belfast on 18th March. He said that the Unionist people must 'take their stand,' and that 1972 would be a year of decision. The following day, two members of the RUC became the first policemen to be shot dead in Derry, by the Provisional IRA. No police officer had been killed in Derry for half a century. Their unmarked patrol car was ambushed on Creggan Road, just outside the Brooke Park Library. One of their killers was reportedly armed with an old American-style Thompson submachine gun. David Montgomery was a twenty year old constable from the Cregagh area of east Belfast. The other victim was Peter Gilgunn, a twenty-six year old sergeant, who had been popular in Creggan. Years later, Brendan Duddy, recalled how the officer would have a cup of tea in his fish and chip shop at Beechwood Avenue, at the end of a shift in the nearby Rosemount police station. I wondered whether Sergeant Gilgunn was the same policemen who, many a day before the Troubles had brought murder and mayhem to Creggan, had patrolled, or should I say ambled, alone along Fanad Drive.

The killing of the two policemen cast a dark shadow over the city and further attacks on the security forces were expected. It was against this background that the Civil Rights march of January 30 1972 took place. Much of the idealism of the heady days of 1968 had been swept away in the spiral of violence that had gripped Northern Ireland. Death and destruction had become an everyday reality. The only reason that the Civil Rights movement had stayed in existence was because the Catholic community believed that all the measures to rid the country of terrorism were being applied exclusively against them. Internment, applied almost exclusively against Catholics suspected of involvement in the IRA, was still an active tool in attempts to suppress terrorism. There was no similar attempt to intern Protestants suspected of involvement in loyalist paramilitary activity. I often wondered why the Dublin government was so critical of internment when it had applied it regularly in suppressing IRA activity in the past.

On that fateful day, which has become universally known as Bloody Sunday, I was busily studying and had made a conscious decision not to go on the banned march, which would have started at about three o' clock. My plans were to take a break from study and walk down to Free Derry Corner for the final speeches around four o'clock. I walked down Beechwood Avenue along Marlborough Terrace towards St. Eugene's Cathedral. The tail end of the march had already passed, but there was a strong and intimidating military presence at Windsor Terrace and Francis Street. It seemed more menacing than for previous marches and I thought that there was a fair chance of trouble. I was not surprised when a man walking back up from William Street told me there was rioting at the bottom of the street. Rather than continue towards the rioting I decided to go back and make my way to Free Derry Corner by a safer route. The simplest way would have been to walk along Little Diamond, but at the back of my mind was the uncomfortable feeling that the soldiers in Francis Street could just as easily use the same route to enter the Bogside, with me as their first arrest. So, I retraced my steps up Creggan Street and along Marlborough Terrace.

The huge wall at the Bull Park had been demolished some years earlier and as I stood by the railings I suddenly heard the unmistakable sound of gunfire coming from the Bogside area. I could see people crouching as they ran, but I was unaware of the exact happenings. The shooting lasted for a few minutes and in all there seemed to be a few hundred shots. And then the shooting stopped. One thing was for sure; no way was I walking towards the sound of gunfire. I walked on along Laburnum Terrace and up the steps towards Beechwood Avenue. Here, feeling safe, I waited to find out what had happened. People coming from the Bogside had few details, but were insistent that the Army had been shooting, and that there were civilian casualties.

I headed home and awaited the News on BBC. First reports confirmed that there had been shooting and that a number of civilians had been killed and injured. The paratroopers had headed into the Bogside, seemingly convinced that the IRA would be firing on them from the Rossville Flats. No one within the army high command seemed to know that of the two thousand shots fired at the British army, in Derry, in the three months before Bloody Sunday, only nine had come from the Rossville Flats. My father came in and was reassured that I was alive, a feeling that was mutual. He had been standing at the Rossville Flats close toe Barney McGuigan a man also from Creggan. They had been sheltering from the shooting. As a former soldier, my father said that the best place to be was with your back to a wall and to stay there as long as possible. He became separated from Barney, who within minutes was shot dead.

In Derry, there was a call for three days of mourning and while I went to school the next morning, we were quickly told to go home. We wandered around the Bogside, which was eerily quiet, the first and only time I have ever seen it thus. With feelings running very high, an emotional John Hume, the Foyle MP and deputy leader of the SDLP, gave an interview to RTE. When what political feelings were now like in the Bogside, he replied, 'Many people down here feel now it's a united Ireland or nothing. Alienation is pretty total…' To outsiders, this may seemed totally at odds with the politics he had been espousing and his unionist opponents rushed to argue that Hume was articulating his own opinions on the political way forward. However, he was simply reflecting the anger and bitterness that was rife in the city. He ended the interview by saying, 'We are all going to have to work very hard to deal with the situation.' I was somewhat astonished when, within a few days of Bloody Sunday, the loyalist leader, John McKeague, from the Shankill Road, in Belfast, appeared in a television programme and proudly proclaimed that for loyalists it was 'Good Sunday.'

A number of commentators have written that Bloody Sunday was the most defining event in the history of the period, when British paratroopers shot dead thirteen men in an anti-internment march in Derry. At the end of that day, there was a literally a queue of young men to join the IRA. Many of them were told to go home. The IRA did not need more recruits at this stage; it needed guns. In the aftermath of the shootings of Seamus Cusack and Dessie Beattie and especially in a reaction to internment, the ranks of the IRA in Derry were full to bursting. It was somewhat ironic that the army, which was increasingly being deployed to suppress subversion, was, by its actions, actually helping the growth and spread of influence of the same subversives. Each side's actions were provoking an aggressive response from the other.

Bloody Sunday was felt like a mortal wound to Creggan, as five of the thirteen men shot dead lived on the estate. During that week, I had played a game of football against Jackie Duddy on the Bishop's Field and on the eve the march I had been talking to John Young, who worked in John Collier's tailor's shop, which was next door to the carpet shop where I had a Saturday job. I had been an altar boy with Willie Mc Kinney's brother and a school friend of one of Barney Mc Guigan's sons. Willie Nash lived in Dunree Gardens, a few hundred yards from me and I had attended the Holy Child Infants' School with him, Betty, a sister and one of his brothers, Frankie. It was numbing to look at thirteen coffins inside the altar rails in St. Mary's Church, the same inner sanctuary where I had so often paraded as an altar boy not that many years earlier. On the day of the funerals, the heavens opened and The Derry Journal summed up the mood with its headline, 'the skies wept too.' A number of Dublin cabinet ministers attended the funerals in Derry. By contrast, Northern Ireland's Prime Minister, Brian Faulkner spoke of mounting hysteria' and called for calm, which was in short supply. In Dublin, a mob burned the British Embassy, in the fashionable Merrion Square, to the ground. There was anger in Derry the day after the deaths, when the Home Secretary, Reggie Maudling, told the House of Commons that the British Army had returned fire directed at them, inflicting casualties on those who were attacking them with firearms and bombs. Bernadette Devlin walked across the floor of the House of Commons and slapped Maudling, much to the delight of Derry Catholics, The subsequent report on Bloody Sunday, later in the year by Lord Widgery, the Lord Chief Justice, was regarded in Derry as a whitewash, as it exonerated the Paras of blame for the civilian deaths.

Within days of the funerals of the victims of Bloody Sunday, both wings of the IRA stepped up their campaign of violence in Derry. There were fierce gun battles, one of which was on Eastway Gardens, just a few hundred yards away from our house. The Provisional IRA abducted Thomas Callaghan, a bus driver, as he was driving his bus through Creggan. He was a part-time member of the Ulster Defence Regiment, the UDR. A few hours later his body was found along the Foyle Road. He had been hooded, gagged and shot in the head. Local priests denounced his killing as a senseless act of violence. There was also revulsion in Derry when, a few weeks later, the Official IRA, in attempting to exact revenge against the Parachute Regiment, killed seven civilians, five women cleaners, a gardener and a Roman Catholic army padre in an attack at Aldershot Barracks of the Parachute Regiment, in Hampshire, in the south east of England. The Official IRA also attempted to assassinate John Taylor, the Minister of State for Home Affairs in the Stormont government. He was shot a number of times but survived. In the centre of Belfast, the IRA carried out a no-warning bombing of the Abercorn Restaurant on a busy Saturday afternoon.

March was a month of complete madness. Two civilians were killed and over 130 people injured. Internment had failed and violence was spiralling out of control. The body of another member of the UDR, Captain Marcus McCausland, was found on the outskirts of Creggan. He had been shot three times in the head. Four IRA members died in a premature explosion at a house in the Lower falls area of Belfast. The IRA exploded a car bomb in central Belfast, killing six people and injuring more than a hundred. It was no wonder that a Methodist minister described the situation as 'the Protestant High Noon.' It appeared as if the IRA was hell-bent on fomenting a civil war and matters were not helped by comments of Harold Wilson, leader of the Opposition at Westminster, that British policy should be changed to seeking a united Ireland in fifteen years' time. The SDLP was moving towards a new policy of joint authority over Northern Ireland by London and Dublin, as a prequel to a united Ireland.

Unknown to us at the time, Bloody Sunday had marked a defining political moment. Two months later, Ted Heath, the Prime Minister, moved quickly to suspend the Stormont Parliament for a one year period. In Creggan, there was no appreciation of just how stunned the Unionist community was by this action, especially as it had been carried out by their traditional allies, a Conservative government. A bond that stretched back to the days of the first Home Rule Bill of the 1880s had been shattered overnight. All Northern Ireland's eleven Unionist MPs, with the exception of Stratton Mills, resigned Conservative Party whip at Westminster in protest to the decision by the Heath government.

For many Unionists, it appeared that violence did pay. As the curtain was drawn down on Stormont, Brian Faulkner lamented, "that those who shout, lie, denigrate and even destroy, earn for themselves an attention that responsible conduct and honourable behaviour do not."

As we had learned through the study of Newton's Laws of Physics, there was going to be an equal and opposite reaction within the loyalist community. Bill Craig's Vanguard Party organised a strike and a rally was organised in Belfast, attended by an estimated 100,000 people. Craig openly and defiantly sent out the message, "If and when the politicians fail us, it may be our job to liquidate the enemy." The seeds were being sewn for a massive increase in violence from all paramilitary groupings, with each being intent on out-doing the other in barbarism and death.

The abolition of Stormont had been a Civil Rights demand for quite some time and there was general satisfaction, if not outright jubilation, in Creggan, when the announcement was made. There were many voices calling on the IRA to cease its campaign of violence but these fell on deaf ears. At that time, Republicans had no concept of attainable political objectives. Martin Mc Guinness, the IRA commander in the Bogside put it succinctly and unequivocally when he said, "Fitt and the rest are wasting their time. We are not stopping until we have a United Ireland." A week later, two Protestant workmen were killed when an IRA van bomb exploded outside the RUC station in Limavady, County Londonderry. In early April, two soldiers were killed when an IRA bomb exploded in the pavilion of the bowling green at Brooke Park, where less than two years earlier we had played football matches against young squaddies.

While Heath was suspending Stormont we were studying Lord Palmerston, Britain's Foreign Secretary in the mid nineteenth century. I was interested in his definition of diplomacy when he articulated that the fundamental objective of British policy was to avoid permanent entanglements. At a time when Europe was erupting in revolutions in 1848, he told the House of Commons, 'we have no eternal allies and we have no perpetual enemies. Our interests are eternal and perpetual, and those interests it is our duty to follow.' I wondered if Ted Heath was applying Palmerstonian logic to domestic rather than foreign policy as, with one single act, he jettisoned the Tory/Ulster Unionist alliance that had been established in the last decades of the nineteenth century.

Meanwhile from our study of French literature, we were introduced to a different perspective on the Troubles from an unlikely source, the life and writings of the French novelist and philosopher, Albert Camus, whose novel, *La Peste*, was on our A level course. In our background reading, we learned that Camus was born in Algeria of extraction that was known as the Pieds Noirs. For centuries, people from Europe, Christians and Jews, had migrated to Algeria, which was under French colonial government. They accounted for about one million people, about ten percent of the country's population and were violently opposed to the Algerian nationalist movement. It was suggested to us by our teacher, Jack McCauley that the Pieds Noirs were very similar to the Ulster Protestants and that they may well suffer the same fate of being abandoned by the former imperial power, which in our case was the British. Heath's decision to suspend Stormont seemed to fit this scenario. However, there were significant differences between Algeria and Northern Ireland, the most important being that Ulster Protestants were in a substantial majority rather than being a small minority. One day in class, we laughed at the suggestion that, on our way home from the College, we should ask the hooded IRA gunmen on Stanley's Walk whether they felt that the Ulster Protestants were in the mould of the Pieds Noirs in Algeria and whether Heath was a British version of De Gaulle. We demurred, realising that the only Black Feet the gunmen may have heard of would have been tribes of Native Americans, then simply called 'Indians,' in any John Wayne western movie!

Politically, it was becoming clear that there was going to be major change in British Government policy and that a restoration of devolved government would only happen if there was a compete change in the manner in which Northern Ireland would be governed. Few grasped this at the time. In the immediate aftermath of the suspension of Stormont, there was much speculation as to what would follow next and there was much talk about a possible re-partition of Northern Ireland, with the west bank of the river Foyle being ceded to the Republic. Such speculation added to Protestant anxieties and accelerated their Exodus to the Waterside and further afield. As the year unfolded, it became clear that there was to be a new government policy. In short, future institutions of devolved government were to be coupled to the establishment of a power-sharing Executive involving the SDLP and an all-Ireland dimension.

At the beginning of March, within six weeks of Bloody Sunday, two teenage IRA members were shot dead in a gun battle with the army on the edge of the Bogside. When I reached school, I discovered that the deceased were Colm Keenan, and Eugene McGillan. I had been through the Christian Brothers with Colm Keenan and he had been at the College with me for our five years up to O Level, when he left. Eugene McGillan had been a neighbour in Carrickreagh Gardens and had also been in the same year as me at the Christian Brothers. Through personal friendships going back many years, quite a large number of students from my year wanted to attend Colm Keenan's funeral, which was an

IRA funeral, complete with colour party, beret and gloves on top of the tricolour-draped coffin. Eugene McGillan had a private funeral. In spite of intense security by the police and the army, Sean MacStiofan, the IRA Chief-of Staff appeared in the cemetery, together with Martin Meehan, a leading Belfast republican, who gave an oration. A volley of shots was fired over the coffin.

Although many students from sixth form went to the funeral, only a small number would have had republican sympathies. Attendance at wakes and funerals was a long-honoured tradition of paying respects, not making a declaration of political beliefs. A few days after the funerals, we were discussing E.M. Forster in our English Literature class and Willie Donaghy reminded us of the writer's sentiments in *What I Believe and Other Essays,* where he had written; "If I had to choose between betraying my country and betraying my friend, I hope I should have the guts to betray my country." A lot of us who were at the funerals could identify with these words and felt no sympathy for the IRA while we mourned two of our former classmates from primary school days onwards.

We were barely three months away from sitting our A levels, which took precedence to anything else in our lives, and stoically endured the Troubles for our remaining school days. One day, we were discussing Camus with Jack McCauley, our French teacher. He reminded us of the final words from *The Myth of Sisyphus*, a philosophical essay written by Camus during the Second World War. Sisyphus laboured to push a boulder up a mountain and each time as he neared the summit he ran out of energy and the boulder rolled back down to the bottom. Camus described Sisyphus as he walked down to collect the boulder in the words, 'il faut imaginer Sisyphe heureux.' The translation, 'one must imagine Sisyphus happy,' aptly summed up our feelings as we knuckled down to our goal of successful A Levels as our passports out of Derry. A line from Don McLean's song, American Pie, rhymed with us, '*the day the music had died*.' The music that was all too common and to which we had become accustomed to hear was a funeral lament.

The one normal activity that continued was our inter-schools debating competition and as a climax to the two turbulent years, we won the *Derry Journal Cup*, with a team consisting of Nigel Cooke, Paul Kearney, Frank Diggin, Martin Tucker, Jim Harkin and myself. The final was held in Londonderry High School and we were duly presented with the trophy and the traditional photograph was taken for posterity. Nigel Cooke recently reminded me that when the picture appeared in the *Derry Journal*, Monsignor Coulter, the College President, acidly remarked that I was the only student wearing a college blazer at the event. Maybe, the others thought they were up for the Dandy Diddler award!

From chatting to our Protestant contemporaries, it was clear that they also wanted to get out of Northern Ireland to pursue university degrees. However, an increasing number of them also said that they had no intention of returning when they would graduate. This was at a time of an increasing exodus of the Protestant community from the west bank of the River Foyle in Derry to the Waterside, on the east bank. Many of the professional and business people had gone further east towards Limavady and Coleraine. Streets such as Clarence Avenue, Crawford Square and Lawrence Hill, which had been almost exclusively Protestant a decade earlier, were quickly emptying of Protestant families. In the three short years from the start of the Troubles, in August 1969, the Protestant population in Derry, on the west bank of the river Foyle, had halved and the Exodus was to continue throughout the 1970s.

As we approached the end of our school days, the deaths of civilians, soldiers, policemen and paramilitaries had become commonplace and people were becoming a bit immune to the news of the latest atrocity. At the time, we were studying Victor Hugo's *Souvenir De La Nuit, du Quatre,* a poem set against the background of an attempted coup against Napoleon III. The first line read; *L'enfant avait recu deux balles dans la tete.'* Children killed was not limited to Hugo's mid nineteenth century Paris. In the middle of May, a fifteen year old schoolboy, Manus Deery was shot dead by an army sniper in the Bogside. The killings continued.

Within a few days, there was one further killing of that period that was seared in to the minds of the residents of Creggan. Willie Best was a nineteen year old soldier, serving with his regiment, the Royal Irish Rangers, in Germany. I remembered him as a gangly youth, who often accompanied his mother to bingo in the Community Centre next to our house in Fanad Drive. He had returned to his home in Rathkeele Way, in Creggan, on leave, in May. He was abducted by the Official IRA, shot dead and his body dumped on waste ground in the Bogside. Over five thousand mourners attended his funeral. Ironically, Willie Best was a neighbour of Mickey Devine, the last hunger striker to die in 1981.

Slowly but surely, the community-based unity that existed in the early days of the Civil Rights movement began to disappear. There was the main division between those who believed in physical-force Republicanism, and those who adhered to constitutional Nationalism. It was a division that was the cause of bitter disputes within families and between neighbours. There was also the inescapable fact that armed force was the policy of the British Government and carried out ruthlessly by the British Army. A few days before Willie Best's death, a British Army sniper shot dead the unarmed, fifteen-year-old Manus Deery. The death of Ranger Willie Best put in sharp focus the divisions that had opened up in Creggan. There were condemnations of the killing, and a sense of outrage that was widely felt. The use of armed force was abhorred by the majority of the people of Creggan, and now it had been visited on one of their own people, by their own people.

There was outrage and over four hundred women marched in protest to the headquarters of the Official IRA, in the Bogside and physically attacked its occupants. A public meeting was called by Fr. Rooney in St. Mary's Secondary School in Creggan. He called on both wings of the IRA to call a halt. I was in the hall as he made a plea, "We must abhor the violence and the beginning of a civil war that we have seen around us." Johnny White, a leading member of the Official IRA was not allowed to address the meeting and he left, looking shaken. Outside, he said that the leaders on the platform were not representative of the people. Women supporters of the Provisional IRA, led by a girl of my own age from Creggan and acting like the proverbial Amazons, hi-jacked the meeting and tried to turn it into one of endorsement of the Provisional IRA's campaign of violence. In the ensuing disorder, the meeting was abandoned. Fr Rooney hardly got a hearing, and was branded as an enemy of the popular struggle. This was the same Fr Rooney who, in the previous September, had sent a telegram to the then British Prime Minister, Ted Heath, calling for the withdrawal of the British Army from Creggan and pointing out that the use of CS gas was making Creggan 'a vast gas chamber'.

That evening, outside St. Mary's, I saw a very senior Provisional IRA figure smirking at the discomfort of his fellow republicans, the Official IRA, for whom the Provisional IRA had little regard. Within a few weeks, however, the Official IRA announced that it was calling a ceasefire. In spite of the announcement, the Official IRA never really went away and was widely believed to continue to be involved in general criminality. The Provisional IRA said they would continue to fight what they called 'British occupation' and remained within the No Go areas. While calling themselves the local police force for the area, they were engaged in criminality at the same time. Seven armed robberies occurred in Derry at bookmakers' premises, immediately after the Grand National.

As the IRA stepped up its bombing campaign of commercial premises in Derry, Martin Mc Guinness, a Provisional IRA leader in the city, said in an interview that the aim of the IRA was to cripple the city economically. Just outside Ferryquay Gate there was a large four story building called Commercial Buildings, which was formerly the Victoria Hotel. My mother was at the hairdresser's on the first floor when the building was quickly evacuated in a bomb warning. As she stood on the landing, tying a scarf around her hair, which was still in curlers, a young British Army soldier said to her, 'Move very slowly away from that dustbin, madam. There's a bomb in it.' She nearly had a heart attack but followed the soldier's instruction. Quarter of an hour later, the bomb exploded, destroying the building. My mother barely escaped being another part of 'collateral damage' in the IRA's campaign to destroy the commercial centre of Derry.

A few weeks later, the IRA placed bombs inside the Guildhall and destroyed one of the city's most beautiful buildings. It had ceased to be seat of Unionist power as the Corporation had been dissolved three years earlier. The bombing smacked of nihilism. One of the bombs was placed at the plinth of the statue of Queen Victoria and removed her head. To prove that the lunatics were taking over the asylum, the IRA began issuing their own press cards to visiting journalists and organized an election, within the area known as Free Derry, for a 'community government.' In what smacked of Soviet–style democracy, it was announced that there were thirteen candidates for the thirteen available seats, thus ensuring that there was no election. It was hardly surprising that republicans had a majority of the candidates. At the same time, the IRA was publicly saying that it was seeking direct talks with the British government. As we finished our last A level, a ceasefire was called that lasted a mere fortnight! In the shop where I worked, one of the carpet fitters had reason to be thankful for this temporary halt to their terrorist campaign. He was a member of the part-time Territorial Army and was abducted by the IRA whilst in a house in Creggan and taken to their HQ at Central Drive. He was carrying his army identification card, which was thrown down in front of him by a senior IRA figure with the words; 'If it wasn't for the ceasefire this would have sealed your fate.' He never worked in Creggan again and considered himself lucky to be alive when he returned to the shop.

Ahead of the A level exams, the football season ended with Manchester United finishing a disappointing eighth in the final table, having started the season well under new manager, Frank O'Farrell. We even topped the league for a while before losing eight games in a row. .June was the sunny month we normally associated with examinations and the papers in my three A Levels were evenly spread throughout the month. Living through a turbulent period of Irish history, I was now answering questions on revolutionary times in the 18th and 19th centuries, assessing Edmund Burke's views on the French Revolution, the leadership qualities of Pitt the Younger, the pros and cons of the Irish Act of Union. We wrote about T.S. Eliot's *Waste Land*, while reviewing plenty of waste lands around us and dissected the clash, in E.M. Forster's *Howard's End,* between the Wilcoxes and the Schlegels for supremacy in Edwardian England, while the hapless Leonard Bast looked on. Shakespeare's *Henry IV Part 2* began with the words, 'O god, that one might read the book of fate/And see the revolution of the times/Make mountains level.' It felt as if we ourselves had just lived through revolutionary times.

In our final term at the College, there were signs that the Secretary of State, William Whitelaw, was making some progress in focusing the constitutional political parties on the need for dialogue. Over five hundred internees had been released since Direct Rule had been declared. At the time, my father was working for the Development Commission, which appeared to be facilitating the integration of some of these ex-internees into society by finding them jobs, sometimes as street cleaners and bin men. Whitelaw's greatly feared Protestant backlash against Direct Rule failed to materialize, in spite of industrial action when the announcement of Direct Rule had been made. Protestant Ulster did not appear to have any stomach for independence, as advocated by William Craig. Northern Ireland was not going to become a new Rhodesia.

The barrier to any political progress was the continuing campaign of violence being waged by the Provisional IRA. Inside the No Go area, the IRA carried out regular checkpoints, usually for the benefit of visiting international news teams. One Friday, Gerry Conway and I were leaving the College about an hour ahead of our official lunch break and had just emerged from the Christians Brothers' gate onto the Lecky Road when we ran into one such checkpoint. 'Are you boys dobbing school?' was the question posed to us by a masked gunman. I was on the point of laughing when he added, 'It's OK, Gerry. I won't tell your Ma on you.' Ironically, apart from the fear of getting caught in cross fire between the IRA and the British Army, life within the 'No Go' area was relatively safe as long as you kept your head down. Derry was not suffering the growing number of tit for tat sectarian murders that were plaguing Belfast. In the majority of IRA bombings in Derry, unlike those in Belfast or other parts of Northern Ireland, adequate time warnings had been given to evacuate the buildings that were targeted.

In the study of British history, we had learned about 'gunboat diplomacy,' practiced so adroitly by Lord Palmerston, the British Foreign Secretary, in 1850. He sent a squadron of the royal Navy to blockade the Greek port of Piraeus in retaliation for the harming of a British subject. I could not but think that it would take more than gunboat diplomacy to end the No Go areas in Derry that were an affront to British sovereignty. I thought it only a matter of time before military action would be taken. One solution being canvassed was that the west bank of Derry would be handed over to the Republic. This appeared unlikely for two reasons. Firstly, Derry had so much significance for Ulster Protestants. The

249

walled city epitomized defiance that it would have been unthinkable for Unionists simply to see the city handed over to the Dublin government. Secondly, no one seriously believed that the Republic would be remotely interested in bringing rebellious Derry under its jurisdiction. It was fine to sing about the Fourth Green Field but it was somewhat else to have to become responsible for governing it and paying the massive British annual subvention!

On the last Monday in June, I sat my final A Level exam at the College. As ever, June had been warm and sunny, what we called exam weather. Dressed in my College uniform, for the last time, I was standing outside the Concert Hall, which was the exam centre, when Fr. Coulter came along. He wished us every success both for the exam and our futures. Our final act in the seven year College experience was to take the third History paper. For three hours, I wrote my answers to the questions on 'Grattan and His Times 1775-1800.' For the previous two years we had been studying this period. The very last question that I answered was; 'Would you agree that the insurrection of 1798 was the product of social and economic grievances rather than of political aspirations?' The question could equally have been posed of what was happening in my own times in Northern Ireland. An IRA ceasefire was due to come into effect at midnight that night. In the hours just before the ceasefire, two British soldiers were shot dead, one of them in Derry. The Provisional IRA issued a statement saying that it would continue to police the Bogside and Creggan. I had little hope that the ceasefire would last little more than a few weeks.

And so my school career ended in the words of T.S. Eliot; 'not with a bang but a whimper.' From my early days at the Holy Child and especially at the Christian Brothers and the College, I had been on a treadmill of exams taking me to the next level. I now hoped that the next level from the College would take me to university and the opportunity to move beyond the confines of Derry. I was hopeful of gaining the grades necessary to gain admittance to Trinity College Dublin to read History and Political Science.

Chapter Seventeen
Waiting for Trinity

Bloody Friday to Operation Motorman as I amble through Windsor and Eton College – The Munich Olympics, dubbed the 'Cheerful Games' become the scene of a massacre.

Samuel Beckett, educated at Trinity College Dublin, wrote *Waiting for Godot*. For me, the summer of 1972 was waiting for Trinity. It began with seemingly strange report in the papers that, during the IRA ceasefire, two British Army captains had been 'captured' by the IRA as they were leaving girls home to the Bogside. It seemed a tad strange to me that two officers were involved. As Tom Dunbar, our French teacher in first year would have said; 'it smells of ancient fish.' It later transpired that, unknown to the general public at the time, William Whitelaw, the Secretary of State had a secret meeting in London with IRA leaders. The two army captains were held as hostage for the safe return to Ireland of the IRA leaders. Whitelaw later told the House of Commons that the IRA made demands for a commitment by the British government to withdraw from Northern Ireland by a specific date and a general amnesty for all IRA prisoners in Britain and Ireland. In his memoirs, he described the meeting as a non-event, given the impossible demands of the IRA delegation. The IRA ceasefire ended within days of the London meeting.

Within weeks, on July 21, the IRA detonated twenty two bombs in and around the centre of Belfast within the space of seventy five minutes. Nine people were killed on that day, which became known as 'Bloody Friday.' It was the worst day of death and destruction in Belfast since the German blitz of 1941. Public opinion was appalled at the carnage and it seemed only a matter of time before the government would sanction a military operation to smash the 'No Go' areas of Bogside and Creggan. The policy of containment was not working and there were mounting military casualties as the IRA engaged the army in regular gun battles and snipers lurked, awaiting any opportunity.

In Derry, the IRA leadership denied rumours that it was planning to assassinate members of the SDLP. However, it stepped up the bombing campaign of the city centre. I had my summer job at Reggie Ryan's carpet shop, in Ferryquay Street, and thus witnessed the results of the IRA's bombing campaign of the city centre when the ceasefire collapsed. The British Army erected concrete barriers around the commercial centre, to seal off direct access to the city centre from the

Bogside, the area of the city from which the majority of IRA bombs were believed to originate. Similar measures were taken in Belfast.

During that summer, as I awaited my exam results, I became involved in an organization called 'Holiday Projects West,' which organized holidays in Ireland and Britain for youngsters from deprived backgrounds. I was an assistant and one of the most enjoyable trips was taking a group of fourteen year olds from Strabane to London, where we were based in Twickenham. Gerry Conway, one of my friends from the College, was also a supervisor. For the youngsters, the highlight of the holiday was a trip to Windsor Castle. One of the boys remarked that he recognized one of the Coldstream Guards as a soldier he had seen on the streets of Strabane! I enjoyed the visit to Eton College and seeing Richmond Hill, that we had sung about many years earlier at primary school. On a day off from supervising, Gerry and I went off to see the sights of central London. Together we wandered along Whitehall and stood upon Westminster Bridge and surveyed the modern scene, much changed from 1802, when Wordsworth penned his famous poem.

I watched on a television screen as the British Army mounted Operation Motorman and invaded the No Go areas of Creggan and Bogside, dismantling the remaining barricades. It was the biggest military operation since Suez. Chieftain Tanks rumbled through the narrow streets. There were over 30,000 armed service personnel involved, which made Motorman one of the biggest deployments of British forces since the Second World War. It was also the largest troop concentration in Ireland in the 20th century, including the Anglo-Irish War 1919-21. It was heralded by the arrival of several Royal Navy battleships in Lough Foyle in the early hours of the morning. At a meeting held in the Bogside to protest against the British Army's actions, Bernadette Devlin said the troops should be 'frozen out and ignored" and Eamonn McCann said they should be 'treated like the lepers they are' The normally moderate John Hume said; 'The British Army is not welcome. The British Army will not be regarded as protectors by the people of Derry.' In a clear reference to the events of Bloody Sunday, he added, 'Memories are too fresh about what they did before.'

With plenty of advance warning of the army's intentions, the IRA gunmen had simply disappeared over the Border into Donegal. Apparently, the Westminster government did not want another public relations disaster like Bloody Sunday on the streets of Derry. The news of Motorman confirmed two civilian fatalities in Creggan, Daniel Hegarty, aged 15 and Seamus Bradley, aged 19. The same news bulletin also told of three no-warning IRA car bombings in the village of Claudy, ten miles from Derry, killing nine civilians, including an eight year old girl. Major incidents claiming multiple fatalities continued that summer. Three weeks later, six civilians and three IRA members were killed in a premature bomb explosion at a customs post in Newry, County Down. The dead civilians included two lorry drivers, who were waiting for customs clearance as the IRA gang left the the 50lb device. Throughout the Troubles, British customs posts were regular target for IRA bombers.

As I watched television pictures of tanks rumbling through Creggan and Bogside, I was sitting in a pub in Whitton, in Richmond Upon Thames, talking to John, one of the Holiday Projects co-coordinators in Twickenham. He was a former paratrooper and had lost an arm in Aden. He still had plenty of mates in the Paras and told me he had spoken to some of them about Bloody Sunday. They told him that they had been briefed to expect sniper fire on that fateful day and believed they had clear orders to return fire. They had also been told that the local army units were regarded by the high command as having been soft on rioters in Derry. His story filled in a few of the missing gaps in that overall picture. The Paras were determined to bring, to the streets of Derry, the same methods they had been using in Belfast in dealing with both loyalist and republican rioters. There were many allegations that the Paras had consistently failed to have a measured response to incidents of riot and shooting and simply regarded the entire civilian population as legitimate targets.

On a very poor telephone line, I received my A Level results, which guaranteed me a place at Trinity, the University of my First Preference, to study History & Political Science. I regarded myself as most fortunate to be able, shortly, to escape from the claustrophobic environment of Northern Ireland and go off to Dublin. Indeed, it was to be a liberating experience. I returned to Derry from London, looking forward to going to the beginning of the academic year. The Munich Olympics, the 'cheerful Games,' as they had been named had just got underway. The exploits of Mark Spitz, winning seven gold medals, and the young gymnast Olga Korbett, are now scarcely remembered. The Games will forever be associated with the massacre of eleven Israeli athletes and a German policeman in the Olympic village. That particular act of terrorism was carried out by a Palestinian terror grouping called Black September. Terrorism was a global phenomenon and not restricted to Northern Ireland. There were terrorist attacks across Spain, Germany and Italy as groups, such as ETA, the Red Brigades and Baader Meinhof, waged their own wars on government and society.

I returned from London to a Northern Ireland, now garrisoned by over twenty thousand British soldiers. However, the level of car bombings, and murders by Loyalist death squads, intensified that summer. The initial effects of Motorman had worn off and IRA gunmen returned to Creggan, having taken refuge, or a holiday, in the seaside resort of Buncrana, in County Donegal. Meanwhile, the Grenadier Guards, about whom we had sung in the Christian Brothers, were had come to town and were encamped on a newly constructed base that overlooked Creggan Heights. The locals called the new encampment 'Piggery Ridge.' There was now constant shooting at the base by IRA snipers and a sergeant in the Grenadiers had been shot dead while working on the camp's construction.

During that long summer I had read a few books and novels in which Dublin was a central location. James Plunkett's *Strumpet City*, set in the time of the Dublin Lockout of 1913, was a modern take on events from the plays of Sean O' Casey. I enjoyed Oliver St. John Gogarty's *As I was Walking Down Sackville Street*, memoirs of Dublin in the 1920s but my favourite reads were J.P. Donleavy's *The Ginger Man* and *The Beastly Beatitudes of Balthazar B*. Donleavy was an American at Trinity in the post-war years and wrote about the adventures of outrageous characters at his Irish alma mater. I was in countdown mode, greatly looking forward to beginning a new chapter of my life away from Derry.

On a sunny Sunday afternoon in October I arrived at the bus depot in Foyle Street, Derry, to begin my odyssey. My father came with me. My mother was both proud and slightly sad as her only child was leaving home for the first time. There were no tears but she reminded me to be sure to go to Mass, work hard and write as often as possible. You would have thought that I was about to embark on an emigrant ship to Boston rather than take a four hour bus journey to Dublin. My father reminded her that when he was my age he was in Shanghai, serving with the Royal Inniskilling Fusiliers! So began a bus journey to Dublin that I would make many times in the coming four years.

My childhood years have been described in many narratives. The concentric circles from local to regional to national and international and global have attracted many writers and spin doctors. I was leaving a city that had seen more political violence in the last twelve months than in the previous fifty years put together. The Stormont Parliament and Londonderry Corporation had been abolished. There was the rise and fall of the Civil Rights movement and the re-emergence of the IRA as the most potent and ruthless terrorist organisation seen in these islands. It was the age of the paramilitaries and Republican and Loyalist violence was to continue for a further quarter of a century. Somewhere stuck in the middle were successive British Governments, which had been sucked into the Irish vortex, having spent a half century scrupulously avoiding such involvement. Northern Ireland, with 'its dreary steeples,' seemed trapped in a time warp and words of William Butler Yeats that sprang readily to mind:

Mere anarchy is loosed upon the world,
The blood-dimmed tide is loosed, and everywhere
The ceremony of innocence is drowned;
The best lack all conviction, while the worst
Are full of passionate intensity.

As the Ulsterbus coach sped along Victoria Road heading towards Dublin, I looked over the river towards the College and Creggan. Clio, the muse of History was staring back at me from the spire of the College as I commenced my odyssey. Horatius was still on the bridge confronting the forces of Lars Porsena and Keats was still looking into Chapman's Homer. Sisyphus was bravely pushing his boulder up the mountain to the strains of gunfire the lingering smell of CS gas hanging over the College. I looked toward Creggan, the hill far away, a place where I had enjoyed growing up. As I reflected on my Maiden City childhood I wondered if I would ever permanently return after my university years had ended. The first chapters of my life had drawn to a close.